If Babel Had a Form

If Babel Had a Form

Translating Equivalence in the Twentieth-Century Transpacific

Tze-Yin Teo

Fordham University Press   New York   2022

Copyright © 2022 Tze-Yin Teo

All rights reserved. No part of this publication may be reproduced, stored in a retrieval system, or transmitted in any form or by any means—electronic, mechanical, photocopy, recording, or any other—except for brief quotations in printed reviews, without the prior permission of the publisher.

Fordham University Press has no responsibility for the persistence or accuracy of URLs for external or third-party Internet websites referred to in this publication and does not guarantee that any content on such websites is, or will remain, accurate or appropriate.

Fordham University Press also publishes its books in a variety of electronic formats. Some content that appears in print may not be available in electronic books.

Visit us online at www.fordhampress.com.

Library of Congress Cataloging-in-Publication Data is available.

Printed in the United States of America

24 23 22   5 4 3 2 1

First edition

Contents

Note on Translation, Transliteration, and Transcription   vii

     Introduction: Equivalence beyond Value   1
1   Transpacific Abstraction   31
2   Sound Translation: Eileen Chang   67
3   Concrete Translation: Theresa Hak Kyung Cha   95
4   Translingual Erasure: Yang Lian   126
     Conclusion: If Babel Had a Form   151

Acknowledgments   *165*
Notes   *167*
Works Cited   *205*
Index   *219*

Note on Translation, Transliteration, and Transcription

This book is about translation and some sideways things that have been done with it; accordingly, I too adopt a range of practices in explaining the texts I study for an English-language academic reader who does not have a working knowledge of the languages in which they were first written. My priority is to communicate my argument and reconstruct its lines of thinking as clearly as possible. This has meant modulating my translation practices to accommodate my argument and the styles of the writer-translators being discussed, taking seriously both the process and product of translation. If an English translation of a relevant text is available in published form, I adopt it with modifications appropriate to my argument (unless otherwise stated); if not available, I translate it myself. My decisions on translation and modification are explained as they arise in the argument, typically in the notes but, if decisive to the argument, in the main text.

To transliterate the Chinese words important for my analysis, I largely follow the current North American English-language academic convention of using pinyin without the diacritics indicating tonal differentiation. Exceptions arise when the argument relies on tonal differentiation: especially in chapter 4 but elsewhere in the text as well, I include diacritics with the pinyin where I judge it necessary to help a reader follow along. When the writing of the main text requires incorporating both the source pinyin and the translated term (which is occasionally also a neologism), I depart from the convention of presenting one or the other term in square brackets, instead electing to present both the source and translated terms in italics and in close succession to one another.

Chinese writing is rendered in full-form (also known as Traditional, Complex, or Standard) characters. I include the source text—including block quotes—wherever the translation has import for my analysis and argument, at times in the notes and at times in the main text. To simplify composition, bibliographical entries for Chinese-language sources are uniformly transliterated.

If Babel Had a Form

Introduction
Equivalence Beyond Value

> Translations, on the contrary, prove to be untranslatable not because meaning weighs on them heavily, but rather because it attaches to them all too fleetingly. —WALTER BENJAMIN, "THE TRANSLATOR'S TASK" (1923)[1]

To Surrender Meaning

What follows is a tale with a meaning less easily grasped. "The Story of Mr. Not So Different" tells of an everyman always settling for substandard alternatives that are merely good *enough*.[2] He is not alone in this stubborn plight. As the fable's author sarcastically scolds, the colloquial timbre of his hero's name stems from its place in the vernacular imagination: Mr. Not So Different is "the most famous person" in the land because "his name is uttered by countless people to the extent that he has come to represent the entire population."[3] So first imagine him as he was written in 1924: a simple bumpkin swimming against the tide of modern life. In an ever more dire series of incidents, he repeatedly fails to learn that minor differences, barely sensible between those scraps of language we may now call *signifiers*, may indeed bear significant consequences. At the bank, a slip of the pen that writes 十 *ten* as 千 *thousand*; at a station, huffing away after a departing train because he cannot believe that those two minutes on the timetable can make such a difference. His misadventures in modern capitalism reach a new low when an illness suddenly takes hold of him. In great pain and unable to wait, he agrees to be treated by Wáng the veterinarian who has accidentally arrived in place of Wāng the village doctor, the *harmophones* of their two names sliding together when he calls for them in a muddy accent too easily misunderstood.[4] The result of the veterinarian's treatment is as one may expect. By the sad and sardonic end, we return only to where we began: the hero is canonized upon his death as a Buddhist legend for his pliant renunciations of will, becoming a role model for a "nation of lazy people" who invoke his name as an alibi for shrugging off their duties.[5] The moral of the story is clear: pay attention to nuance; educate the people; never settle for an approximation.

Few of sound mind would enlist Mr. Not So Different as a translator. Useless as a reader and hopeless as a comparatist, his lamentable qualities of mind make him not long for the modern nation that his creator wished into being—and indeed this world that is now ours too. After all, in denouncing one national character, the fable tacitly recommends another one: a perfectionist precision of technique for a work ethic necessary in a developing industrial-capitalist world, indispensable for a world in which so much can be made out of so little. In *this* world, to be a good translator is to ground oneself in a readerly and activist ethic, paying close attention to even the slightest linguistic, formal, cultural, and any other intelligible differences between myself and another in order to ultimately transform us both—and in that metonymic process remake the objects and systems that have brought us into relation.[6] Little wonder that the story leaves behind a world that is, in the end, not so different: on a subtler reading than the screed against a lazy nation's character, Mr. Not So Different dies not because he cannot *perceive* the fine differences that create meaning in language but because he does not take those differences seriously *enough* as meaningful agents that may themselves make a difference in the conditions of his material world.

Those differences so formative for meaning and context call for closer examination. In this book, they go by the name *value*. Value is a concept that functions in many guises across linguistic, economic, and ethico-political registers; drawing its explanatory power from that overdetermination, the concept of value at once anchors the meaningful gaps crucial to processes of signification and points to the bitter fruits of capitalist accumulation. Yet more than a simple concept, value—and particularly exchange-value—is the broken logic of capitalism that continues to uphold the power of empire and globalization. From the racialization and extraction of human labor for *producing* value to the subtler coercions that arise from *assigning* and *distributing* value unevenly across a globalizing world, the cruelty of this abstraction acts *upon* lived experience, carving out our actually existing particularities through processes of material and social differentiation, blocking the passage into those never existing arenas of solidarity and universality. *Because* of value and its uneven operations across global political economy, our experiences of power and life are incommensurable to one another, singular and even untranslatable. In living with value and its cognate logic—the Marxian system of *general equivalence*—"we are being exposed to a catastrophe of meaning."[7]

I hope to stay with this catastrophe of meaning for the short while of this book—and to embrace its difficult lessons with Mr. Not So Different by my side. After all, when thinking about *translation*, crises of meaning and incommensurability are never far away, perpetually present as an occupational hazard of sorts. May the strange work of translation and literary language steal quietly away from those regimes of exchange-value? For thinking about meaning in this context, an important touchstone for my argument has been the work of Lydia Liu, whose critique of equivalence moves with alacrity from a model of political economy to a model of *semantic* economy by trading on metaphorical associations between the linguistic and the economic in Marx and Saussure. Where for Saussure, money is an analogy for the structure of language, for Marx, language is an analogy for the economy of money: Liu's reading then sets Marx and Saussure into a chiasmus wherein economics *and* the structuralist conception of language are isomorphic structures that attain a powerful "figurative equivalence" (both are at once vehicle and tenor), integrating them into a dialectical whole.[8] That chiasmus of a *semantic* political economy animates what Liu captures in her term "meaning-value." Akin to Marx's account of surplus-value, meaning-value is generated and compounded through exchange in circulation. Where commentators have often implied a fundamental or even ontological difference between literary translation and a more culturally oriented mode of critique that moves beyond the level of the word and text, Liu's diagnostic work instead powerfully frames them as a set of concentric circles orbiting the same problem: the derivation of meaning and experience *from* structures of value, as those structures span registers from the political to the economic and semantic.

Insofar as Mr. Not So Different dies by a materialist theory of linguistic value, he is also a precocious theorist of the linguistic static at the heart of this book's argument. From those harmophonic resemblances that misrecognize the veterinarian as the doctor to a thousand that becomes ten by eliding a single stroke: this is the chaos of meaninglessness that ensues when words are mere sounds and images bleeding into one another, seeping through the fading lines of linguistic and cultural difference with no regard to any commensurability of meaning and reference. What form *can* translation take when it becomes, in a recent telling, "a constant reassessment of the sign in its flexibility and versatility" in our age of neoliberalism?[9] For on yet another reading, our protagonist dies from a failure to understand a central precept of structuralist linguistics: what bonds the signifier to the signified and referent—which is also what gives the linguistic sign its integrity *and* ability to refer to something in the world—is the contingent arrangement of an internally coherent culture, within which meaning is derived from the relations of difference between one sign and another.[10] What is more, he even intuits and dies by the poststructuralist radicalization: the signifier has always been decoupled from the signified, acting as the *primary* driver of meaning-making in a network of infinitely differentiated signifiers. If this lonely protagonist were to be resurrected in a different place and time, he might well find that his habit of collapsing so much into indistinguishable wisps of language could have a strange potency unknown to his creator and the many readers who would follow in time. But like so many early and naive readers of poststructuralist thought, he would be gravely mistaken to think that *that* was all he needed to do. Which is why it remains funny to scoff at his misplaced confidence that nonrepresentational and nonconceptual dimensions of language will function conceptually, based on a mere resemblance of the senses: as the fable warns, just because two words or sounds *look* or *sound* almost the same in no way implies that they *are* the same—or that they *work* and *mean* in the same ways.[11] No sameness of ontology and meaning, or indeed sameness of function, intention, or even understanding: there are many important things that these bits of language cannot be and cannot do. Yet the small miracles of such alignments have captured the attention and directed the energies of the translators studied in this book. Put in its simplest form, my question is to ask why and how this has been so—and to follow their surprises wherever they may go.

Soft and tender as it may be, that sameness is at the core of this argument's power. With translation studies as my method and comparative literature as the first site of intervention, I return these fields to an old chestnut—equivalence between source and translated texts, languages, cultures, times, and sociopolitical formations—in order to think its politics anew.[12] My argument's opening move surrenders a translator's ethos of meaning and interpretation in order to measure the force of a nonsignifying sameness. At stake is a praxis of translation reinventing its conceptual debts to value and the formal principles of colonial capital. Where recent work sees translation as setting interpretive difference and textual singularity into systems of circulatory exchange,[13] I instead pursue an equivalence by other means: a startling poetics that contests the differentiations of exceptionalism and ethnic typologies in a Sino-US context defined by a long Pacific century of imperialism and reifications of cultural incommensurability.

Equivalence, first understood as the translator's making of "two equivalent messages with two different codes,"[14] has come under scrutiny by postcolonial theorists who point to the unequal systems of capital that create, assign, and arbitrate value through epistemological and material processes of cultural translation.[15] Such critiques of meaning and value underscore the naiveté in taking any semblance of equivalence as a model of translation: a series of false equivalences that point only to the impossibility of having any real ones.[16] Whence the drive in recent translation theory to an interpretive heuristic of difference, finding meaningful gaps embedded in interconnected yet unequal cultures or metabolized across circulatory systems that spit up the waste we may call the untranslated and untranslatable. Thinking with the untranslatable does not lock one into a static position,[17] and indeed keeps one "as far as could be from such a sacralization of the untranslatable, based on the idea of an incommensurability of languages and linked to the near-sanctity of certain languages."[18] Rejecting the logic of value implied in sacralizing the commensuration of languages, Barbara Cassin instead suggests that the work of the untranslatable is an even stranger one: to show how "the universality of concepts is absorbed by the singularity of languages."[19] Is it possible to trace an equivalence in those singular languages and all that melts into their air?

Before such an undertaking may be possible, a tangle of questions remains to be asked. After all, perhaps the greatest surprise in the story of Mr. Not So Different is its unspoken skepticism that such an ethical lesson of difference may be quite so easily learned. The story's main literary device is an open form of differentiation along the lines of what can be seen, understood, calculated, and heard—*and* the ways in which those forms of differentiation nevertheless become compressed into approximations of one another in that space we call literature. In turning to this poetics of sameness on the level of the signifier, I describe a theory of translational equivalence that at once answers to its debt in the abstractions of capital *and* raises demanding questions by adopting literary language as its instrument of endeavor. What powers do we unlearn *and* occupy when we find equivalence in the tangles of language rather than in meaning and culture?

To write about translation theory from this angle is thus also to attune oneself to a history in which managing linguistic and cultural *meaning* has always been coupled with assigning and making *value*. A long history and future of translation may well be written as a polyphonic epic about where meaning may lie and what to do with it: transfer, decode, echo, reconstruct, interpret, multiply, relay, circulate, cannibalize, transcreate? As Maria Tymoczko argues, "The most empowering activity translators can undertake . . . is to explore and reflect upon the nature of meaning in general and the nature and role of meaning in translation in particular, thus liberating their translation practices from the false dictate to preserve meaning."[20] In other words, Tymoczko suggests that the translator is best empowered when they instead thoughtfully reckon with the very grounds of meaning—and how shifting those grounds may in turn shift the parameters of their practice. Those possible histories thus encapsulate the translator's possible relationships with meaning as the fundamental measure for their work, calling one to a necessary conviction that finding and playing with processes of signification always entails transforming them in unforeseen ways, so that such transformations are not only necessary but even indeed of *value*. Taking meaning as a loose theory of value then sheds new light on a translator's unending shuttle between the level of the word or text and their systems of language and culture.

In the same breath, rethinking meaning as value also prompts a closer examination of *how* we anchor translation in the formation of meaning, a sturdy precept of translation studies from the oldest and most conventional theories of transferring meaning to newer arguments that transform and circulate it. For even as being vested in meaning is an indispensable political and pragmatic orientation for thinking about translation, it has also sustained a deep-seated habit of thought that bears down on works of translation as exercises in failure or perpetrators of inequity. In these accounts, the inadequacies of meaning accrue normatively to the traitorous translator or—more justifiably—to the world systems of circulation and exchange in which meaning can only be progressively diluted or distorted in the drive to reconstruct it anew. To be sure, the problem with this situation is not the heuristic of meaning itself but the unequal institutions and forces of institutionalization through which it circulates and is produced. Yet those conditions continue to function in no small part by restricting what counts as translation and what operates as critique. To place meaning at the center of our critical and interpretive practices has made it difficult to recognize unintelligible modes of translation percolating in these same realms of violence and in plain sight.[21]

In this analysis, the most potent gesture may be a calculated withdrawal from relying on meaning at all. Finding the immense depths in the very smallness of this gesture has been the defining challenge and reward of writing this book. Doing so sets the stage for a striking politics of translation: a new equivalence that contests the differentiating systems of value by suspending its protocols and confounding its logics. In this reduction, I probe an unexpectedly radical implication of Gayatri Spivak's turn toward the rhetoricity or process of meaning-making in translation. For her, such a turn enables a seductive readerly identification in translation, a gendered agency that "ha[s] to turn the other into something like the self in order to be ethical."[22] Where Spivak would surrender the translator's *self* in the name of ethics, I further surrender *meaning* and suspend its processes of making in order to encode that ethical resemblance as a poetic one. In this move, I step away from the existing semantic or cultural dyads of translation defined and measured by their relation to meaning—sense-for-sense or word-for-word, freedom or fidelity, domestic or foreign, coercion or resistance, circulated or untranslated—and step toward fragments of language that align provisionally to give invisible acts of translation: a sound for a sound, a letter for a letter, or indeed an echo for an echo—a citational poetics of "incorporation without interpretation."[23] Dislodging the old thesis that translation seeks *semantic* equivalents between source and target, I uncover the muted stakes of *nonsemantic* equivalence in loose constellations of sight and sound across unassimilable worlds.

Yet where do such idealizing gambits leave you and me and those who worry that doing away with meaning as a sine qua non for the translator's craft—even doing away with the agency of the translator herself—may risk devaluing the field twice over or further disempowering translators in unforeseeable ways? To this I would suggest, perhaps a little paradoxically, that a vision of literary translation as being determined by more than any one translator's labor, intentions, or intelligence may indeed invite *more* people to locate themselves in a field that was never about *accumulating* value but always about transforming the material and epistemic conditions through which value is created and comes to be known as such. To delve into the work of translation requires a fierce commitment to knowing how the politics of language may carelessly shape us just as we carefully shape it—an agency grounded in commitment and made the more robust by a sustained confrontation with all that is out of one's hands, what cannot be controlled after all.

Such a vision—the task of working to transform the processes of value in which meanings live and are remade—then invites readers and practitioners to take seriously a counterintuitive heuristic and ethic of translation: more than intentionally cultivating meanings in a new text, the writers studied in this book narrow their worlds and even their selves into shards of language that approximate source to target, availing themselves of an literary equivalence made possible by those fuzzy habits of mind. Neither a nihilist denial of meaning nor a refusal of its worldly dimensions, translating through those dissonant harmonies of language—and even relinquishing the intentionality of the translator—turns a translator's disinheritance into the locus of her response. Unlike the lightness of power familiar from the Foucauldian paradigm, our translator inhabits a lightness of *liberation* scattered across those not so different shapes and sounds of language, enabling her to write another myth of equivalence through all its difficulties and difficult joys. Working across a geopolitical imaginary that at once prohibits and weaponizes it, I invest our inherited concept of equivalence with a renewed speculative force. To *become* the same was never the *goal* of translation; instead, and only in its lightest and stealthiest forms, sameness is an instrument for the translator's craft.

Transpacific Inheritances: A Prehistory of Literary Equivalence

The impetus for this argument lies in a transpacific age of abstraction: a crucible of translation that met the need for an ever newer literature by fusing the colonial dynamics of capital with a vivid promise of conceptual amplitude. Across the volatile history of the Sino-US sphere, flashpoints between the Chinese and English languages continue to inflect how we see translation to the present day. Writing on the transpacific literary upheavals of the twentieth century, critics have argued that this "age of translations" demanded a new vision of what it means to translate at all.[24] In the same spirit, I look at the work of Sino-US writers who take translation as a theme and formal principle for navigating their transpacific spaces across the long twentieth century, tying its work to counternormative ideas of what literature was—and what it could be. The book begins with the turn of the century, when a need to manage linguistic and cultural difference for a renewing modernity led thinkers across the Pacific to frame language as a technology of mobile fragments. As those fragments moved with and across languages—from speech to writing and back again—they became that intricate machine of poetry that caught Mr. Not So Different in its gears. As I argue, those gears continue to turn as a formal principle of transpacific translation. Later writers gravitated toward those fragments as an antihermeneutic model for translation, thereby chancing on the surprising theories of translingual translation at the heart of this book's chapters. A series of transcriptions made in error are sound translations, their echoes freighted with the vernacular politics of a home left behind. Wandering images of language are superimposed and even compressed in order to create the semblance of a translator—bringing us from concrete poetry to a concrete translation. And finally, in a long concerto of grief, a translingual fugue distributes its sounds and images to recast their abstractions as an activity of erasure, stubbornly insulating meaning from its referential possibilities and ending the argument's arc in a minor key. Together, their efforts come to define acts of translation that begin in privation, separating language from its assigned meanings in order to release *un*assigned passages of equivalence.

The transpacific is typically defined through the geopolitical construct uniting the many countries located across the Pacific Ocean, bridging Asia with the many colonial dependencies and independent nations that form the Americas, New Zealand, Australia, and the Pacific Islands. An edited collection by Janet Hoskins and Viet Thanh Nguyen offers a systematic treatment of this subfield, tracing decades of work on Pacific networks of exchange that typically (though not exclusively) adopts the methodological frameworks of area and cultural studies. As a term, however, "transpacific studies" is credited to the literary critic Yunte Huang whose work focuses on the visions of Asia that define American poetry's most provocative self-actualizations.[25] In similarly taking the Sino-US axis as a synecdoche for the geopolitical whole, my approach follows an earlier critical history with two related impulses. First, commentators sought to understand Asia beyond the paradigm of transnational capital after the financial boom of the 1980s and 1990s; further, they worked to decenter the exceptionalist narratives that drove the wars of US imperialism and especially the Cold War.[26] Closer to the present, those critical impulses have even been rendered into economic policy in the Obama-era Transpacific Partnership, a free trade bloc safeguarding US interests by providing an alternative to Chinese funding across Asia and Latin America.

At the same time, the latest preoccupations in the field suggest a wider range than its political-economic origins may imply. Scholars have increasingly sought to decolonize the Pacific by eschewing capitalism and neoliberalism as points of reference for knowledge production, affirming noncommensurability and incomparability as a bypass around the mediating reach of major powers.[27] Other critics highlight resistant and minoritarian epistemologies: from studying indigenous self-determination and Asian settler colonialism to charting solidarities for anticapitalist justice across the Global South and highlighting the dialectical immanence of intra-Asian comparison, critical accounts of the field bespeak the abundant fissures—in capitalism, emancipation, even comparative reading—shot through these transpacific worlds.

Presented as a fable of attending to language to survive within globalized conditions of industrial-capitalist cruelty, the life and world of Mr. Not So Different sits somewhere in between the two facets of this account. Moreover, his invention in 1924 would have been impossible if not for the formative decades of translation earlier undertaken by many Chinese intellectuals. Spurred to self-transformation by an ongoing discourse pathologizing China as the "sick man of Asia," they saw in translation an inexhaustible means of bringing literary tradition into modernity, offering fresh modes of historicity in the material praxis of literature.[28] For a mode of resistance against the colonial traumas of the late Qing—the multiple wars and invasions leading to the dissolution of feudalism and the 1911 revolution for the Republican era—and determined to assume an equal and greater role in the new world order, those translators sought inspiration from texts as wide ranging as abolitionist tracts and speculative fiction, domesticating the cultural power of American and other western texts with little concern about introducing significant differences in order to suit their context.[29] Their translations thereby created temporary spaces of "self-authorization," untethered to the originals, as a gesture of critique—and Mr. Not So Different would have sat amiably at the very same table hosting their collaborative and improvisatory processes of textual making.[30] For them just as for him, sameness and differences of meaning were simply less important. Yet unlike our protagonist, they elided those distinctions not because they were careless but precisely because they were so concerned with what those translations may *do* as vectors of power: the democratic cultures and national characters at stake, the readerships to be made and found, the political impulses slowly germinating, and the socialist revolution first fomented and then overturned.³¹ Self-styled proponents of *shijie zhuyi*, or *cosmopolitanism*, in the quest to look beyond the nation and establish China's place in a fractious global community, the thinkers around that table would have fully and even uncritically embraced its normative ideal.³² Yet cosmopolitanism was also more than an idea; it was an experience shaped by unprecedented encounters with the tokens of the world in cities exploding with travelers and industry, and even a higher degree of international mobility and exposure to western education due to new semicolonial schemes like the Boxer Indemnity scholarship. In these ways, Chinese cosmopolitanism may be understood as a variable set of sensibilities that are "located and embodied[,] . . . [inviting one] to measure such critical, normative power as may remain to it."³³ To adapt the terms of translation theory, one may even imagine the recent history of Chinese translation as the use of domesticating strategies with a foreignizing agenda: a cosmopolitical quest for a *political* equivalence.³⁴

The movement from a political equivalence to a *literary* and *poetic* one is far from a simple gesture. To be sure, as an apparatus of Chinese modernity, the Chinese *language* as it is known today has been constituted by transpacific translation and the cosmopolitical ambitions indexed therein.³⁵ At a time when translation was transforming the political landscape, it was translating the literary culture too. Mr. Not So Different was the creation of Hu Shi, a catalyst of the New Culture Movement whose ideas can be traced to his time studying philosophy and political science in the United States under a Boxer Indemnity scholarship, eventually mentored by the American pragmatist philosopher John Dewey.³⁶ Hu's literary experiments exemplified a movement seeking to elevate the vernacular languages of China, codify its speech, and modernize its script via western alphabetic print technology.³⁷ Hence the reliance on those untranslatable fragments of script and sound in his parable of literacy: a central prong of Hu's reformist agenda was to teach the common people—identified with Mr. Not So Different—how to read and write in the interest of progress. To loosely adapt Roman Jakobson's theory of translation, the making of the modern Chinese vernacular language may well be an unstable process of consolidating interlingual and intercultural dynamics into an *intra*lingual and *intra*cultural code beyond paraphrase.³⁸

Investing transformation in semiotic detail also has a second dimension. At the same time as Chinese intellectuals lamented a stagnant culture, their counterparts across the Pacific instead found inspiration in that ossified image, learning the lesson that Mr. Not So Different could not. Anglo-American modernists parsed ethnographic sources to forge a new ideograph from the annals of Chinese poetry, and in this phantasmal invention, they instilled a powerful contradiction: a so-called nonsignifying language would simultaneously be an unbreakable and enduring vessel of representational meaning—unbreakable because it is an abstraction that has thereby encapsulated the "concrete" essence of a new modernist poetry.[39] Some subtlety remains in debates over that translated essence and if it even deserved that name. "It is hard alone to wring song from philology," intoned Hugh Kenner in a scathing assessment of the Sinologist Arthur Waley's contemporaneous translations from the Chinese.[40] Using the classic faithful-or-free dyad, Kenner set the earliest terms of critical engagement in which the translations of his Pound era could only be castigated for not being correctly Chinese—that is, lacking in philological or ethnographic value through a positivist lens—or praised for literary value on the grounds of aesthetic judgment. Yet later critics took this problem as inherently formative, reading their intersection "not as coincidental but as causal" and crafting paradigms such as textual displacement and formal dissection to describe the force of Asian ideas in American literary history.[41] A longer afterlife may even be found in experiments of belonging across ethnic American poetry, wherein the foreignizing acts of modernist translation are reframed as resolutely domesticating gestures whose reparative aesthetic powers strain the normative borders of the American experience.[42] Across this book, the ideograph charts a similarly kinetic itinerary: from its origins in the imagistic "translucencies" of Pound to the "trans-immigration of image and memory" in the anti-indexical poetics of Theresa Cha and the fractured "transletters" of concrete poetry, its many tasks of translation across the facets of poetic language shed new light on the dictum, "Every generation must translate for itself."[43]

As even this short prehistory suggests, the *time* of equivalence is always divided. I have integrated debates on translation and literature in China and the United States into a single transpacific unit of analysis—a paradox of equivalence—without assigning priority to one over the other. Yet they create a syncopated history of their own. For this narrative could not have been a teleological one: just as networks of modernity are classically connected to a multidirectional sense of translation, Chinese modernity was not simply a *product* of transpacific encounter. Rather, as Shu-mei Shih notes, it is the torque of a false teleology requiring the self-described moderns to proleptically *assume* a future equivalence to which they would one day catch up, such that appropriating the mantle of modernity is the a priori condition for temporally grounding a historical narrative of self-development.[44] If translation represented a shock to the system, then that shock also *allows* equivalence to be posited as a goal to be reached. When considered through the historical conditions in the transpacific, any claim to equivalence must be haunted by its unfinished work and unforgettable violences. Thus, critics charge, it remains a naive and asymmetrical equivalence grounded by nothing more than a specular tautology.[45]

Few of the foregoing accounts have ever left the abstract realms of thought and discourse. Nonetheless, their thoughts and words were lived—and they exerted a powerful force throughout the history treated in this book: a tension between pathology and utopian fantasy that animated a host of transpacific intimacies and bent the shapes of translations to come. Can they help us to think that specular tautology of equivalence otherwise? In thinking about abstraction as a comparative axis for the transpacific, I seek to account for the capitalist logics of translation through *and* beyond their material and philosophical grounds. If comparison has a purpose, that moving target might just be translation. And through the test of translation, equivalence emerges for a new contestation.

Abstraction and Exception, Asia and Beyond

Abstraction has recently become a powerful diagnostic frame for critics writing on transpacific Asia and America. Understood in my argument as a conjugation of aesthetic nonrepresentation with the forces of economic and social differentiation under global capitalism, abstraction is also important for its central role in the formation of value and mystification of labor time in the Marxian analysis of capital: in this model, there can be no equivalence—indeed, no translation—without abstraction. The draw of this framework may also be explained via two critical-discursive tendencies that, for the purposes of my argument, stand in productive tension with one another: first, the centrality of labor as a biopolitical analytic for Asian presence across North America, the transpacific Americas, and the Caribbean; and second, a robust critique of particularism and exceptionalism in the theoretically inclined corners of Asian studies. Particularism is the attachment to a national or ethnic group—a work of reifying cultural and historical difference to give shape to those abstractions that we know as *Asian* or *Chinese* or *America*. Exceptionalism is the related political doctrine that holds a particular group or nation above the law and other regulative functions. Where the first critical tendency would insist on parsing the differential *effects* of capitalism's abstract power upon the lived experiences of persons through the destructive processes of racialization, the second would insist on situating and analyzing Asia and its constituents within a framework coeval with the capitalist West, suggesting that eschewing the exceptional place of Asia vis-à-vis the West—arguably the result of capitalist divisions as well—in fact paves the way for historically rigorous and theoretically refined studies of Asia and its discontents.[46] To state it in somewhat reductive terms: where transpacific Asian American studies has been historically invested in processes of subject and racial formation, Asian studies has been invested in processes of cultural formation (with all the problems that a term like *culture* may imply). Yet despite their divergent historical and intellectual contexts, I would argue that what *unites* the two critical tendencies is how both bodies of thought continue to understand abstraction as a biopolitical mode of regulating difference, resulting in an image of Asianness as an avatar of linguistic and cultural opacity fluent in global capital—the very dream of abstraction itself.

To state the point another way: the structural logics of global capitalism—accompanied by liberalism and neoliberalism—have produced a contradiction of *cultural* difference always at work in the constitution of Asian studies. Branching out from Rey Chow's observation that "the ethnic as such stands in modernity as the site of a foreignness that is produced from within privileged societies and is at once defined by and constitutive of that society's hierarchical divisions of labor,"[47] theorists like Aihwa Ong and Pheng Cheah have been especially attentive to the transnational and unevenly global dimensions of that division of labor in Asian contexts, examining the metamorphic logics of flexibility, exceptionalism, and indeed humanity under neoliberalism—always with an eye toward the vanishingly small exertions of everyday sovereignty enabled by their mutable structures.[48] In literary studies, a version of this critique may be found in a sensitive study of Chineseness at once racialized and disembodied by the economic and philosophical gears of Western modernity. In the figures of bodies that labor without pain and hypothetical mandarins whose distant lives are put at stake to ignite crises of ethics, Eric Hayot finds that the abstractions of language and capital are historically lived and dialectically alive, even undead—a series of universals "*that retain the instance in fossil form*" while continuing to exert unmeasurable force on the particulars from which they emerge.⁴⁹ In the discursive formation of Asian studies as an area of study, abstraction is the means by which the capitalist logic of value is transmuted into an epistemology of culture, marking Asia as both avatar and exception.

In working through processes of economic, social, and epistemological differentiation, the act of abstraction also thereby upholds narratives of particularism that *deny* universalism in uneven ways, enabling, in oft-cited words, "somebody's way of saying 'not yet' to somebody else."⁵⁰ The wider consequence for theorists in Chinese studies has been a critical pull toward the universal in myriad and concrete forms, motivated by an antihegemonic politics that does not wait its turn. Abstraction in this context is then not exactly totalizing but particularizing in a total fashion. Whence the cogent critique of particularism in Rey Chow's essay on the disciplinary apparatus of Chineseness, an abstract category of the nation-state under which a complex of vernacular languages and cultures has been subsumed, functioning as a tactical diversion to paradoxically ossify China's power in a formidable past, deny the conceptual power of contemporary Chinese critique, and mask the colonizing influence of the West.⁵¹ Thus it has been necessary to push back on these tendencies, as exemplified in Shu-mei Shih's method and theory of the Sinophone trenchantly refusing the claims of ethnicity. Arguing that there is no such thing as a Chinese ethnicity because of the plural ethnic groups that comprise the Chinese nation and its imperial worlds, Shih instead takes Sinitic *languages* as a frame for analyzing cultural productions on the margins of nation-states and their hegemonic claims.⁵²

The need to write such antihegemonic and concrete universalisms—what Lydia Liu theorizes as "competing universalisms" that have subsumed their particularities⁵³—sits alongside a recent turn to the decolonizing possibilities within an Asia writ a bit larger. While critics like Harry Harootunian and Arif Dirlik have influentially observed that imagining Asia has been generally undertaken from a pro-capitalist, neocolonial, and Cold War-centric American or Western point of view, it has also been an arena in which decolonizing thinkers like Kuan-Hsing Chen and Wang Hui intervene on precisely those grounds of epistemological method. For even as "Asia itself, as an object, simply doesn't exist" (being unevenly constituted by Western thought),[54] the very history of its formation also offers lines of flight that compel thinkers to "deimperialize" or "de-Americanize" that abstract theoretical creation, arguing instead for a method in which "societies in Asia can become each other's points of reference, so that the understanding of the self may be transformed, and subjectivity rebuilt."[55] This does not naively fall prey to the fallacy or fetish of a "native Asian" intelligence, which is after all still adumbrated in relation to the Western imagination. Rather, the work of decolonizing that Asian abstraction—the work of thinking *within* Asia—stems from a full-throated recognition of its dialectical and fundamentally derivative character: Asia is "at the same time colonialist and anti-colonialist, conservative and revolutionary, nationalist and internationalist, originating in Europe and shaping Europe's image of itself, closely related to visions of both nation-state and empire, a notion of non-European civilization, and a geographic category established through geopolitical relations."[56] Somewhat pace Harootunian, Asia is a little more than a discursive nothing; it was emptied when it landed in our laps already translated.

Not so coincidentally, the abstraction of the "Asiatic" has similarly been a key speculative instrument for formulating and maintaining the ethnic typologies that uphold US exceptionalism. Yet in the context of thinking through Asia in American studies, the *aesthetic* principles of abstraction as a nonrepresentational tactic also come to the fore, beginning the complex work of parsing if not resolving the contradiction of a cultural opacity fluent in global capital. Though beginning with the necessity of anticapitalist critique, close attention to the specific character of abstraction and its manifestations has nevertheless enabled a slow drift toward a reparative—and still critical, still historically active—mode of formalist reading across these contexts. Writing against the overreaching force of abstraction as a subterfuge for power as well as a transhistorical leveler, Colleen Lye explains that focusing on what she calls racial form "discloses the ways in which US colonial and race relations are marked by power's more totalizing reach and increasing abstraction in the twentieth century."[57] As Lye's book goes on to note, much of that long century took place in the long shadow of the Chinese Exclusion Act, which promulgated xenophobia against Chinese immigrants driven across the Pacific by the declining conditions of the late Qing dynasty and reduced to disposable labor and ethnic typologies.[58] At the same time, Lye also argues powerfully, via the Marxist critic Raymond Williams, for moving beyond a representational paradigm and grappling with the realization that "the formalist desires of Asian American literary criticism today are also deeply at heart historicist desires" insofar as they respond to the exhaustions of an identity-centered heuristic by embracing a materialist and historically active theory of literary form.[59] Working in the wake of Lye's argument and with a clear-eyed grasp of the violences of abstraction onto itself, Steven Yao coins the gesture of "ethnic abstraction" to explore how a nonrepresentational approach in Asian American writing may yet "transform familiar protocols of 'ethnic' signification in an effort to rethink existing conceptions of identity and difference, as well as to trouble the arrangements of power that have fostered their constitution and ongoing maintenance."[60] Taking a step beyond the Althusserian reading of Marx, abstraction is at once a situated *and* systematic formalism, inflected by the materialist mechanics of dialectical critique so that it is neither purely destructive nor simply salutary.[61]

Given its contextual motility and explanatory power, abstraction is a mode of reductive *and* historically active formalism that retains the scars of history and whose laws govern the material world—whence the Marxian formulation of a *concrete* abstraction fashioned from the dialectical methods of materialism. To understand abstraction as itself a clustering of concrete particularities has far-reaching implications for my account of equivalence, which aims to conceptualize it beyond the signifying differentiations of meaning and its cognate in value. In a helpful extension of Colleen Lye's insight on the growing abstraction of power, Iyko Day further "defines social differentiation [including the production of racial difference] as a form of destructive abstraction anchored by a settler colonial ideology of romantic anticapitalism."[62] The all too attractive ideology of "romantic anticapitalism," the key diagnostic term for Day's argument, begins by divorcing the sensual and concrete thing from the abstractions of capitalism—and the particular from the universal—in an often well-intended misreading of the Marxian method. Unfortunately, that antinomy of romantic anticapitalism does not so much dismantle capitalism as enable its ongoing mystification, especially by erasing the socially necessary labor time that creates value and defines the dual nature of the commodity. More than that, persistently framing abstraction as *separate* from social life may drive its lethal manifestation in the social *deaths* that inhibit racialized persons from being recognized as persons rather than labor. By identifying Asian migrant labor *solely* as abstract labor when triangulating Asian life with Black and Indigenous death under the logic of settler colonialism—Day's comparative study argues—the logic of romantic anticapitalism drives Asian labor ever deeper into the value-making machine of capital, rendering Asian humanity and personhood unthinkable outside the labor function.

And there is more. By comparing the *indisposability* of African American labor to the *disposability* of Asian American labor in the settler colonial paradigm, Day's framework changes the terms of Lisa Lowe's argument that the abstraction of the Chinese migrant names an epistemic crisis and failed connection to the forms of violence from which it has emerged.[63] Instead, focusing on settler logic reveals that the abstraction of Chinese migrant labor possesses a kinetic and unpredictable force of mutability that—in contradistinction to the death-bound experiences of African American and Indigenous lives under settler colonialism—turns out to align the Asian alien with capital. In a twist of the model minority knife, Asianness emerges as what she calls a "new Jewishness" in which Asianness is not death-bound precisely because, in its abstraction, it is *developable*, indeed translatable into something else.

Such is the intellectual context and political power of understanding Asia as at once subject and object of abstraction. While the scope of this book means that it cannot with any intellectual honesty be seen as decolonizing our paradigms of abstraction and translation, its argument may nevertheless position the transpacific as a would-be translation of a derivative and dialectical understanding of "Asia" and that (also but not equivalently derivative) political exception named "America." To move from the end of the "American century" into the rise of the "Pacific century"—the yellow peril that has again come, this time from the future, to steal yet another American lunch[64]—is after all only a claim of false equivalence if one accepts that the two were different to begin with. Given the critiques rendered thus far, that argument is less tenable: at least at the level of abstraction on which these terms are operating, they are instead nonexceptional apparitions of the very same capitalist order. Via the heuristics of translation studies, I take seriously the ethicopolitical ramifications of treating China as a synecdoche of Asia and the US-China relation as a catachresis for the broader transpacific: what might it mean to imagine a nation not as complete unto themselves but as an original incomplete without translation, whose very exception and dominance thereby *demands* translation into something else? Through the agile thinking of translation, I attend to the ideological trope of the Pacific century not to rehabilitate it but to operationalize what Hoskins and Nguyen call its "change of tactics" toward the complexity of a transpacific Asia in which dyadic narratives of global power have never fully obtained.[65]

Unlearning a Literary Epistemology of Value

Which brings us right back to where we began. What kind of a thing is that linguistic, aesthetic, political, and economic phenomenon called translation—and how does it fit in this narrative of abstraction, antiexceptionalism, and transpacific labor? Once again, the familiar tale of Mr. Not So Different may help light a path through these questions from his particular place and time circa Republican-era China. After all, the story sacrifices his life to secure a sure-footed literary epistemology of meaning-value: his lazy eye and lazy tongue at once index a lazy nation *and* make us more competent and observant close readers whenever we too may have to go to a bank, catch a train, call for a doctor, or be anything more than lazy people who settle too easily. Its false choices and faulty equivalences are consistently framed and *enabled* by an abstracting logic of semiotic detail, tying its little Taylorist moral to those very literary achievements of cultural and linguistic translation across the transpacific world. Transposed into a minor key, the fable may even hint at the gallows humor of a neoliberal program to come: pragmatism is wielded like a whip, and compromise is rewarded by a menu of small ways to suffer and/or to die. Within the diegetic and ideological frame of the story, the character as we know him simply cannot survive.

Yet survive his spirit does—in the peculiar poetic equivalences that may well enable a translator to play a central role in *unlearning* the violences that attend any gesture of abstraction. To do so is to hew to a strange proposition: a translation with no value, a translation that functions at the limits of translation. Perhaps one of its virtues is that it cannot easily fall into the romantic trap of an anticapitalist capitalism rooted in sensuous particularity as critiqued in Day's account: after all, the project of any translation is to hold multiple levels of concretion and abstraction together—be it from word to meaning or from sense to sense or indeed from sense to person. More than that, an important precept of my argument is that one cannot rely on the process of translation to recognize and distinguish those levels that separate word from meaning or culture or person: the curious effect of the new equivalence I am describing here is to *collapse* the concrete into the abstract, and the abstract into the concrete, especially when trading in the name of poetic writing. Because of this insecure distinction between concretion and abstraction, abstraction does not function in my argument as translation's "third term" between source and target to offer a mediating equivalence that can only be in the realm of simulacra, as is often diagnosed in anticapitalist and anticolonial critiques of equivalence. That is, I am not arguing that translation is a passage from one concrete reality to the abstract realm of the ideal and back again to yet another concrete real—which after all tacitly replicates the conventional model of meaning transfer. Rather, I seek to deepen and multiply the abstract character of translation, understanding its (nontemporally) pre-signifying frame as a feature rather than a bug. Each situated abstraction I pursue in this book then necessarily relies on how and why they take place: in each case I think with *and* against the problematics it encodes.

Abstraction also supplies a clarifying heuristic for approaching recent work in translation studies, giving a name to anecdotal and pervasive anxieties about how actual translations, real translating, or working translators do or do not appear across the range of our archives and approaches, imagining the object of knowledge in translation studies as alternately only producer, product, and process. While the surfacing or suppression of translations legible and intelligible as such may at first suggest the timeworn contest between an aesthetic and ahistorical formalism versus cultural studies and its ideology critique (to which cultural translation and intersemiotic adaptations are sometimes assimilated in order to be dismissed in favor of translations proper),[66] I would suggest instead that translation is operating at plural and divergent planes of abstraction across the field of translation studies—and serves to mediate across those differentiated levels in this book as well. A reader alert to translation in its abstract dimensions may then ask, What makes a translation intelligible as such? What renders a translation into an object for knowing? Are the conditions obscuring my view of a translation a set of material conditions, epistemic conditions, both, or yet else? If the hand and labor of the translator is not visible, does that mean that there is no translation? And how indeed do we move from that subject called *the translator* to its active work of *translating* and only then to the abstract noun *translation*?[67] To be sure, thinking about translation without translators may fall prey to a historical tendency to deny translators their due in both material and conceptual terms—and certainly, the argument I am making here should not be taken as a call to stop that work of restitution around which much of the field of translation studies is centered and in which many working translators have gained much hard-won ground on the frontlines (and from which, it should be said, I myself have professionally benefited by being hired as an academic specialist in the field). Yet the idea that there must therefore be no translation outside of the intentional hand of the translator—that it simply would not be translation—is another thing altogether, no longer a counter-gesture of reparation that rises to meet a long forgetting but a mystifying reification of a new rule that regulates intelligibility: in other words, it is not so much a category confusion as it is a rigidity of the category itself—and a rigidity that I would argue should be undone.

Focusing on the striated possibilities of abstraction in the transpacific context further invites a wider reassessment of a long-standing division in translation studies between literary and cultural translation—a division founded historically on long-standing disciplinary assumptions about literature and cultural studies. That distinction too operates in part through increasingly unstable *objects* of translation, calling attention to its bounds and limits: am I translating a poem, the Bible, an old photograph, a ship's ledger, democracy writ small and large, a colonized self?[68] In each example, translation becomes more difficult to recognize let alone produce, requiring ever deeper critical excavation and remediation. In this account, the cultural translation of persons and ideas may *seem* to operate on levels of abstraction beyond the poetic or literary. Yet one precept of this argument is that detail is abstract, too: when translation works in close reading, we are *already* in the realm of abstraction typified by what Pound calls the "luminous detail," never far away from the ship's ledger or colonized self.[69] Contra Pound, however, I would suggest that detail does not have to be luminous—that is, ideationally far-reaching and transhistorical—to be historically active: instead, thinking with abstraction may also "ask us to conceive of details more broadly and more variously as those parts of the text, of potentially any scale or size, that seem prosaic, beneath notice, or simply mechanical," to borrow Rebecca Walkowitz's helpful invitation to what she calls "close reading at a distance."[70] The array of forces named by the term *abstraction* renders an inchoate world *available* for recognition and translation: its overdetermination as at once a condition of thought, modality of aesthetic power, site of contradiction, and metacognitive possibility exerts a volatile power that needs to be carefully parsed and rigorously described.

Arc of Chapters

To those ends, I look at translators and writers animated by a paradox: how reducing transpacific life to the abstractions of literary writing does not erase worldly conditions but instead sharpens their consequences. Contrary to the term's definition, it is not only possible but indeed important to speak precisely about abstraction and its effects: it dehumanizes, captures, measures, rationalizes, disciplines, and exerts other untellable vectors of force on its many objects in ways that exceed intention or individual calculation. As I have argued in the context of translation, these forces are at work in the making and shaping of meaning through the political economies of translation. Contesting the translator's relationship to that meaning—and its cognate, value—is the task of the chapters that follow. While this introduction foregrounds the central theoretical project, that argument has been derived through the process of writing and reading for these chapters—and listening for *their* paradigms of equivalence in which meaning is an accident waiting to happen and value may never materialize. By embedding the relationship between meaning and nonmeaning in contingent *and* abstract practices of assignation and recognition, my turn to abstraction is not a turn to or from meaning per se; rather, it is a turn from hermeneutic praxes of translation that retain meaning as a sine qua non for equivalence. What I seek to leave the reader with is not a prescription on *whether* one *should* think with terms like *meaning* and *value*—a prescription that would itself be indebted to Orientalist and colonial logics—but how momentarily thinking without that banister helps one to describe new or hitherto illegible dimensions for the open question of equivalence.

The book's arc is formed in two broad moves. The first is concentrated in the opening chapter, where I ground my sense of translation in a twentieth-century history and theory of abstraction tying the Chinese language with the English language and Asia to the United States. Under the sign of abstraction, that first comparative move brings together two counterpoints of transpacific translation, vernacular speech (sound) and ideographic writing (image), arguing that these sites of translation and translingual practice serve as the locus for theorizing a politics of formal resemblance. The argument's second move then takes up sound and image as conceptual resources for the next three chapters. Taken as a whole, they organize a starting heuristic for a radical literary translation—a set of proposals for what to do with an equivalence of formal resemblance, using the unlikely tools inherited from our transpacific context. Looking at three writers compelled by circumstance to live between places and in translation across the Pacific, the chapters probe their entanglements with the aesthetics of abstraction, unfurling translations coiled around the untranslatable flesh of language—formal likenesses that only loosely wear the marks of origin, language, and identity without following through to any recognizable cultural meaning. Where the writers treated in the opening chapter use resemblance to *preserve* the cross-cultural and national differences (that is, value formation) uniting their respective projects, these later writers instead use those same resemblances to speculatively engage—misdirect, contain, mitigate, eliminate—the violent processes of differentiation within which they find themselves. If their acts of translation and retranslation are seen as *subsuming* the realities of social differentiation, then that subsumption still does not homogenize experience but stanches the wounds of an exceptionalist and ethnocentric world. Equivalences are to be found not so much in codes or *systems* of target languages or receiving cultures, but in the wreckage of those systems and unlikely acts of salvage.

After the introduction establishes the conceptual questions guiding this argument, the first chapter goes on to catalog the historical intersections and literary materials grounding its claim. Literature and poetic writing are the terrain on which old equivalences were mapped *and* newer equivalences may be shifted and gleaned. But how and why did this come to be? In the chapter, I examine how the didactic efforts and literary theories of two men—the American Sinologist and ambassador Ernest Fenollosa and the architect of Chinese modernity Hu Shi—set crucial precedents for reforming their respective literary traditions and found vital sounding boards that aligned the intellectual and material history of Chinese writing with the founding ideals of modernist poetics. While Fenollosa's essay *The Chinese Written Character as a Medium for Poetry* was a well-known touchstone for Ezra Pound and later commentators on modernist translation, the surprise of the chapter is the delicate resonance between his theories of nature and empiricism—as embodied in ideographic thinking—and the literary theory of Hu Shi, advocate of the Chinese *baihua* or *plain speech* vernacular movement whose Mr. Not So Different opened this introduction. Hu was one of few Chinese thinkers who came to be directly interested in the reformatory possibilities represented by Anglo-American modernist poetics, as recorded in his essays on language reform and diaries as a Boxer scholar in the 1910s.

The chapter's readings contest the conventions of the ideograph as a word picture of nature or the visual bearer of meaning, finding in its antechambers a series of unexpected technologies of translation that thread Hu's self-named "poeticempiricism" [*sic*] with Fenollosa's lost insistence on the diachronic character of the ideograph as a kinetic allegory for transpacific relation. The interest of this technology of translation lies in its *fleeting* relationship to meaning: in their concordant efforts to "bring language very close to things,"[71] or even to infuse speech into writing to develop a backwater language and culture beyond its property of *youyinwuzi* or *sound without writing*, both Fenollosa and Hu must paradoxically break language down into its abstract dimensions. Their arguments thus afford two concrete abstractions explored in the remainder of the book, forming the basis of my newer sense of equivalence: (i) the concept of speech (sound) as a natural given and the driver of ideological change toward vernacular writing; and (ii) the contested writing of the ideograph (image), understood as an *arranged* complex of ideas that visualize their inconsistencies and even contradictions. The chapter anchors this argument in the granular transformations of a modernism that was always on the move and in circulation: whereas the myth of ideographic thinking is typically seen as the catalyst for a renewed modernist emphasis on *writing* as the concrete and enduring dimension of language, that idea is translated across the Pacific as an emphasis on *speech* as a similarly natural and unmediated resource in the quest to realign the future power and cultural capital of China in the world. In developing the chapter's key concept, abstraction, through an iterative conversation between the two thinkers, I finally elicit the paradox at stake in the book's transpacific and comparative framework: how an untranslatable poetics of sound and image directly participates in the relay translation of literary modernity across the Pacific.

If the opening move of the first chapter is to imagine the crafting of equivalence *as* capital and value formation, then the next three chapters go on to narrate the heart of this book's claim: to argue for a poetics beyond meaning and value in the writing of an equivalence with fewer ontological connections to capital. As the first chapter argues, the untranslatable elements of writing do not sit out of the game of translation but rather are an enabling force in its formation. In the wake of their invisible logic, how may a sound or arrangement translate at all—let alone create arcs and abysses of equivalence? How may this book's propositions be set into motion? The three chapters each develop an argument on equivalence in unlikely quarters: the substitution of sounds in the second chapter, the compositional arrangements of image in the third chapter, and, finally, in the fourth chapter, commingling sound with image to force a vanishing of meaning-value in the midst of translation.

The second chapter finds Hu's ideas tellingly transformed over the course of Eileen Chang's late career, tracing an aesthetic of translingual modernism to glean her politics of translation. Held as one of China's great modern writers, the lifelong bilingual Chang began to take a serious interest in translation after she left mainland China in 1952, writing for the United States Information Service (USIS) first in Hong Kong and then in the United States. Although she stopped her work for the USIS after several years, Chang would continue to live and write in Los Angeles for the final forty years of her life. This chapter focuses on her lesser-studied essays, translations, and correspondence written after her move abroad. Where critics working on this later period tend to focus on the propagandistic realism or aesthetic complications of her English-language writing and translations in the Cold War context, I instead recover a lively kinship between that same US-based turn to translation and the earlier Republican-era interest in vernacular writing.

Departing from poetry, I extend the first aspect of transpacific abstraction—*speech and sound* as they guide the vernacular reform of writing—to Chang's casual habits of sound translation throughout her late reflections on vernacular language reform. The chapter begins by situating those reflections within her two translations of an innovative late Qing novel from its vernacular Shanghainese Wu into standardized Mandarin Chinese (1981) and English (unfinished in her lifetime), with Hu Shi as an important interlocutor in this project. Yet evasively marked by Chang with a conjugation of reading as not-reading, her mercurial approach to these translations theorize a striking break from a long tradition of translation as an act of exegesis or careful parsing. In this light, I then turn to other short essays written in the United States in which Chang mediates between those three languages by lighting on disembodied sounds that substitute one word for another with no attention to their semantic relations. Through accent and accident, these translingual encounters create often humorous (and sometimes bathetic) results across her essays and translations, producing dissociative calques of sameness and substitution that echo across memories of her childhood, adult, and exilic homes. In her hands, a distantly remembered sound of a street vendor's cry—analogized to the radio that plays across the city in every home—comes to hallucinate a translating harmonium rendered through the forgetting of his body. Elsewhere, a misheard, misread, and misbegotten transcription of an archaic Wu word in one of her screenplays sets her off to obsess over a vernacular philology that may or may not even exist. These examples see Chang departing from the conventional view of sound translation as a minor avant-garde curiosity, which status as translation lies in question because its ludic approaches are seldom semantically driven. No less ludic and at times even funnier, Chang's sound translations ultimately emerge as a nostalgic force that confronts the linguistic sediment of her transpacific exile. Compelled by her equivalences of substituted sound, I take a closer look at those antihermeneutic sparks of language that may yet take shape as translation.

Where the second chapter examined sound translation as a political vector, the third chapter looks to its twin in language—a seemingly counterintuitive *concrete* translation in the transmedial work of the Korean American artist and writer Theresa Hak Kyung Cha. Born in Korea and having migrated to the United States at the age of thirteen in 1963, Cha was an avant-garde Berkeley-educated performance artist and writer who left behind a small corpus of art and writing on her untimely death in 1982. Critics have read her expansive and most influential work, *Dictée* (1982), as a sharp rebuke to any possibility of translational equivalence, most often citing its scene of colonial pedagogy in the titular French dictation exercise requiring translation from French to English. To make sense of its set-piece sequence, one must compare two parts of the bilingual text to detect its differences. That is to say, *Dictée*'s rebuke relies on positioning the reader in an actively hermeneutic pose, adopting the text's aphasic voice as a participatory heuristic necessary for reading its doomed translations at all. It is through these differentiations that Cha emphasizes the opaque yet remediating role of language in the struggle that is translation: a nonrepresentational stage of critique that can only approximate the dissociative loss of identity for a feminine colonial subject.

Perhaps because translation is typically understood in a linguistic and hermeneutic register, critics have not yet connected Cha's critiques of translation to her visual and process-based artwork outside of *Dictée*. Intriguingly, however, Cha's very earliest meditations on translation were intended for a visual medium and indeed provide striking counterpoints to the hermeneutic modes of reading demanded by *Dictée*. In this light, the chapter recasts the stakes of equivalence and translation in her work by looking at her minor poetry, performance art, notebooks, and diaries before returning, with fresher eyes, to a reading of *Dictée*. In proposing this argument, I am partially drawing on the principles of concrete poetry, the avant-garde movement from 1950s Brazil.[72] Practitioners of concrete poetry typically emphasize the visual, typographical, or other nonlinguistic and nonsemantic arrangements of writing (e.g., a poem about a mouse with its words arranged in the shape of a mouse's tail), stretching the nonsignifying limits of language into an instrument of formal possibility—and in the process exploding the poetic conventions inherited from Eurocentric and colonial pasts. By fully investing meaning in the abstractions of form, concrete poetry inherits the ideographic fantasy of words as pictures of things—but with a newfound awareness of its mediated and mediating role. While Cha does not directly reference concrete poetry (as is consistent with her anticitational and antidocumentary practices),[73] its influence on her many objets d'art is abundantly clear. Her innovation extends the principles of concrete poetry—attention to how a poem is arranged on the page—toward an anticognitive theory of translation and equivalence. Of particular interest is what she sees as an early inspiration for *Dictée*: an unfinished documentary about Korea that she titled *White Dust from Mongolia*, imagined as a (nonconventional) cultural translation for a US audience. The broken measures of *Dictée* look different in Cha's earlier planning notes for *White Dust*, in which her translators' images and voices are to be "superimposed" on one another so as to be distinct yet virtually interchangeable. Similar arrangements of near-sameness are peppered throughout Cha's earlier work, from a singular body incrementally riven by time in her poetry to a video-poem recounting two time zones on either side of the Pacific overlaid on a long shot of an unchanging plane window. None of these minor translating functions look anything *like* translations, yet their very arrangements lay bare the labor time that underwrites translation. Finally returning to *Dictée*,

I examine the textual placing of a pseudo-ideographic Chinese-English translation that keeps source and target nineteen pages apart with no clear explanation—finding in this textual crux a concrete translation that quietly but actively restricts the recognition of meaning within translation.

Far from happening in isolation from one another, homophonic and concrete strategies converge and interact in translations unguided by meaning. The fourth and final chapter returns to poetry and poetics to present a stringent test for the arguments of the foregoing chapters, transposing their ideas for an exilic epic by the contemporary Chinese-language poet Yang Lian. A lifelong dissident who had been barred from mainland China after the 1989 Tiananmen protests, Yang has only recently returned to the mainland after a long period of exile in New Zealand and Europe. Often identified as a member of the *menglong pai* or *Misty school*, so named for their often-obscure writing, Yang is especially known for his demandingly abstract style, balanced by a willingness to explain his work in essayistic commentaries. Moreover, critics have looked to translations of Yang's work into English as themselves exemplary of the wider challenges of literary translation writ large. For these reasons, he is often cited as a proponent of a world poetry that inherits and transforms Ezra Pound's tradition, calling into question the borders between national languages through the power of poetry.

Building on these critical arguments as well as Lydia Liu's concept of translingual practice, the final chapter recasts the transpacific abstractions of the first chapter as an intricate thought of translingual *erasure*, which Yang develops via a harmophonic and visually driven poetics. Writing on the occasion of his long poem *Tongxinyüan* (1997; lit., "circles with the same heart") being translated into English as *Concentric Circles* (2005) by Brian Holton and Agnes Chan, Yang draws a surprising connection between that English translation of his own work and Yunte Huang's Chinese translation of Ezra Pound's *Pisan Cantos* (1998). Both Pound and Yang are poets of *shishi* or *epics*—a genre that traditionally compounds *history*, or *shi* in the third tone, with *poetry*, *shi* in the first tone. Yet for Yang, Pound's epic is not one of history but of *erasing* its epistemological dimensions in order to arrive at another truth already contained therein: as he writes, "the *Cantos* is not an *epic*, i.e. a poem about history, but on the contrary, it aptly uses *shi*, poetry to efface the fantasies of *shi*, history," and here Yang most especially has in mind its diachronic relationship to *time*, *shi* in the second tone.[74] This insight sets the stage for Yang's provocation that the Chinese translation of the *Cantos*—and implicitly his long poem as well—both inherits and *replicates* that Poundian erasure: more than that, because of the Eurocentric commonplace that the Chinese language has no linguistic tense, he even argues that Pound's desire for a "timeless" *Cantos* is "completed" by the Chinese *Cantos*. In this chapter, I raise the stakes of such an erasure translation through its implied identification with Yang's own *Circles*, which persistently returns to an unspecified leitmotif of *sizhe* or *the dead*. Written in the wake of Tiananmen, Yang's translingual erasure conjures a politics of death and survival that demands concerted questioning of what it means to write in the Chinese language. The chapter's set piece examines how sound and image come to mirror and translate one another in poetic signification, looking at Yang's sensitive work with the quasi-ideographic possibilities in the character that may be translated as either *poem* or *poetry*. In his hands, its possibilities are dissected for an epic of political grief: the word is a composite of several radicals meaning speech, soil, inch; as well, it is a homophone for a long "disappearance" borne out across the long poem, sounding a persistent monument for the life of the dead. Tarrying with the transpacific abstractions with which we began, the chapter transforms the untranslatable elements of poetic form into a translingual elegy, resurrecting the ghosts of equivalence, culling its dispossessing foundations, and salvaging the forms by which it may yet survive.

Finally, the conclusion generalizes the argument for an equivalence beyond value made throughout the book, positioning the broader argument within existing theoretical debates in translation studies and comparative literature, and with a special focus on postcolonial critiques of equivalence and the recent turn to untranslatability. Yet this is only the final step in a long process of earning the claims at the heart of this book. In building the chapters, I have sought to reconstruct and refine the theoretical insights at the heart of each enigmatic moment I read, refraining as far as possible from introducing any conceptual grids of intelligibility that do not come from the author or the required secondary literature. In these immanent readings, each chapter has its own timbre, each inviting a sea change in your and my minds about what we can be and do in translation. In a book about sameness, the last thing I want to do is elide the *contingencies* of their sameness, for it is attending to that contingency that allows this new equivalence and its unexpected sameness to shimmer as brightly as it does. Each author is at once a translator *and* a theorist of translation who thinks rigorously in their own lexicon yet also beyond the immediate confines of their life and writing, promising a radiant particularity that shines its light beyond itself. How does that light fall on the fields of translation studies and comparative literature, and what shadows might it carve out? The conclusion finally stands as a metacognitive reflection for the methods and domains that produced *this* equivalence, recasting the argument as an open heuristic for a new epistemology of translation.

In returning to equivalence, I have been committed to the totality of that inheritance, the density of its conceptual formation, how it gathers—without unifying—several historical origins into an ungainly matrix: the violations of colonial ways of knowing, the metamorphic re-creation of meaning, the positing of abstract value, the circulation of exchange, the joyful and cruel contingencies of encounter. And these contradictions take shape around a lacuna still held to be axiomatic: the categorical impossibility of a *poetics* of equivalence—echo for echo a transformative yoking of sounds, forms, and textures across different languages that begin to look and sound the same. In that space—there where a translator may lose herself—is where this book lives. By relinquishing that axiom and writing its impossibility into being, and in asking what happens when we actively reduce our field of attention to the level of literary language and the signifier, I seek in the end not to contest materialist critiques of equivalence but to confront the persistent closeness of our textual involvements—a closeness that goes by the name of *abstraction*.

1   Transpacific Abstraction

Modernism's Abstraction: Equivalence as Capital

Thus far, I have outlined the theoretical and political stakes of a new equivalence compelled by poetic fragments of language. These fragments at once encode their meaning-value—that is, they are themselves produced by abstraction as a conceptual process—while suggesting alternate arrangements beyond meaning and its dialectical economy of semantic accumulation. Translating with attention to those fractured pieces of sameness—with all the imprecision implied therein—would seem to fly in the face of foundational assumptions in translation studies and literary theory, both of which take difference as a crucial predicate for thinking about language and its embodied politics. Yet such an approach may still tune in to quieter forms of entanglement that themselves participate in the work of translation. Abstraction makes language at once imprecise and supple, creating schematic likenesses that parse and translate the facets of "Chinese writing" into a literary and political modernity for its stakeholders across the Pacific.[1]

In this chapter, I assemble a comparative archive for the book's framing account of abstraction: a theory and technology of translation at the turn of the century principally exemplified by two writers who aligned Chinese writing with modernist poetics—and who in the process formalized the means by which the abstractions of literary equivalence acquired the semblance of cultural capital. The first touchstone is Ernest Fenollosa, an American expatriate art historian and Sinologist who wrote the influential *Chinese Written Character as a Medium for Poetry* (*CWC* henceforth; manuscript dated around 1906). After Fenollosa's death, his manuscript was edited and installed in literary history by Ezra Pound in the service of Pound's own project of modernist translation around 1914–16. Alongside Fenollosa's essay, I examine the literary theory and experiments of Hu Shi, a reformist advocate of the Chinese *baihua* vernacular movement in the 1920s—and one of few Chinese thinkers who was directly interested in the reformatory possibilities represented by the free verse of Anglo-American modernist poetics, recorded in his diaries as a student at Cornell and Columbia in the 1910s. Through close readings comparing the theories of linguistic and cultural confrontation at work in this transpacific archive, I argue that their translations divide *and* unify speech with writing—and sound with image—to authorize the ideological formations shaping a Sino-US transpacific politics of translation.

Even at this early point in the argument, alert readers may observe that my articulation of transpacific abstraction bears some resemblance to contemporaneous accounts of modernism. Indeed, any account of literary vernacular reform in China may well seem all too easily assimilable to what is by now an old saw, that "what we call artistic or aesthetic 'modernism' essentially corresponds to a situation of incomplete modernization."[2] To be sure, the most canonical instantiations of Anglo-American and European modernism have been historically tied to the aesthetic principles of abstraction qua antirealist and antirepresentational modes of writing, amply treated in earlier moments by eminent critics of poetry such as Charles Altieri and Charles Bernstein, who were influenced by the visual art of the same moment as curated by the art theorist Clement Greenberg.[3] A later generation of critics variously sought to understand how abstract experimentalism afforded tactics to evade the protocols of racial inscription and ethnic intelligibility themselves generated in an age of abstraction, which in recent years has become a special preoccupation for theorists working in Black studies, such as Fred Moten, Stephen Best, and the art critic Darby English.[4] At the same time, recent work attending to the transnational and global origins of that modernism has looked to translation and its circulatory modes of production, finding in them a critical vector for a metamorphic field with a rich archive. Critics like Rebecca Walkowitz, Marjorie Perloff, and Jacob Edmond have repositioned the *longue durée* of modernism—including its poetic principles of abstraction, translation, and iterability—as it bleeds into contemporary practices in experimental avant-garde writing and new media across the globalizing world.[5] As Walkowitz presciently asks, what happens if we take for granted that "translation is not incidental or secondary" to the contemporary world literature that she calls *born translated* but rather is "a condition of their production"?[6] Written as a diagnosis of the present, Walkowitz's words nevertheless offer a precise articulation of the past and lingering conditions of a Chinese modernity predicated on cosmopolitan ambition. For Edmond too, such an ethos of affirming and recouping the so-called derivative can easily be read back into the earliest moments of modernism.[7] Building on these arguments that dispatch with notions of authorial origin and originality, my argument affirms their collective insight that working in a modernist idiom compels one to recognize the ways in which that name was always distributed far and wide, such that "copying and mimetic desire are not signs of non-Western derivativeness but qualities shared equally by non-Western and Western modernism."⁸

Why then treat modernism under a different name, and why embed it in the transpacific dimensions of abstraction? Even as my argument displaces *modernism* for *abstraction* qua aesthetic principle of capital and a close kin of US imperialism, my intention is not so much to dispatch with the former as it is to disclose the questions dormant in the latter—in other words, to diagnose the uncanny kinships knitting the two terms together. Embedding my discussion of abstraction in a transpacific literary theory takes seriously the spirit of Fredric Jameson's oft-cited hypothesis that "the structure of imperialism also makes its mark on the inner forms and structures of that new mutation in literary and artistic language to which the term modernism is loosely applied," up to and including his corollary insight that those literary forms and structures are everywhere elastic and themselves mutate along with the restructuring of our existing political formations.⁹ Writing a more capacious theory of translation shadows two cruxes of modernist translation—the aesthetic economies of circulation and the epistemic and representational anxieties of the ideograph—with ever more severe and often cruel forms that come into sharper view under the name of abstraction. In cataloging some moments of equivalence *as* capital—and in locating them at the heart of the modernist aesthetic project—I trace a global modernism defined by neither origin nor identity nor circulation but by the translating logics of exceptionalism, ethnic typology, and manufactured futures that shape our transpacific economy of abstraction.

The Ideograph and the Ideologue

In a more affirmative register, taking seriously the formative work of abstraction may also enable, in Andrea Bachner's helpful formulation, "the freeing of the Chinese writing system from any burden of cultural essence or purity."¹⁰ Bringing these two translators into a conceptual room together may indeed seem to promise just such an impure surprise lurking around the dialectical bend. On the one hand, to compare a writer closely associated with the modernist invention of ideographic reading with a contemporaneous author of the ideology of China's New Culture Movement might well be taken as positing a flattening equivalence between the two—an apologia for Fenollosa's liberties or a naive assertion of the power of appropriating Western thought for Chinese reform that Hu had overestimated in his own lifetime.[11]

Yet the equivalences they forge are far from flattening. Perhaps the most striking convergence between Fenollosa's and Hu's accounts of language—and the primary motivation for my comparative treatment of their work—is their common attraction to an inchoate and often contradictory sense of empiricism as a resource for their new linguistic orders formed through translation. Reading Hu and Fenollosa together finds and permits some surprising frictions within those differentiating structures of value cast throughout their work as "natural," that is, philosophically given and ideologically fraught. In this analysis, the consonance between the two writers rather serves to deepen and even ossify the aporias of sound and image that frame my account of poetic equivalence. Some of this surprising convergence may well be attributed to a common interest in American pragmatism however tenaciously or loosely held,[12] or indeed their shared but bifurcating interest in Buddhism as an aggregative force for the work of cross-cultural translation. For Fenollosa, the Buddhist reconciliation of nihilism with a commitment to the systemic nature of material life paved the way toward the restless yet integrative ontology so central to his poetics,[13] whereas Hu's complicated takes on Buddhism were continually tied to his nationalist concerns for the development of Chinese history.[14] The many possible causes of their convergence become meaningful most especially for its future effects. Hu's ideas took shape via Pound's and Amy Lowell's accounts of imagism, vorticism, and the "direct treatment" of "the thing" in its "natural state" exemplified in the ideograph,[15] leading him to become especially taken by what he coined as a "poeticempiricism" in reforming the Chinese language to privilege the vernacular.[16] In both thought and practice, this claim of empiricism not only triangulated the imaginary relationship between the self and the foreign, but would even be the catalyst of political progress. More than a trope of colonial ethnography seeking to define the uncultured other, or even the deconstructive insight of finding the foreign lodged unknowably within the self, nature functioned for both Hu and Fenollosa as the future-oriented promise of a radical modernity: a fantastically unmediated engagement with what they both idealized, with nuance and variation, as the "language of man."

That is to say: in both of their accounts, nature affords a literary theory of equivalence. This chapter represents the opening move in my book's project to rethink translation's general orientation toward meaning and value: to locate equivalence not in meaning and its related structures of value but at least partially in what Christopher Bush—critically diagnosing the force of Western-invented China—has called the abstraction of meaning into "the parasemantic dimensions of language: its gestural volume, its performative effects or inscriptive force, its iconic glamour, mimetic charge, or mute persistence,"[17] and indeed a version of what Bachner (writing about French theory's Chinese example of the 1960s) calls "a symptom of a profound turn in thought: the reworking of signification under the sign of death."[18] To be clear, I am not arguing that one ought to uncritically adopt the ideographic mythos for thinking about translation, or that it should be ventriloquized through non-Western voices. Rather, I follow Bush and Bachner in provincializing the— as it turns out largely European—modes of quasi-universal literary theory and modernist aesthetics that have grown out of the ideographic imaginary. What Bush helpfully captures as the ideograph's paradoxical history-of-never-being-able-to-become-historical—that is, its persistent shuttering by European thought in the European prison of ideational abstraction—is, *because* of that cumulative history, far from reversible in simple terms. To the contrary, at stake in the ideograph and its Orientalist mythology is an irresolvable contradiction, compelling us to undertake "an analysis of how Western modernism used Chinese writing to figure modernity's simultaneous demystification and magical estrangement of language: language's reduction to a reified, almost technical medium, on the one hand, and the revelation of its material being in an explosion of textures, tones, and shapes, on the other."[19] A technocratic reduction of language *and* its hyper-specified and hyper-embodied materialization, each subsuming and interrupting the other: this is the derivative contradiction that I build on in thinking about abstraction as a technology of translation. As a contradiction, it is neither reversible nor resolvable but simply *repeatable in another context*. For if the deconstructive and Eurocentric exception of the ideograph is caught up in its meta-dialectical character—provincial *and* universal, partial *and* totalizing, charged with meaning *and* only meaningful when illegible, "Chinese" *and* European *and* "the fundamentals of all aesthetics"—then my thought, stated bluntly for now, is that a comparison of the European-provincial ideograph via its Chinese translation may (ironically) bring out the dynamism at the heart of translation and how uncertain that concept may be—and the ways in which its "transletters" may well continue to signify after all.[20]

In short, the ideograph—in only this regard akin to the Chinese language it represented without recognition—was never dead or invested in metaphysical plenitude, as its mythmakers wished to believe; its life resides in the contradictions that attend its abstraction. I am not alone in tracing the lively inheritances of this invention. Working at that very conjunction of language's technocracy and the determination of its material being, while tracing its vicissitudes across global reinventions of Chinese script, Bachner conceptualizes the *sinograph*, denaturalizing "what binds languages, scripts, and medial expressions to cultural and national identity . . . [and] the ways in which the confluence of the digital media revolution and the reshaping of global power structures impacts our understanding of the Chinese script in particular and of writing in general."[21] Granting a historical and materialist polyvalence to a mythology foreclosed from it, Bachner's emphasis on the many lives of writing traverses many realms, tracing Fenollosa's "medial take on signification" to its resurrection in the Brazilian tradition of concrete poetry and, especially, to the digitization of writing writ large—a process that began *avant la lettre* with the advent of the sinograph.[22] Just as Bush provincializes the European ideograph qua translation, Bachner in turn *de*-provincializes the sinograph.

In the wake of these arguments, I suggest that in contrast to long-held discourses asserting the ossified difficulty of the Chinese language (said to hinder literacy and political progress), both Fenollosa and Hu instead theorized an even more confounding obverse: ideologies of easy translatability and plainspoken equivalences between the Chinese and English languages. By reducing the Chinese language to image, sound, and the myriad processes that relate and distance them—that is, by treating it as a prototype of its contemporaneous structuralist linguistics—the authors of this archive bestowed upon the ideograph the speed of modern progress through translational processes of abstraction. More than a critique of the ideograph, their conversation affords a critique of translation and its obscure internalizations of ideographic thought.

"Can you ideograph it"

It may be simplest to begin this story at its historical end. In 1941, Ezra Pound brought two questions to Kitasono Katue, the Japanese avant-garde surrealist who was also one of his longtime correspondents. The writers had bonded over their shared investments in the modernist avant-garde and had long been particularly interested in translating classical Chinese poetry in order to revivify their respective languages and literary traditions in both parts of the world[23]—a work of translation that had even deeper colonial debts in Japan than in Pound's transatlantic milieus. By this point in his uneven Sinographical career, Pound had been stung by the critical reception of his Chinese-ideographic translations in the collection *Cathay* and had thus turned his attention to the more validating pursuit of Japanese poetry read via and with Japanese interlocutors, finding in it a mediated resource for what he still believed was the Chinese essence of English verse.[24] The broader context for Pound's two questions was thus a simple one: he was burrowing deep in the work for his *Cantos* and wanted to know what his friend thought of a few lines of material. These lines, he proffered, may either "go to the VOU Club without explanation" or "go into Canto 72 or somewhere."[25]

Yet Canto 72 (LXXII) was not just any canto, and in hindsight this was not just any offer, despite its characteristically flippant delivery. By this point in the war, Pound's anti-Semitic views and fascist sympathies were publicly known. Both the letter to Kitasono and Canto LXXII were written from Rapallo on the Italian Riviera; the canto was to be an ode and poetic vessel for the futurist Filippo Marinetti at the height of World War II, a memento of Pound's slow and certain turn toward the fascist agenda of Benito Mussolini. Along with Canto 73 (LXXIII), Pound's new work was to become one of the two so-called Italian Cantos, named for the fact that Pound wrote them in Italian to address their muses, translating only LXXII into English and leaving no surviving translation for its companion piece.[26] Their status as outliers in the textual history of the *Cantos* belies the forcefulness with which their ideas are presented, so much so that when they were finally included in the text of the *Cantos* proper, they took their place as its most noxious wound, marked by the anti-Semitic vitriol that would eventually commit Pound to a mental institution in his home country for twelve years. In the event, the lines sent to Kitasono did not wind up in their intended home in Canto LXXII when it was completed on the occasion of Marinetti's death in December 1944.

Yet the most striking aspect of this encounter is not so much its context and content as it is Pound's casual implication that his homeless fragment may have been equally at home in a journal cofounded by his Japanese modernist interlocutor *and* one of his own most racially violent pieces written in the Italian—and that the distinction between the two possible homes may be made with something of a simple shrug "or somewhere."[27] To be sure, the lines in question traverse the poem's imaginary Japan and Italy quickly, moving from a scene of agricultural syncreticism—bamboo clacking against olive trees—to a more immediate scene on the Italian Riviera. Yet Pound himself seems to doubt its connective tissue, inquiring of Kitasono if Japan even has olive trees and if they are harvested by beating bamboo sticks against the tree as his poem imagines. The lines end with an everyday scene on the Riviera that coalesces into a characteristically Poundian complex image.

> The sexton of San Pantaleo plays "è mobile" on his carillon
> "un' e due . . . che la donna è mobile"
> in the hill tower (videt et urbes)
> And a black head under white cherry boughs
> precedes us down the salita.
> The water-bug's mittens show on the bright rock beneath him.[28]

Pound is especially taken with the final line, calling his friend's attention to it with a footnote.[29] In the footnote, he seems dimly aware that his request would be neither innocent nor isolated, nor *simply* about the *Cantos*' ambition to be an epic for the totality of the world.

> If I were 30 years younger I would call 'em [the "water-bug's mittens"] his boxing gloves. I wonder if it is clear that I mean the shadow of the "mittens"? and can you ideograph it; very like petals of blossoms. All of which shows that I am not wholly absorbed in saving Europe by economics.[30]

A strange alibi surfaces through this account: that Pound's imagination remains, after all these years, with the ideographic "petals of blossoms" would seem to be a pleasant aesthetic distraction from his infamous wartime career in "economics." The term "economics" conceals a multitude of sins in the

Poundian context: especially focused on an abstracting reading of money skewed from the Marxian account, Pound's theories moved from a concern with monetary policy and the role of the state (especially around the time of the Great Depression) to, increasingly, the form of money itself, which he disparaged as a toxic convention separated from the material world.[31] A number of commentators have carefully historicized the complex relationship between Pound's fascism and economic theory, noting that his interest in monetary policy—and especially what was called Social Credit during the Depression—were in place long *before* his turn to fascism in the public eye. Through this chronological narrative, some critics have suggested that Pound's theories are rooted in a Jeffersonian mode of economic populism decrying the overreaching power of banks, with one even going so far as to present Pound as a heterodox anticapitalist *avant la lettre*.[32] Yet such efforts to redeem Poundian economics remain difficult to reconcile with his overwhelmingly anti-Semitic association of Jewishness with the toxicity of money, unreliable, ephemeral, and always in need of correction or epistemic stability at the hands of a strong state—a longtime racial abstraction of capitalism *and* a toxic political populism, from which the fascisms of Mussolini and Hitler gained sustenance and momentum in the economically depressed interwar years.[33] Indeed, the indissociable link between his economics and anti-Semitism is made clear via Pound's two models for strong and effective government developed later in his career: first, an especially fecund body of thought in Confucius emphasizing the importance of a stable state as manifest in poetic structure, which in his worldview eventually correlated with a hard and fast attachment to Italian fascism identifying the fiscal ideas of Jefferson with those of Mussolini.[34]

This is the fraught context in which critics have tended to reconcile Pound's economics with his poetics of ontological translation, even if the results continue to offer some cause for skepticism: as Paul Morrison explains, "Pound's economic project, which is to return the signs of wealth [i.e., the convention of money] to their material basis in human productivity, in work done and goods produced, is one with his aesthetic project, which is to reestablish the lost connection between the order of words and the world, to repair the chasm between the signifier and the signified."[35] Giving the lie to Pound's separation of the two realms, Morrison's observation further points to the possible connection between his absorption in the wartime European economics of 1941, on the one hand, and the strange processes of translation by which poetic images become at once loaded with meaning even while being reified as opaque and fragmentary.

That process of translation, in Pound's hands, seems to go by the name "ideographing." But what does it mean to "ideograph it," and what is at stake in this formulation of intralingual translation? Pound's question to his friend renders visible—and uncertain—a process that much of his earlier work has taken for granted. In a radical ontological twist, he transforms a noun into a transitive verb: the ideograph was first made, and then it becomes the maker. *Can* you ideograph something that isn't already an ideograph? To ideograph something may simply be consonant with the project of Pound's modernism in toto: to find its dynamic, concrete, and visual principles in places other to itself. After all, Pound's small question to Kitasono, despite its characteristic oddity, is at bottom a twofold request: for (a kind of) *translation*; and, which here amounts to the same, a theoretical operation. Stepping partially away from the context of Pound's letter—and in the context of what this chapter will soon study about the Fenollosan ideographic imagination—we may deduce that to "ideograph it" implies a formal and imaginative operation upon a given image or metaphor. Such an operation would likely rearrange the image in such a way that the consonance between its constituent parts would be readily apparent: in this case, to underline that somewhere between the thing (water-bug's mittens), light, and a bright rock, a shadow emerges to relate and unify these parts—a way of gathering petals in order to construct blossoms. Whether or not such an operation is even possible remains an open question. After all, Pound's offhand "can you ideograph it" may easily be read as a questioning of possibility rather than a request per se: "*can* you ideograph it." Yet what is most suggestive here is the break from translation in its conventional sense as a transmission of semantic content between two implicitly equivalent languages. In its stead, Pound begins to frame translation as a manipulation or perversion of writing *qua* script: a translation that itself abstracts the interlingual into the intersemiotic, newly governed by the organization of language.

Even more particular, however, is the translational axis implied in this moment. In the first direction, and most banally, moving linguistically from English to the ideograph may loosely be understood as a translation from one language to another; but the particularity of this translational vector, and the context of Pound's ideas, is suggestive in that it impels a movement from one theory of language into another, and even (if one momentarily assents to the ideographic account) from abstraction "back" into concretion. To "ideograph it" is thus also a theoretical operation that takes place *prior to* and *in* the threshold "material" of script. (A quick contrapuntal to illustrate this point: if one desired a translation from Chinese to English, requests for a friend to "alphabetize it" or "phoneticize it" would bear idiosyncratic—though no doubt interesting—results.[36] The point here is simply that the two directions of transliteration or translation make their respective appeals to different aspects of the linguistic system: translating the medium does *not* translate the message.) Moreover, if we provisionally abide by the posited rules of the ideogram, the translating— or even quasi-ekphrastic—movement of "ideographing" would therefore also require not exactly a restoration of the concrete, but an infusion of the semantic truths of alphabetic syntax into the visual dynamics of the ideograph, reminiscent of Jameson's resonant definition of the modernist gesture as one "in which an appearance of meaning is pressed into the service of the notation of a physical perception."[37]

At the heart of any claim about concrete writing and "the thing itself" is thus a necessary process of abstraction.[38] This chapter explores how and why my book indirectly takes up Pound's marginal invitation for a series of objects that he likely never expected—in the process betraying the contradictions at the heart of this idea and exhuming the promises buried when an objectified ideograph morphs into a transitive weapon and verb for "ideographing." So much depends (to borrow another old saw) on "it": can you ideograph it—a metaphor, China, Pound's untranslated Italian, and the world? If *China* is the aporetic limit point for the ideographic imagination of modernist writing—both its very instantiation and the point at which knowability necessarily falters—such that it is operating within modernism as already and merely a metaphor, what may one achieve by "ideographing it" anyway? Indeed, what may it mean to extend the ideographic logic beyond its associations with Chinese script and Asian aesthetics into a global realm, and how would that even be possible? What kinds of political gestures and implications may attend such a movement?

In turning from Pound and instead foregrounding two of his close contemporaries who held similarly strong investments in the manifold politics of Chinese script, I seek to reevaluate the place of the ideograph and what was arguably its *re*translation into the foundations of (Anglo-American, European, transatlantic) modernism. To the extent that Pound's work has served—and continues to serve in this book—as an indispensable frame for these critical conversations because of his role as a public mouthpiece and translator of the foreign for the Pound era and into "our time," it also casts a complex critical and ethical shadow that has tended to obscure the agility of translation as strategy and practice in the modernist moment. Concerned with neither accuracy nor intimacy, Pound's mode of free and imaginative translation eschewed the possibility of error and came to be seen as a lodestar for the transformative potential of modernist poetics. Yet this chapter's premise—and indeed the premise of translation studies as a field—is that the stakes of this paradigm for modernist translation reach further and wider than the constitution of a modernist praxis or the contested politics of Pound's career. Foregrounding and juxtaposing the far-reaching insights of Ernest Fenollosa and Hu Shi—and finding their points of alignment and divergence as cultural ambassadors abroad in Japan and the United States, respectively—draws out the wider political stakes of Pound's work and attends to modes of modernist translation for which Pound is a marginal specter rather than moving cause. Both Fenollosa and Hu thought deeply—through their own attempts at thinking about language and its forces—about what it means to reform oneself by making the other a mirror, yet their similar gestures would lead them to different conclusions with sharply different stakes.

The Exceptions of "Poeticempiricism" in Hu's "Dream and Poetry"

Literature—and its peculiar kinds of political operations—operates across this chapter as a first principle, yet as a first principle, it is unusually kinetic and manifold. Contextualizing it—a little reductively for now—offers an inroad into the layered conceptuality at play. The classical concept of literature in the Chinese context generally begins with *wen*, variously translated as *civility, writing, poetry, pattern,* and *literature*; more recently, it has been associated with *wenhua* or *culture* and *wenxue*, the scholarship of *wen* as an object of knowledge.[39] *Wen* is classically taken to be at the heart of order and governance in the universe, marking an integration of writing with the world in which it lives and which it organizes. In the turn to modernity generally located in the late Qing and early Republican era (around the turn of the century), this broad picture of the Chinese context has been complicated by a continued interest in the political work of literature as well as a growing interest in the Western and post-Romantic tradition of literature as a radically singular expression or event tied to a notional subjectivity or genius, in which the political dimensions of literature are less readily assumed and indeed are often open to question, inviting the possibility of a literature that is either autonomous from the world or against instrumentalism.[40] What then might it mean to discuss a concept of literature through and under comparison, conceptualizing it across a transpacific context—and what might it mean to integrate these senses into a manifold conceptuality?

This is the context in which Hu's modern paradigm of skeptical and positivist empiricism was less easily translated into the realm of poetry, a fraught genre for his ambitious literary reform because, unlike novels, no poems had as yet been written in the vernacular. Hu thus became the first of many to accept the challenge of filling this void. In 1918, he published his vernacular poem "Dream and Poetry" in the pages of *Xinqingnian* or *New Youth/La Jeunesse*, a journal he had helped found and a leading venue for progressive political thought. The same poem was collected in his volume of poetry *Changshi ji* or *Experimental Verses* published in 1920 and widely cited as the first volume of vernacular poetry in Chinese literary history.

"Dream and Poetry" is also often cited for its final couplet that would seem to indicate the birth of a new Romantic individualism fueling the New Culture Movement. Yet in Hu's account, individualism always encompassed more than the individual and indeed was intimately conjoined to the Kantian notion of the categorical imperative: this new sense of self was thus not so much a liberal atomism as an enabling condition for poets to reject the burdens of literary tradition and allusion, to create a wider sense of a modern nation rooted in self-determination rather than bureaucratic governance, to reject the political pathologies of the nation's past, and (per Kant) to act as if one's own actions are to serve as a universal guide for all. These ideas play out only partially by the end of an extended parallelism that imagines writing poetry as a form of dreaming.

All is commonplace [*pingchang*] experience,	都是平常經驗，
All is commonplace impression.	都是平常影像，
By chance they rush into a dream	偶然湧到夢中來，
They are transformed into many new patterns [*huayang*].	變幻出多少新奇花樣！
All is commonplace sentiment,	都是平常情感，
All is commonplace word.	都是平常言語，
By chance they meet a poet	偶然碰着個詩人，
They are transformed into many new poems [*shiju*].	變幻出多少新奇詩句！
Only after being drunk does one know the wine is strong,	醉過才知酒濃，
Only after having loved does one know the depth of love.	愛過才知情重：—
You can never write my poems,	你不能做我的詩，
Just as I can never dream your dreams.[41]	正如我不能做你的夢。[42]

This conclusion appears definitive: you and I have the right to and are the guardians of our own unique subjectivity; you and I have ownership over our poems *and* our dreams, and indeed that ownership is granted for those very reasons—never shall my poems be the same as your dreams. What is at issue here is not communication or communicability (or indeed translation) but the seemingly simple act of two distinct persons who are writing and dreaming at all, here powerfully analogized over the course of the poem. Perhaps in order to name those acts with precision and to draw his conceit as carefully as possible, Hu uses the same verb to mean both the *writing* of poetry and the *dreaming* of dreams, an idiomatic play possible only in the vernacular Chinese; this verb *zuo* can be translated more generally as *making* or *doing*, firmly connecting writing and dreaming to a materialist register of social action.

Yet the making of both dreams and poetry is also rendered in an elegant metapoetic syllogism in which "I" and "you" (i.e., poetic speaker and addressee/reader) are explicitly asserted for the first time only at the end of the poem, and in terms that may not be as stable as the poem's formalistic qualities may imply.[43] In particular, the final couplet introduces a subtle yet seismic shift in the form of the poem, whose meticulous construction is characteristic of the *wenyan* or classical literary training that most Chinese intellectuals would have received and whose deadening influence Hu sought to reform. At first glance, speaker and addressee, writer and dreamer are presented as equals in two similar acts of fiction-making that the poem works to conjugate, and that sense of equivalence is preserved almost throughout the poem: the first stanza considers how dreams are made, and the second stanza then repeats the first in form and diction with the only differences marked by substituting dream for poetry, experience for sentiment, impression for word, and so on; that is to say, the first two stanzas share the exact same form but for their subjects and objects, which are presented as readily substitutable in order to draw the poem's parallels as closely as possible. Yet the final two lines break that tightly woven spell of allegory by introducing a logical conjunction *zhengru*, translated here by *just as*: aptly, this conjunction that marks an analogy is the only word or phrase in the poem that is not formally repeated in an analogical way. That syllogism tacitly reframes a parallelism as a loose hierarchy, in which the dream is not the equivalent analog of the poem but more precisely (and unsurprisingly given Hu's training in philosophy) its logical predicate and didactic ground—an argument filled out too by the fact that the stanza about dreams comes before the stanza about poetry. By the same token, "you" are not simply the direct and projected addressee of "I" and my poem but are revealed to be "my" logical predicate and didactic ground. In this reading, it becomes clearer why the act of writing is assigned to the poetic speaker and the act of dreaming assigned to the addressee: each takes ownership of the mode of fiction appropriate to their place in this discursive whole. Substitution happens on the level of language but importantly stands at significant odds with the poem's content.

After the poem's conclusion, Hu appends a short "self-analysis," in which he argues that the poem represents his *shi de jingyan zhuyi* or *poeticempiricism*, a quasi-compounded term that he coins in both Chinese and English (with the English term provided in-line in the original Chinese text). Hu's analysis insists stringently that the material common to dreams and poetry is experience. They are fashioned from its raw materials *by chance* [*ouran*] and are thereby *transformed* [*bianhuan*] into something new.

> [Self-analysis] This is my "poeticempiricism" [*shi de jingyan zhuyi*].[44]
> Simply put: if even dreams must be made from the basis or substrata [*dizi*] of experience, then what more [can one say of] poetry? The greatest problem of today is writing poetry without the basis [*dizi*] of experience.

Hu's poem and analysis would seem to hew closely to the critical commonplace that both dreams and poetry were socially transformative for the May Fourth optimism that he inspired in the early moments of his career as a public intellectual. Moreover, they suggest that the core of the poem's political appeal lay in its recourse to the fact of experience—which for Hu was coterminous with empiricism—and the ways in which experience functions as a gatekeeper to any social compact. What begins as a descriptive empiricism—dreams are made from the dreamer's unique experience—is subtly transformed into a prescriptive norm: this is how poetry must be written. Indeed, upon closer examination, these facts of experience are deeply mediated, to the extent that the exception of individualism is predicated not on experience per se but on its poetic and oneiric transformation. In this regard, then, it may be helpful to consider another text in which the conditions for exceptionality encounter a related crisis of literary language.

Fenollosa's Nature and the Exceptionalism of Metaphor

Fenollosa's translating movement between the English and the Chinese is grounded in an even more prior articulation of an always potentially universalizable "nature," variously constituted by his own reading in (depending in part on which critic is reading) the American Transcendentalist and essayist Ralph Waldo Emerson, the German idealist philosopher G. W. F. Hegel,[45] and the classical Chinese writing he studied in Japan. Yet just like Hu's notion of a "poeticempiricism," Fenollosa's universalizing enterprise (as well as the long tradition of the Poundian modernist ideograph that continues and develops from his essay) also founders on its articulation of "nature," which then yields further implications for his syntactical calque between English and Chinese. Deeply indebted to and yet pulling away from Hegel and Emerson, Fenollosa saw *his* "nature" as manifested *specifically* in the unique mode of textuality offered by the Chinese character. In his ideographic account, the Chinese character offers a mimetic visual representation of the natural world and its active relations, to such an extent that it even offers a visible *etymology*, thus laying bare the modalities of its signification. Because it is first a photographic picture and metaphorically cinematic, its visual and visible character renders it legible to anyone who can perceive nature's forces.[46] Turning the Hegelian reading of Chinese writing on its head, Fenollosa's ideograph is not so much impossible to remember (per Hegel) as impossible to forget, because it—that is, its attendant natural relations—can always be apprehended and understood anew.

As the argument up to this point may already suggest, there are several complicities invoked in any deployment of the term "nature," thus calling for disambiguation. Even more than a false possibility of universalizability, the concept also occupies a fraught place within the Western philosophical tradition. Its problems may be understood in two ways. First, the advent of nature as a category historically coincides with the invention of the Enlightenment subject, turning nature into an epistemological object posited as exterior and distant, often tacitly racialized within the booming colonial sensibilities of the time. Thus radically estranged, nature became a locus of melancholic nostalgia that is ultimately irrecuperable for the thinking and remembering subject. While such a historical account of a radical break at the time of the Enlightenment perhaps does justice to neither pre- nor post-Enlightenment thought (nor indeed even the variegated Enlightenment itself), nevertheless, the ensuing deconstruction of such a subject thereby also unsettles the category of nature. It is in this deconstructive vein that recent work in eco-criticism has called instead for alternative philosophical accounts of ecological enmeshments and withdrawals to reconfigure the dialectical divisions of subject and object structuring the concept of nature.

Second, "nature" also names an intractable givenness that is always predetermined. The problems here are most obvious when one considers ideological and essentializing appeals to the term as a biological category, or even the social consensuses so formative for "human nature" serving as pretexts for normalizing (pathologizing) behavior. Yet the aspect of givenness might also be taken as mobilizing a promising point of departure for materialist philosophy: the Deleuzian plane of immanence, as derived from Spinoza's elaboration of nature as the substance of God, suggests the ideal possibility of a politics and ethics of immanence where, if we are all embedded in the same material, we might begin to think and act in ways that materially affect one another, through ways that may or may not be knowable to each agent (distinct from the subject of knowledge and reason). We may, in other words, *sympathize* with one another in the most literal sense of the term.

Indeed, the philosophical and historical debate over "nature" subtly parallels Fenollosa's articulation of the ideograph as the material and aesthetic representation of nature. For example, one crucial difference between Fenollosa and Pound resonates with the Deleuzian approach to materialism: their conceptualization of the conditionality of "the thing." As Jonathan Stalling explains, Pound's reading of the "verbal precision" of Chinese characters as shorthand pictures of things leaves him in significant disagreement with Fenollosa's emphasis on "their clearly aggregative character in order to dismantle 'thingness' itself by showing the dependency of contextual causes and conditions."[47] Refusing the independence of the thing and positioning it within the theoretical register of poetics and the ideograph thus accounts for Fenollosa's seemingly odd slippages between what he calls "nature," "Chinese writing," "sentence," and the "universal," adding up to a legible articulation of the relationships between them. While he might primarily attribute "the dependency of contextual causes and conditions" to nature, all his other terms become also simultaneously governed by the causality and conditions to be found only in nature and mimed only in Chinese sentences. Fenollosa's essay thus presents itself not just as a theory of language or an imagination of the Chinese ideograph; it is also simultaneously a materialist theory of nature wherein referentiality is insistently claimed but yet to be achieved, and the materiality of language is necessarily affirmed through its relation to that nature.

Yet the materiality of language that Fenollosa affirms can only be a qualified one, bound as he is to metaphysical presuppositions of what language can do. As Robert Kern observes, the "nature" that Fenollosa employs bears a considerable resemblance to the "nature" deployed by Ralph Waldo Emerson. In this regard, Kern argues that nature in Emerson's writing functions as a transcendental signifier in the Derridean sense: that is, it is posited as a master term that dominates and unites difference from an impossible prelinguistic state but which thereby becomes endlessly referred and never referential.[48] The resemblance is perhaps most stark if one considers the Fenollosan appeal to the natural "likeness of form" between English and Chinese sentences serving as a central metaphor for this book. Yet Fenollosa also develops this universalism through recourse to a further mode of poetic language similarly indebted to Emerson: metaphor.

Aptly enough in a discussion of metaphor, the means by which Chinese and English sentences may yet become united for Fenollosa are precisely what presently set them apart: coded as nature, the project of East-West reconciliation hinges on what the primitivity of the Chinese language has always had in abundance, which is also what Western thinking has too woefully abandoned and must now seek to recover in order to regain parity with their transpacific counterparts.

> [Now] **you will ask** how could the Chinese [ever] have build up [this] **a** great intellectual fabric [out of] **from** mere picture writing?[49] To the ordinary Western mind, which believes **that** thought [to be] **is** concerned with logical categories, and which rather contemns the faculty of direct imagination, th[e]**is** feat seems quite impossible. [And] yet [it is quite clear that] the Chinese language, with its peculiar materials, has passed over from the seen to the unseen, by exactly the same process which all ancient races [and tongues have] employed. This process is metaphor; the use of material images to suggest immaterial relations.
>
> The whole delicate substance of [human] speech is built [upon] substrata of metaphor. [Our most] abstract terms, [when] pressed by etymology, reveal their ancient roots still embedded in [this soil of] direct action. But the[se] primitive metaphors, which created our vocabularies, spring not [as some may suppose, out] of arbitrary, subjective fancies. They are possible only because they follow objective lines of relation in nature itself. Relations are more real and more important than the things which they relate. The forces which produce the branch-angles of an oak, lay, potent, in the acorn. Similar lines of resistance, half curbing outward-pressing vitalities, govern the branching of rivers, and the branching of nations.*[50] Nature thus furnishes her own clues. Had the world not already been full of homologies, sympathies, and identities, thought would have been starved, and language chained to the obvious. For there would have been no bridge to cross over from the minor truth of the seen to the major truth of the unseen.[51]

An important interlocutor who goes unnamed here is Hegel, whose skepticism of the possibility of Chinese progress and disparagement of the matter of Chinese writing becomes displaced onto the haplessly Hegelian "ordinary Western mind."[52] However, Fenollosa's departure from Hegel lies in his conviction that the Chinese language has indeed "passed over from the seen to the unseen"—that is, per his host of accompanying binaries, from concretion to abstraction, from matter to spirit, and from "minor truth" to "major truth"—through what he calls a process of metaphor.[53] Remaining still within an implicit hierarchical binary, Fenollosa's ostensible recuperation of Chinese writing comes via the commingling of material with immaterial in the structural coupling of metaphor. The unseen is asserted as the dominant necessity for progress, such that, as the gloss on metaphor momentarily suggests, material images are only the furnisher or mediator of clues to the more originary immaterial relations that they conceal.

Yet when Fenollosa offers a closer look at these immaterial relations, they turn out to not only be "follow[ing] objective lines of relation in nature itself," but furthermore the lines of relation are "more real and more important than the things which they relate."[54] The appeal to reality here is difficult to parse: while it makes explicit that it is not treating a *material* notion of reality, it also invokes a quantifiable sense of that reality ("more real," "more important") that appears again to edge the relations over the thing. Why then would relations be "more real" than things themselves? The claim may partly be attributed to Stalling's observation of Fenollosa's interest in aggregation over Pound's interest in precision and directness, but another clue may lie in the passage's flagrant metaphors of potentiality and immanent force: an acorn is nothing if not the repository for "the forces which produce the branch-angle of an oak." The reality of these relations thus lies in their vitalist resistances, which "half curb" and "govern" homologous things like rivers and nations, which would themselves be impotent without the immaterial forces lying dormant in them, revealed only through the metaphorical nature of Chinese writing.

As Robert Kern observes, it is at this moment that Fenollosa most radically departs from his conceptual alliance with Emerson: his interest in the ideograph as a snapshot of forces, actions, or processes (perhaps in a more linguistic register, it may be called a synchronic representation of diachrony, calling to Yang Lian's theory of translating history and time, discussed in chapter 4) fundamentally rejects the Emersonian understanding of words as static facts of nature. Nevertheless, Kern points out too that Fenollosa's reliance on Emerson "coheres around the assumption that language, in a way still visibly exemplified by Chinese, was originally a direct reflection of the world."[55] Further, Fenollosa also differs from Emerson in that the reality of *his* natural world is constituted specifically through transference and agency on the part of the things themselves; more than "homologies, sympathies, and identities," we also have "resistances," governances, even forces of production that are dormant in the acorns at rest.[56]

I would suggest that these resistant forces and transferences at least partially account for the strange and unstable status of "[human] speech," marked by Pound's editorial hand in Fenollosa's long discussion on the processes of metaphor. Removing "human" as it modifies "speech" unavoidably raises and implicitly answers a swath of philosophical questions. Broadly, Pound's editorial move can be read in two mutually exclusive and ultimately undecidable ways. In the context of the passage, the formulation is that this "speech," human or otherwise, is a "whole delicate substance" that is "built [upon] substrata of metaphor." The analogy is then as follows: as the wholeness of substance is to the substrata on which it rests, so is "[human] speech" to the process of metaphor. Yet given Fenollosa's consistent collapsing of nature and substance with language (and Pound's implicit acquiescence to that), what seems to be at stake here is a differential admission into the "whole delicate substance" of speech and then, implicitly, the relegation to the substrata of metaphor on which it rests. On the one hand, Pound's implication may quite simply be that "human" is redundant because "speech" is, by its very definition, exclusive to humans; this would then suggest that the by-definition-human speech rests on and emerges out of the substrata of metaphor, which is identified with nature. On the other hand, however, Pound's editorial hand may well be divesting Fenollosa of the anthropocentric bias that keeps speech exclusive to humans, making room thereby for "a whole delicate substance of speech" attributable to persons and nonpersons alike, growing to become "whole" expressions of nature-as-substrata.

The Unity of Speech with Writing in Hu's "Modest Proposals"

In the first part of this chapter, I suggested that "speech" and its companionate "experience" function as the site of ideological contestation, especially as they conceal their abstract and derivative character: they are not so much the *substance* from which a new linguistic order is formed as they are the tangled linguistic order itself. This then brings us to the vernacular movement and its centrality to the work of Hu Shi. Hu first became interested in the political possibilities of imagism and free verse via the work of Amy Lowell, who, writing in 1916, laid out a series of dictums in the vein of Pound's well-known manifesto "A Few Don'ts by an Imagiste" (1913) from three years before. Upon reading about her preface to "Some Imagist Poets" in the *New York Times*, Hu faithfully copied into his diary her six principles of imagism and noted to himself that "there are many points of convergence between this school's principles and my own."[57] It was most likely Lowell's work that led Hu to Pound's "A Few Don'ts." The discovery of this work may well have been a major intellectual development for the young Hu, especially on the heels of an award-winning student essay he wrote on the Victorian poet Robert Browning in 1915. Hu's interest in Browning's poetry largely dwelled on what he identified as a philosophy of optimism and self-determination, giving short shrift to the genre of the dramatic monologue or formal questions of blank verse that are typically considered Browning's primary poetic innovations.[58]

To be sure, poetry for Hu and in the common understanding of Chinese tradition was never *not* philosophical—and for him, poetic language (more than fiction) came to represent a vexed category of social and political life that would be something of a crux for national reform, even isomorphic for the then-inchoate Chinese nation writ large. Indeed, his volume of vernacular poetry would eventually lead to renewed interest in vernacular writing and translation from European languages across China. And as Hu's diaries confirm, it seems to be the special encounter with the burgeoning modernist movement, marked by his several excited references to "the so-called modernists," that draws his attention to Western ideas as something more (or other) than the ideational or philosophical—and indeed, as worth translating at all.[59] After all, despite his physical location at Cornell University, Hu's primary intellectual circle continued to consist of many other Chinese students who were, like him, intensely involved in the tumultuous changes happening in China and who held sharply divergent views about the role of Western ideals in Chinese modernity. Yet when Lowell writes that poets are "to use the language of common speech, but to employ always the exact word," she echoes the terms for Hu's future thinking, articulating two elements of modernity—"common speech" and analytical precision—that he would champion for much of his career as a nationalist reformer. In this unexpected conjunction, Lowell's modernist formulations provide vital context for the enigmatic and important ways in which Hu's calls for reform translated and transformed the radical empiricism of John Dewey (widely thought to be second only to Marx qua Western intellectual influence in the Chinese context).

Hu looked toward poetic language as a manifestation of the scientific-rational ideology and culture he saw in Dewey. The work that he discusses in his diary as being closely connected to the poetics and philosophy of imagism was likely his important essay, "Some Modest Proposals for the Reform of Literature," written and published in Chinese in January 1917 shortly after Lowell's manifesto and the record of his reading in the diaries. The same essay has recently been translated into English for scholarly use by Kirk Denton. To read this essay as a cultural translation of US modernism rather than Hu's self-spun doctrine, I argue, opens a host of interpretive and comparative cruxes: more than a theory and ontology of Chinese literature, the essay also records its partial genesis in Hu's careful management of the relationship between the two traditions.

Written with what one can only imagine was conscious pragmatism in the classical *wenyan* style (since this was still the expected language of intellectual discourse at the time) and published in the pages of *New Youth*, Hu's "Proposals" for intellectuals to write in the vernacular, so named in their modesty topos to "underscore the sense of their incompleteness and to respectfully seek the redaction of my compatriots," were widely read and debated when first published and eventually became shortened as a series of punchy *babu zhuyi* or *Eight Don'ts*, claiming in full view its debt to Pound's "A Few Don'ts" and, in hazier view, to Lowell's later preface.[60] Inaudible in the English translation is also a sly pun on Hu's part: *bu*, a negating adverb meaning *don't*, is a homophone of the word for *steps* or even (here a bilingual pun) poetic *feet*, so that quietly audible in its negative prescriptions are also eight *poetic* steps for the progress he aims to effect with this work.

1. Writing should have substance
2. Do not imitate the ancients
3. Emphasize the technique of writing
4. Do not moan without an illness
5. Eliminate hackneyed and formal language
6. Do not use allusions
7. Do not use parallelism
8. Do not avoid vulgar diction

Hu's ideas in these "modest proposals" paved the way for what was known as the Literary Revolution, central to the May Fourth Movement of modernization that took place only two years later in 1919. The essay advocated clearly and passionately for a new kind of plain-spoken writing, bringing together the *wu*, substance of *qinggan*, *feeling* with *sixiang* or *thought* in the realm of the vernacular. The result would supplant the literary and poetic tradition of China even while remaining steeped in that long history, renarrativized in Hu's hands as a history of the vernacular and its people.

The question of how to attain this new method, however, was a fraught one, legible in the negative proscriptions as a necessary strategy to clear the ground for modernization. Furthermore, it required conceptualizing and presenting readers and the Chinese people with a dynamic sense of vernacular language that was, on the one hand, intuitive, familiar, and rooted in historical and local experience *and*, on the other, an abstract and transcendent idea around which an emergent Chinese nation may potentially rally. Indeed, and much like Pound's approach, this empiricism itself had a history and was thoroughly mediated, a "direct speech" construed by the least direct possible means of translation: if Hu is championing the bare speech of the people, it has still been stripped bare by many hands, his own and those of others. The result for Hu and for Chinese modernity was thus a qualified naturalism that sought to theorize the new literary language as a "unity" of its historically sundered spoken and written components—not so much a dyad of speech against writing as a perfect marriage of speech with writing, bringing vernacular speech into the fold so that one may write as one speaks (and not speak as one writes).[61] The new literature is thus more than the static historical inheritance of literary *wenyan* or the social use of the vernacular as *parole*, instead braiding the two in order to produce a future from historical memory.

The most extensively elaborated of these prescriptions is the sixth one, which enjoins writers to avoid *dian* or *allusions* to the corpus of tradition, which had thus far served as a key literary and formalist strategy in the *wenyan* mode against which Hu is arguing. This idea, Hu hastens to add, is offered in a circumscribed sense, as he distinguishes between "broad" and "narrow" senses of the term, where the latter is understood as a subset of the former. Two related aspects govern this initial distinction. First, the broad sense of the term aims to describe how language operates in a systematic and transhistorical way by connecting words to objects and common experience: many of these *piyu* or *metaphors* are universal; that is, they mobilize objects from common experience that are not exclusive to the literati class and should certainly remain in use "if employed appropriately" and if they "do not lose their efficaciousness with time."[62] Conversely, the narrow sense of the term names those times "when men of letters are incapable of creating their own words and expressions to write about what is before their eyes or in their hearts and instead borrow, in part or wholly inapposite, anecdotes and hackneyed language to do it for them."[63] In other words, the difference between a broad and narrow allusion is that a broad allusion uses language that invokes *objects or experience*, whereas the narrow and undesirable allusion uses language that invokes *prior language*.

And the problem with allusion runs even deeper than that, drawing upon a second aspect that operates the distinction between the two forms of allusion: that of a metaphorical use versus a substitutive use. But what then differentiates a metaphor from a substitution? For given the above discussion, one may certainly wonder what exactly constitutes an appropriate use of allusion: for these purposes, Hu provides a series of five examples from antiquity to the present—including one of his own poems inspired by reading a translation of Walter Scott's novel *The Talisman*—in order to argue that the best uses of allusion "use [it] to say something that cannot be said more directly" even as the limitations of a formalist tradition meant that "their metaphoric use of allusion changed toward a substitutive use. The problem in using allusion is that it causes people to lose the original meaning behind the metaphor. Crude uses of allusion are when the host and guest are reversed [*fanke weizhu*]."[64] Upon closer inspection, metaphor and substitution are distinguished by the extent to which they rigidly maintain and adjudicate the lines between origin and deviation, host and guest: allowing one to exist and function alongside the other (metaphor) is not the same as allowing one to take the place of the other so that the original object motivating the metaphor becomes invisible or irrelevant (substitution). To use narrow allusions as a weak substitute for a considered metaphor that provides a meaningful access to its first or original context is the undesirable symptom of a literary tradition that shackles the imagination and prohibits the writer from crafting a universal appeal. In this way, a problem of crafting an exception also edges into a complex typological ambition.

One may also ask how a metaphor is best composed in Hu's implicit theory of language. At stake in this question is how literature has been understood and how it should be understood in Hu's account. A helpful resource for this lies in Hu's commentary on his first aphorism: writing should have *wu*, *substance*, understood as an alternate motivation, intention, or force to poetry that would provide an antidote or antithesis to the tradition of *wen*, here best glossed as *form*.⁶⁵ In seeking to decouple the idea of literature from the strictures of form, Hu follows in the steps of modernists the world over who simultaneously sought to understand the politics of literature's formalist endeavors: here, it is a politics that does not have to be claimed or justified but rather—and no less strenuously—assumed from the beginning and wrestled with throughout. Symptomatic of this is the fact that Hu begins this short section with a citation of Confucius, a traditional literary gesture par excellence, in which Confucius is quoted as saying, "If writing is without form, it will not travel far."⁶⁶ Embedded in this quote is a tacit claim of use-value, communicability, and perhaps even translatability, predicated on a distinct sense of "form" as it regulates and systematizes language as poetry. Hu takes issue with the Confucian doctrine not because he disagrees with its content but simply because Confucius has nothing to say about substance, or indeed the function of form per se beyond its capacity to "travel far."

Importantly, "substance" does not begin as something material or physical awaiting form and shape but is rather a force unto itself. Hu insists that substance inheres in only two concepts: *qinggan* or *feeling* and *sixiang* or *thought*, both interesting intentions reminiscent of his "poeticempiricism" of experience and tellingly rendered as metaphors by Hu. Feeling, he writes, is the soul of literature, and thought is its guiding intelligence or mind—"as the brain is to man's body, so is thought to literature."⁶⁷ In this way, then, "without these two kinds of substance, literature is like a beauty without a soul or a brain; though she have a lovely and ample exterior, she is nonetheless inferior."⁶⁸ And earlier in the essay, he writes that "literature without feeling is like a man without a soul, nothing but a wooden puppet, a walking corpse."⁶⁹ Within the parameters of Hu's argument, these metaphors underscore his claim that "the harm of an overly formalist literature lies in this so-called language without substance."⁷⁰ Yet in an odd twist in which metaphor implicitly theorizes metaphor, and in the estranging light of Fenollosa's and Pound's only partially human "speech," Hu also presents the possibility of a new literature in which a metaphor's tenor is not an everyday *object* but rather simply an everyday *feeling* or *thought*—yet also one in which feeling and thought cannot but be rendered as metaphorical bodies that serve to theorize literature. This then is perhaps the roiling core of Hu's self-named and translated empiricism: one in which literature must come to be personified through acts of gendered embodiment, inhuman metaphor, *through* metaphor, in order to fulfill its claims on the experience and knowledge of the senses.

Like Forms in Fenollosa's "Exceptionally Easy" Translations

And even as metaphors operate within a space of dynamic differentiation, they may well also collaborate with other aspects of literary language in order to produce a zone of poetic equivalence. What I have in mind is an elliptical moment that would likely be surprising to anyone familiar with both the English and Chinese languages: a remark from Fenollosa that "the likeness of form between Chinese and English sentences render [*sic*] translation from one to the other exceptionally easy. The genius of the two is much the same."[71] Tellingly, this is one of very few moments in Fenollosa's essay that remains completely untouched by Ezra Pound's typically heavy editorial hand. What might be at stake in their unusual consensus?

To begin answering that question, one may first wonder if Fenollosa's dismissal of the labor of translation ought to be taken quite so seriously. Even leaving aside the sheer volume of his translations, cribs, and notes, his posited "likeness of form" lies between English and Chinese *sentences*. The point Fenollosa makes here is thus a structural and syntactic one. For, as he quickly goes on to note in his very next sentence, "frequently it is possible, by omitting English particles, to make a literal word-for-word translation, that shall not only be intelligible in English, but even be the strongest and most poetical English. (Here, however, one must follow closely what is *said*, not merely what is abstractly *meant*)."[72] Buried within the parenthetical afterthought is what seems like the familiar principle of literary theory with which I have been grappling for some time now, which begins by parsing the difference between the exactitude of poetic saying (the signifier) and the routes it takes (signification) toward the abstracted meaning (signified). Here, however, the mysterious locution "what is *said*" is not simply to be followed closely; it is also presented as differing from the abstract and, further, implicitly possesses a "likeness of form" to English sentences that are "the strongest and most poetical English"—as long as one removes consideration of the particles of English, considered to be weak and functionless for these purposes. For

Fenollosa, "what is *said*" in Chinese poetry is "word-for-word" alike in form to the most poetic English there can be. Yet the concomitant failure to account for the English particles that he conveniently excises in his easy translation suggests already that the claim of a literal "word-for-word" translation of sentences, by way of a cross-linguistic "likeness of form," is a troubled one, even within the artificial parameters of his account.

Such an unusual claim about linguistics and grammar is inflected by the sociopolitical situation in which Fenollosa studied the Chinese language and its poetry. Writing in 1906 as something of a cultural ambassador of the United States to Japan (where there had been a long history of intercultural influence and even rivalry with nearby China) and in his official capacity as an expatriate academic lecturer of art history, sociology, and philosophy in Tokyo, Fenollosa uncannily opens his essay with the stirring declaration that "the future of Anglo Saxon supremacy in the world is probably bound up with the future of that East,"[73] going on to note that "this Chinese problem, alone, is so vast that . . . [n]o nation can afford to ignore it; we in America least of all. We must face it across the Pacific, and master it—or it will master us."[74] His demands for poetry to be wrenched into this dubious political service belie the claim that insistently follows this problem of geopolitical diplomacy: if the American and Anglo-Saxon worlds, as conflated by him, are to retain their dominance, they must first go "beyond a sentimental sympathy" in summoning a "patient sympathy,"[75] which is part of developing an "aesthetic sympathy"[76] with the Chinese—modes of sympathy that are all momentarily lacking but are ostensibly achievable through an education in Fenollosa's ideographic Chinese character.[77] If Fenollosa is to be believed (along with Pound, who also takes this up wholeheartedly for a time), the ideographic mode and its exceptional *legibility* for the attuned Anglophone Anglo-Saxon can heal and transcend the linguistic, epistemological, and political divides of the Orientalized Pacific by provoking this enchainment of sympathies.[78] He, the embattled Anglo-Saxon in danger of losing his mastery of the Pacific, must move beyond the sentimental, toward a suffering patience learned from an aesthetic education in the roots of the ideograph—a transcendental signified par excellence.

Yet more accurately, however, that transcendental signified is only a clutch and aggregate of signifiers. After all, it takes the form of a *sentence*, a linguistic entity typically defined by syntactical hierarchy and conceptual wholeness but vexed by incomplete signification in Fenollosa's account. By nestling comfortably together in his like forms, the Chinese and English languages *and* epistemologies most readily translate into each other. Yet at the same time, the like form of the sentence is also a point at which the unquestioned identification of nature with language begins to suffer a crisis when it must consider the very different "forms" and modalities of the English and ideographic sentences. Their "likeness" is then riven by historicity: where the English sentence is presently prescriptive, linear, and freighted with Western thought, the ideographic sentence presents the proleptic future of English in its very primitivity, unencumbered as it gives visible nature homologically in a single line. The English sentence, now sternly admonished, can only achieve this likeness if it integrates the lessons of the ideograph. Perhaps this may partially account for the attention to the problem of incompletion throughout the discussion of the sentence.

> On the one hand, practical completeness may be expressed by a mere interjection, as, "Hi, there!" "Scat!"; or even by shaking ones fist. No sentence is needed to make ones meaning more clear. on the other hand, no full sentence really completes a thought. The man who sees, and the horse which is seen, will not stand still. The man was planning [for] a ride before he looked, and the horse kicked [up] when the man tried to catch him. The truth is that acts are successive, even continuous; one causes, or passes into another. And though we may string never so many clauses into a simple compound sentence, motion leaks everywhere, like electricity from an exposed wire. All processes in nature are interrelated; and thus there could be no complete sentence but one which it would require all time to pronounce.[79]

On a literal level, Fenollosa is criticizing the conventional grammarian's criterion of the sentence as being the expression of a complete thought; he has previously arrived at the topic of the sentence by wondering why the sentence "seems so universally necessary *in all languages*," wondering if it might not therefore "ought to correspond to some primary Law in Nature."[80] One may reasonably ask, what is this natural law that the sentence aspires toward? Yet at the same time, the passage, in ostensibly providing the answer, seems rather to be concerning itself with what exactly a sentence might be. Beginning with some examples of "practical completeness," wherein completeness seems to reside in a successful communication of meaning wherein "no sentence is needed to make ones meaning more clear," Fenollosa nevertheless closes the passage with the suggestion that completion on the level of the sentence would be ultimately impossible. Because the sentence mirrors nature and because nature is made up of interrelations that cannot be set apart, the sentence can therefore only be complete if—and this is the real fantasy—there were "all time to pronounce."

The unfulfillable promise of a full sentence thus partly accounts for the two strange and difficult examples Fenollosa gives to illustrate the causal interrelations and transferences of nature. The first example of the restless man and similarly restless horse, perhaps an allegorical rebellion of the seen in response to the seeing, appears at first glance to be a meditation on the succession of "acts" as well as what he later calls "motion": to put it as baldly as possible, the man cannot be still, therefore the horse also cannot be still. Framed in a relationship of seen and seeing, the man and the horse are subject and object caught in an apparently linear relation of act and response: in other words, they seem to be functioning as figural stand-ins for a conventional sentence. Yet the second example throws one for a loop, as we learn that motion does not just leak from the polarities of man to horse, seeing to seen, subject to object, but furthermore it "leaks everywhere, like electricity from an exposed wire," such that the man-horse process of causality is only one of "all processes in nature" and their interrelations. Yet as we broaden our views from man to horse to electricity, this series of displacing examples all remain incomplete precisely because where there is interrelation, there is also interruption (as figured in the exposed wire) and thereby the unassimilable and uncontrollable residues of causality that "leak" into nature and constitute it. The sentence, then, also "leaks everywhere": because of this, it is *and* is not like nature, and because of this, it too escapes exemplarity, conceptuality, and the conventionally hierarchical relations of seeing, being seen, and being unseen but nevertheless felt (such as in the case of electricity).

It is in this unusual context that Fenollosa explains the form uniting the ideographic and English sentences.

> The sentence form was forced upon primitive man by Nature herself. It was not we who made it; it was a reflection of the temporal order in causation. All truth has to be expressed in sentences, because all truth is the *transference of power*. The type of sentence in nature is a flash of

lightning. It passes between two terms, a cloud and the earth. No unit or natural process can be less than this. All natural processes whatever, are, in their units, as much as this. light, heat, gravity, chemical affinity, human will, have this in common, that they redistribute force and their unit of process can be represented by the following diagram;—

O >———> O

... [Now] it seems to me that the normal typical sentence, in English, as well as in Chinese, [**just**] expresses just this unit of natural process. It consists of three necessary words;—the first denoting the agent, or subject, from which the act starts; the second embodying the very stroke of the act; the third pointing to an object, the receiver of the impact.

For example

Farmer   pounds   rice

[It thus appears that] the form of the Chinese transitive sentence, and of the English ([barring] **omitting** the particles **a, the, etc**.) exactly corresponds to the universal form of action in nature. This brings language [very] close to things; and in its strong reliance upon verbs erects all speech into a kind of dramatic Poetry.[81]

This enigmatic account of causality cuts to the heart of Fenollosa's claim of a likeness of form between the sentences of the two languages. The claim is that there is an exact correspondence between the Chinese transitive sentence, the English transitive sentence, and the "universal form of action in nature." Here, Fenollosa seemingly rehearses the previous example: indeed, we may well replace "Farmer pounds rice" with "Man rides horse." However, the focus is not simply on causality and forms of action, but how they might "redistribute force" and constitute a "transference of power" through a rather stunning list of processes: "light, heat, gravity, chemical affinity, human will." The form of action Fenollosa supposes here is obscure; departing from the form in his diagram, things like light or chemical affinity do not generally take an object in any obvious way, nor do they act in the same way as "human will" (one can hope). Moreover, unlike a horse that can kick a man, rice cannot pound a farmer, even if it might affect them in other ways that do not take direct cues from their own actions, such as making them less hungry or wealthier. All of which is to say that the present and implicitly dialectical model of a redistribution of force or transference of power, which is also that crucial point of convergence in nature for the English and

Chinese sentences, remains unable to account for the leakages and interruptions invoked in the previous example. Or perhaps the sheer proliferation of absent objects here might be a hint to read these natural processes as *in*transitive verbs, positing sentences that are themselves always incomplete, exposing a wire that can only leak "everywhere" and nowhere at once. Fenollosa's claim of absolute equivalence is thus posed through a textual moment of radical intransitivity, or at least a redistribution of force whose directionality remains unclear.

Translating Hu's "Hope"

In connecting his unusual theories about sentence- and metaphor-based translation to a future-oriented transpacific politics of his time, Fenollosa invites a test of his claim. In finally turning to one of Hu's own poetic translations, I argue that the future takes on a more complex form than either Fenollosa or Pound could have imagined.

Hu's translated poem, simply titled "Hope," was eventually collected in the same volume as "Dream and Poetry," the poem discussed earlier in this chapter. There, I argued that the poem staged a tension between the interchangeability of speaker and addressee and its invitation to a general "experience"—a tension that attends what Hu called his "poeticempiricism," a theoretical term he developed especially in relation to that poem. One wonders, however, if this hierarchy is a static one. Its vision of two separate subjects, who each must make their respective writerly or oneiric worlds of experience even as they lean tacitly on one another, finds a surprising pendant in "Hope," this one less invoked and less well known in the critical reception and literature. Translated from a Victorian-era English translation putatively of the Persian poet Omar Khayyam's *Rubaiyat* by the Sinologist Edward Fitzgerald (1859), Hu's retranslated poem was consciously staged *as* a translation—that is, published in a bilingual format alongside his English source text—in the pages of *New Youth*, where it was first published with another of Hu's poems in the April 1919 issue.[82]

Hu's finished translation bears some resemblance to the Fitzgerald translation—most notably in the structure of the quatrain and his effort to replicate Fitzgerald's AABA rhyme scheme—but also makes at least two important departures from it. In lieu of leaning on Fitzgerald's translation (i.e., Hu's source), I have retranslated his translation into English to highlight the distance between his work and its source while remaining attentive to the form of the quatrain and rhyme.

XCIX
Ah Love! could you and I with Him conspire
To grasp this sorry Scheme of Things entire,
Would not we shatter it to bits—and then
Remould it nearer to the Heart's Desire!
—Trans. Edward Fitzgerald: *The Rubaiyat of Omar Khayyam* (1859)

「希望」

要是天公換了卿和我,

該把這糊塗世界一齊都打破,

要再磨再煉再調和,

好依着你我的安排,把世界重新造過! [83]
—Trans. Hu Shi, *New Youth* (1919)

Hope
Love, were you and I to take the place of Fate,
This sorry world we must together break;
Remold, refine, re-align
To fit our designs—a world newly remade!
—My retranslation of Hu Shi's translation

Hu gives his translation a new title that suggests the acuity and reach of its ambition: Hope, his allegory suggests, resides in the shattering of a messy and confused world in order to ceaselessly remake it anew. In a political moment when his reformist zeal was beginning to take shape and find its strongest expression, it is not difficult to see why Hu may have lighted on this particular poem in a long sequence of more than a hundred quatrains for the *Rubaiyat*, translating what was first a love poem—and importantly working from an Orientalist reiteration of that poem, although he does not seem to recognize it as such—into an allegorical call to arms for Chinese modernity. Indeed, the poem may even be something of an allegory for translation itself, contingent after all on the breaking of one world to reconstruct a newer one.

Yet the poem-translation also conceals more than allegory: published alongside its English source in the pages of Hu's Chinese-language periodical *New Youth*, the poem's status qua translation and transnational reading also tacitly makes the case for the necessity of learning English and other European languages to mine their cultural and explanatory power in regard to the then-plight of China—bringing it back in a full and elliptical circle with Fenollosa's insistence on mastering the language across the Pacific.[84] Hu's "Hope" and its paratextual apparatus and design appears alongside its English resource as a demonstration of what is to be done in the face of such foreign power: it is to be broken, learned, and thoroughly transformed. For inasmuch as the poem draws its rhetorical power from the positing of equivalence between the Fitzgerald translation and Hu's own—an equivalence locating them in a loose contemporaneity and equating Chinese with Persian and Victorian poetics[85]—it moreover draws its metadiscursive power from the radical breaking of that equivalence (as promised in the poem itself and the act of translation too) *and* from mobilizing the way in which the English would only have been partially available to its Chinese readers, mediated through the difficult and utopian middle of Hu's own translation, and remains thus to be approached and learned. More than a didactic or prescriptive translation that presumes to remake the reader in a given image, Hu's translated "Hope" may equally be understood as something of a Socratic mechanism, a means of exposing and indeed realizing what one's interlocutor may not know—and the uncertain future of their knowing as such. Such a reconstructed equivalence, the poem whispers, becomes possible only in the untimely future of reading.

The poem's metadiscourse—as implied in its print medium and titular framing—thus raises the stakes for the considerable changes that Hu makes in his translation. Central to its cosmopolitical aspirations is the translation of Fitzgerald's "Scheme" as *shijie* or *world*, which would seem to highlight a sense of the status quo as a kind of systematic arrangement—even while erasing the secondary sense of a conspiratorial scheming of such a plot.[86] Perhaps because of its new status as "world," such a "Scheme" no longer needs to be "grasp[ed]"—which is to say, seen and demystified as an object of knowledge—in Hu's version: indeed, the action of grasping is silently elided in his translation. In its place, Hu offers a series of three incantatory, sloganeering actions that extravagantly translate Fitzgerald's lone "remould": after breaking a sorry world, the poem's interlocutors are exhorted to *zaimo, zailian, zaitiaohe*—that is, *remold, refine, re-align*—an object that we can only interpretively guess is the old world. The repetition and necessary stress of *zai* (a word attached to verbs in order to indicate a repeated action), translated here with the prefix *re-*, creates an internally regulated line that marshals both the residue of *wenyan* poetics and the trochaic rhythms of English verse, its very form yoking the poem's several inspirations for reform. The first verb, which I have translated as *remold* in a nod to the Fitzgerald translation, may well be better translated as *regrind* or *rehew*—an action in which repetition erodes an object. Yet as the next verb indicates, this action also sharpens or refines, most usefully understood through the logic of a refining fire. Amid these tropes of strenuous improvement, however, is the final action that Hu prescribes: the action of *tiaohe*, an active and instrumental seeking of harmony, balance, reconciliation, rationalization, or even compromise which I have sought to express as *align*. Alignment, in Hu's account, is the final step of reform (and of translation's work of reading): to bring these actions into harmony and to regulate them for a newer world order—even and especially as readers are shown what they do not know and who may even themselves be the material to be refined.

Which alights on the last verb in Fitzgerald's translation that Hu gracefully sidesteps: where Fitzgerald's speaker and addressee are said to "conspire" with "Him" in order to effect their world-changing aspirations, Hu instead insists that his speaker and addressee are to "take [His] place." For Hu's account and translation, the agents of world-making are solely the speaker and addressee, who work in concert to realize their common design; "Fate" or *tiangong* is decidedly substituted—and indeed substitutable, out of the picture. The trope of shattering and remaking a world anew then stems from a moment of substitution, in which the poetic speaker and an intimately addressed other or addressee come to take the place of a deity-like character (personified in the Chinese folk tradition as *tiangong*—lit., *heavenly father*, understood polytheistically and as regionally rooted in the Southern folk and vernacular tradition). In a telling metatextual moment, his translation allows Hu to think of a utopia possible not simply by shattering the existing world but by proleptically putting *us* in place of *Fate*.

The Future of Reading

What then of the ideograph and the ideologue with which we began? Across this detour that sought to assemble—if not unify—two disparate thinkers within a singular transpacific analysis, I have suggested that their conjunction calls to the fore a series of abstractions that function as eccentric modes of translational equivalence. Upon this return, we may well repeat a version of Pound's question: can you ideograph—that is, read and translate—it? As Steven Yao notes in his reading of the *Cantos*, Pound eventually departs from his early thought that any given Chinese writing can and should be translated for an English-reading reader and that the work of translation is itself powerfully generative for the poet's originality—a position that he held in the 1910s around the time of *Cathay* and in the wake of editing Fenollosa's essay. After his wartime move toward fascism, Yao argues, Pound comes to emphasize the effect of an exclusionary and encoded *differentiation* of readers, wherein the Chinese characters, cryptically studded with little explanation throughout the *Cantos*, "automatically excluded the 'lazy' or the 'unworthy,' while remaining open to anyone possessing the right [Fenollosan] 'sensibility.' . . . In this respect, they underwrite a politics based on a hierarchy of abilities, which has its connection to Pound's attraction to Fascism."[87] To "ideograph it" has always been a task with moving goalposts that not everyone "can" do: it is to make apparent the dynamic relations between things—only to render them secret and to withdraw their availability for reading. And insofar as my argument in this chapter has carefully and insistently shifted those goalposts beyond even Pound's reach—through a thoroughgoing comparison of the ideographic imagination and the conditions of its thought—the next three chapters raise the stakes yet further: toward forms of translation with no reading and no future available to them.

2   Sound Translation
Eileen Chang

Hearsay; or, The Revenge of the Translator

The literary experiments championed by Hu Shi found an avid heir in a young Eileen Chang, long before she too became one of China's foremost writers of twentieth-century cosmopolitanism and modernity. Beyond his own experiments in *baihua* or *vernacular* verse, Hu also sought to revive public interest in vernacular novels by penning opinion essays, which were published in the periodicals of the time. As a wide-eyed child among the reading public that Hu sought to reach, Chang took a special shine to two such novels: the well-known Qing classic *Hongloumeng* or *Dream of the Red Chamber* (hereafter *Dream*) and a lesser-known novel published almost a hundred years in its wake, Han Bangqing's *Haishanghua liezhuan*, commonly translated as *Biographies of Shanghai Flowers* (hereafter *Shanghai Flowers*). In several letters to her friend and champion C. T. Hsia as well as her *sanwen* or *literary, occasional essay* written on the occasion of Hu's death in 1962, Chang recalls that Hu's reading of *Shanghai Flowers* had been decisive in awakening her interest in it: after reading Hu's essay, her father purchased a copy of the novel, swiftly devoured by a precocious young reader. This life event was so cherished that the very same reader would eventually return to those texts as a critic and translator, when China and her childhood were an ocean and a lifetime away.¹

In that later part of her career, Chang's work on translation operates along two linguistic axes. In addition to translating between Mandarin and English after moving abroad to the United States, Chang also writes and thinks between the vernacular Wu (from her hometown, Shanghai) and Mandarin Chinese in its evolving forms of standardization.² That is to say, then, that many decades deep into her exile and even after China has moved into its postsocialist era, Chang inhabits a surprising relationship to translation allowing her to tarry with the principles of the vernacular movement as championed by Hu Shi and his contemporaries, even amusing herself and her readers by rhyming it with the English idioms of her new home. Such was the origin story for her decades-long, unremunerated, and largely unrecognized project of translation amid a peripatetic existence, first from the novel's Wu vernacular to a Mandarin translation eventually published for a Taiwanese readership in 1981 and, finally, to an unfinished English translation that was posthumously revised, completed, and published by Eva Hung under Chang's working title, *The Sing-song Girls of Shanghai* (hereafter *Sing-song Girls*).

Thus compounded, Chang's trilingual approach to translation grounds the curious origin myth for this chapter and its argument on sound and substitution: an endnote that appears to have been misplaced between one translation and the next, lost as it were *between* translations. In endnote four in the second chapter of the Mandarin translation,[3] Chang purports to explain a layered circuit of translingual mishearing that gave rise to the term *sing-song girl*.[4] Her reasoning goes as follows: the English term stems from a mishearing of *xiansheng*, a precisely chosen phrase that, in context, would have denoted the social hierarchy of courtesans and is typically reserved for learned men. Women addressed as *xiansheng* are understood to be of the elite—the most educated, refined, worldly. When the term is spoken with a Wu accent, Chang explains with her characteristic undertow of ironic humor, *xiansheng* sounds somewhat like *sing-song*—at least according to foreign observers, who then rationalized their mishearing as a metonymic description of a courtesan's musical entertainment. What is more, Chang attaches the endnote to a moment in the text in which two male client characters discuss a subtle distinction of class: the first wants to know why they did not stay at a party to which they were spontaneously invited, and his companion admonishingly points out that the party had many elite courtesans in attendance, making it a faux pas to call for lower-class women for their own entertainment (implying that they would not have been able to afford the companionship of the elite courtesans at the party).[5] This is what Chang takes as an occasion not only to explain the hierarchical distinctions between courtesans but also to speculate on the mishearing of *xiansheng* as *sing-song girl* from Wu to English.

For Chang to imagine any would-be Anglophone translator substituting a local index of a courtesan's social status in place of an aesthetic transaction for those who patronize her—and mobilizing a calque often correlated with a primitive folksiness—is a telling prelude to the hallucinated philology of sound examined in this chapter. Her little excursus may well have made some sense in an *English* translation but is the more bewildering for being located in a Mandarin translation of the novel, in which that English word does not appear at all. More than that, all three English translations available in print—two short excerpts in the Hong Kong literary journal *Renditions* and the standard full-length edition by Columbia University Press—are in fact missing any explanation of the *Sing-song Girls* working title in the main text.[6] This is especially surprising given that Chang's frequent editorializing—often on similarly tangential matters and not always factually reliable in their wry humor—is most often retained by her editors. Nevertheless, in the mere act of recording this pseudohistorical factoid of sound translation that eventually migrates from endnote to title, Chang quietly alludes to much more than the unruly nature of hearing something and repeating it in writing—a wisdom captured in the common description of the vernacular language as something so embedded in social change, so volatile, that it is *xiebuding* or *impossible to secure in writing*. Transliteration is not a mere transit into a different script or from speech to writing; here, it is demystified as a close kin readily identifiable with the exchange-value of translation—and a domesticating and colonizing translation too.

That Chang would even go on to put the very same invented mishearing front and center as the working title for her English translation suggests that her translingual poetics are quite a bit more than meets the eye. With her, I linger in those untranslatable—and unexchangeable—calques embedded in the sound of speech, developing my argument toward a sense of translation that falls away from its association with reading and interpretation. In the first and framing chapter of this book, I situated the formation of Chinese literary modernity within a transpacific framework. Tied to the same fates, Chinese modernity and the language of modern Chinese are at once the mediating site *and* product of translation. Forging modernity required stabilizing and abstracting the plural body of Sinitic vernaculars into a singular standard system of writing; yet in Chang's subtle take on that idea, even the singularity of that target system may well always have been a translingual and polyphonic one. What imaginative cultural equivalence that may have existed for an ambitious nation's desire to take its place in the world, I argue, was transmuted into an abstract poetics of equivalence characterized by dissociating speech from writing, sound from image: inseparable antinomies of transpacific abstraction. As this chapter moves into the next part of the book's argument, I take a closer look at the first half of that antinomy: the confounding refusals of meaning that emerge when *sound* takes the lead in translation, with writing following in its wake. The result in Chang's case is a mode of almost willfully antihermeneutic translation that looks a lot more like a simple and indeed *unvalued* substitution.

Chang is a particularly interesting catalyst for this argument's turn because her place in the narrative of Chinese literary modernity has always been uneasy, upheld as both exemplar and exception. In treating her as a transpacific writer, I show how her Cold War–era writing on translation captures, ex post facto, both the limitations and revelatory possibilities of Republican-era translation and its cosmopolitan ambitions transplanted across the Pacific. Beyond her short but celebrated early career concentrated in the wartime period from the late thirties to early forties, Chang's lesser-read later writing is generally understood as work stemming from the period after she left her native Shanghai for Hong Kong in 1952 and subsequently settled in the United States from 1955 until the end of her life in 1995. It is only after leaving the mainland that Chang turns to translation, including translations of her own earlier writing, with substantial focus: it is how she makes a living as a writer—at least in the initial moments of her exile working for the USIS and applying for research fellowships in American institutions—but also becomes, as I will argue, an emotive and noninstrumentalist means of reviving some older and fraying attachments to texts that have been influential for her own work. Her metareflective remarks on translation proper are sparse and tend to hew close to expected narratives (itself unsurprising given the circumstances under which she wrote and delivered most of them), centering often on questions of reader-friendliness or the importance of making Chinese culture and civilization known to a wider (American) audience: they consist mostly of paratexts for her Mandarin and English translations of *Shanghai Flowers*, a series of lectures delivered to academic audiences at several host institutions,[7] as well as some of her other self-translations written after moving to the United States.

In discussing Chang's relationship to translation and self-translation, critics have varied in their assessments of its center of gravity in her corpus; such critical inconstancy may well be symptomatic of Chang's own ambivalence on the question. At times, translation is an instrumental expediency—what she morosely calls, in 1964, a "mechanistic work" that if nothing else pays the bills and stays out of the way of her more creative work.[8] Or it may be an index of her belated aesthetic debts to both the Chinese and Western literary traditions, occasioning an interest in self-translation between Chinese and English as a decisive mode of rewriting her own work; the latter is an idea with important antecedents in Chinese literary history, wherein translation was seen as a reconstruction of an open-ended text, commonly coterminous with editing and collaborative approaches to literary production. In the latter regard, critics have traced the delicate and far-reaching effects of Chang's revisionist tendencies, articulating the contingent forms she transmits through self-translation for feminist, translingual, and transnational states of being: as Tsu Jing notes, some of Chang's Cold War–era writing "raise the bar of a possible theory of translation in light of the larger context of Chang's obsession with rewriting and its psychic maternalization of language."[9] A related approach seeks to extend this line of thinking about psycho-historical origins and transmission toward the geopolitical necessities that undergird them, paying particular attention to the ways in which the Cold War inflected her literary production and even epistemic and aesthetic sensibilities.[10] Centering primarily on quasi-epistemic political tropes such as betrayal, collaborationism, information, and truth, recent critical work has deployed Cold War frames of reference to reflect on Chang's perennial interests in the ascetic qualities of love and desire in the face of politics.[11] Indeed, even as Chang's later work is most often considered secondary to the work she produced in her Shanghai youth, it has more recently—especially with the posthumous publication of her thinly veiled autobiography, *Xiaotuanyüan*, and its English translation as *Little Reunions* by Jane Weizhen Pan and Martin Merz—become the subject of critical revisionism and even revival.[12] Moreover, in seeking to assess the role of translation in Chang's writing, critics have largely been confined to her self-translations between English and Chinese (in both directions); with the notable exception of *Shanghai Flowers*, they have largely overlapped with her bread and butter work for the USIS. To put this another way, critical attention has typically focused on her translations in the more literal and intelligible sense of the term.

    Building on this work, I suggest that Chang's commentary on language reform and the Wu vernacular in her literary essays invites a more expansive understanding of how translation surfaces and functions in her work: as a translingual and intersemiotic substitution of speech with writing—and a sound translation that gives way to a gestural equivalence between two levels and registers of language (imperfectly mapped onto *parole* and *langue*). In identifying Chang's throwaway gestures of sound translation with a more legible act of literary translation, my goal is to take seriously—and put to the test—the more capacious definition of translation set out in this book's argument: one in which the processes and contextual terrain of the translator's interpretation are called into question in order to transform ways of assigning meaning when making and reading translations.

Such an argument stands in a complex relation to existing conceptualizations of homophonic translation via the twentieth-century American and European avant-garde. Taken as a self-conscious authorial experiment in the poetic autonomy of language, homophonic translation has thus far been understood as the act of crafting ludic processes of translating purely for and through sound with no regard for sense or meaning. The idea came to prominence with the Objectivist poets Louis and Celia Zukofsky's lush homophonic translation from the Latin, simply titled *Catullus* (1969)—though the Zukofskys may certainly trace their inspiration back to Pound's translations of Catullus and other Latin sources. Within that discursive domain, homophonic translation is generally regarded as an aesthetic curiosity, possible only with languages with common ancestry (typically imagined as European and descended from the Latin). It is not clear if the experimental American poets recognized their work as linked to the transliteration of nouns and proper names in many modes of colonial and semicolonial translations, although much more recent experiments like Jonathan Stalling's—blending Chinese with English along similarly homophonic and transliterating lines—suggest intriguing descendants of a similar practice.[13] If, as Yunte Huang argues, sound translation "changes every word to a proper name and invokes the indexical," then it may well also raise the political and poetic stakes for such a gesture—even if that indexicality may always be doomed to a perpetual historical emptying in the realm of poetry and poetics.[14] In her epic lyric *Commons*, the poet and critic Myung Mi Kim probes the abstracting force of such a gesture, accumulating a connotative cloud surrounding the ideas of translation, translatability, transliteration, and transcription.

> Bit, part, scattered phoneme, suggestion of sounds, a glitch of ear and tongue occurring in unrecognizable patterns: for a long time I dismissed (or could not fold in or hold) these random, skittish stutterings. However, once perceived as (made audible and tactile as) potential sounds in Korean or, for that matter, any number of languages (Middle English, Latin, French) that constitute "English," these roaming fragments fall into the writing. . . . It is not the actual

translation or even the state of translatability between the two texts that is intriguing but the possibilities for transcribing what occurs in the traversal between the two languages (and, by extension, between the two "nations," their mutually implicated histories of colonization, political conflicts, and so on). What is the recombinant energy created between languages (geopolitical economies, cultural representations, concepts of community)?[15]

What is especially striking about the "recombinant energy" that Kim suggests is not only the urgent colonial politics surrounding it but also the fact that she locates its antecedent in "these random, skittish stutterings" that finally could no longer be dismissed when they take their place as "potential sounds" within a given linguistic order. That is, transcription and transliteration between languages—*especially* between a hegemonic Western language like English and a language from another family such as Korean—is a means of signposting those unintelligible *registers* of language rooted in a homeless "glitch of ear and tongue occurring in unrecognizable patterns." Following Kim's lyrical argument, I am interested in sound translation *not* as a non-Western derivative of an existing concept drawn from the Euro-American avant-garde, that is, as a paradigm of cultural drift over cultural difference. Instead, I argue that its very ordinariness, even banality, is the core of its translingual critique against interpretation. Indeed (and in a rather different register), David Bellos observes in his writing for a popular audience that professional translators often make recourse to sound and loan translations, such that refusing to count sound translation as translation would be to narrow the existing liveliness of translation and even—tongue firmly in cheek—"to throw out the baby *instead of* the bathwater."[16] What interests me about Chang's transliterating and sound translations is then not exactly the arbitrariness of meaning to which they give rise. Rather, I want to take seriously the *vernacularization* of those properties as enabling an estranged and eccentric equivalence: one that even more fully realizes—and surprises—Charles Bernstein's distantly related claim that homophonic translation "can symbolize the revenge of the translator: no longer invisible but through the text's opacity [to meaning and interpretation] making the 'original' invisible (or occluded)" by standing in its place.[17]

Embracing a more accommodating sense of translation in turn allows us to recalibrate what we know about Chang's political relationship to translation *and* her relationship to the earlier moments of Chinese modernity, which can only be one of belatedness. In what follows, I recover that surprising kinship between her US-based turn to translation and the earlier May Fourth Republican interest in vernacular writing, arguing that her playful mock-philologies forge vectors of equivalence on the level of the word and its sounds. First, I examine the conditions for this claim in the rapport between Chang and Hu, centering primarily on their readings of *Shanghai Flowers* and the unlikely ways in which the novel's disappearance in literary history comes to be conflated with Chang's translation and substituted with its literary antecedent, *The Dream of the Red Chamber*. Then, turning from these works to three of her short literary essays written in the United States (for a devoted Taiwanese readership that sustained the second part of her career) and which continue to make reference to the Wu of her childhood and of *Shanghai Flowers*, I trace how her sonorous descriptions of cross-linguistic, transnational, and transhistorical echolalia are equally stolen from nostalgic memories of Shanghai street encounters, the tradition of Chinese literature, her long life in letters, and sharp observations of her new home's idiosyncrasies. Together, they along with Chang reject logocentric diagnoses that the vernacular properties of *youyinwuzi* or *speech without writing* were a premodern pathology of China. More than a simplistic nostalgia for home from exile, the abstractions of speech—found then lost in writing—come to enable granular connections of equivalence between languages and times, at and through the limits of signification and even the work of reading.

On Not Reading the Mandarin *Shanghai Flowers*

Published sporadically across her later career as occasional pieces of writing, Chang's idiosyncratic accounts of translingual transfer and equivalence—substituted particles of speech between English and Mandarin, between Wu and its regional variants as well as Mandarin—owe a debt of influence, undetectable webs of memory, to that translingual literary experiment that was *Shanghai Flowers*. What looks like simple, incoherent nostalgia gains a remarkable consistency, I argue, when contextualized by her loving and ultimately hopeless labors of twice translating that text. Often heterodox in her commentary, Chang sought to establish the historical lineage for *her* translation within the narrative of Chinese literary tradition—especially as a self-conscious rebuttal of Hu Shi's claims about the novel's modernity. In 1981, the Mandarin translation was published in Taiwan by her longtime house,

Crown Publishing. This would be only the first of two translations—the first into modern Mandarin Chinese and the second into English—that Chang undertook for a novel that had lingered with her throughout her life and whose aesthetic lessons are ensconced throughout her work. Unlike the other translations that Chang undertook on her move to the United States, however, her work on *Shanghai Flowers* did not seem to be motivated by the need to break into the English-language market in order to support herself; as early as 1968, Chang herself ruefully noted in reference to an English translation of the novel that such a translation project was certain *not* to turn a profit, suggesting thereby that her motivations for translating it lay elsewhere than its commercial appeal.[18] (The novel was also a commercial failure when first published in China in 1892.)

Translation into Mandarin was necessary because *Shanghai Flowers* was written by Han Bangqing with extensive swaths of dialogue in the Wu dialect widely spoken in Shanghai, in part to create a sense of verisimilitude for a novel set in the working courtesan district of a city on the cusp of cosmopolitan modernity. The novel was published in installments in the literary magazine *Haishang qishu*, known also as the *Wonderbook of Shanghai*, which was owned and operated by Han himself. At the time, the print culture would have collapsed the distinction between classical and vernacular fiction, often printing them alongside one another and reflecting their shifting registers. Yet Han took this one step further: his commitment to naturalism was so strong that he invented characters and plotlines for the specific purpose of incorporating the Wu.[19] These innovations of realism were matched by narratological inventiveness: Han rigorously theorized his major aesthetics of *chuancha*, a form of *interweaving*, as well as *cangshan*, which literally translates as *hidden flash or twinkle* but is better translated as an *intermittent revelation*, an opaque foreshadowing that defers explanation for the reader. As these rich terms suggest, Han was also highly invested in the narrative's coherence, and he thought deeply about the powerful slowness of progress and delay made possible by publishing in installments.[20] As a result, this challenging novel reads as a discontinuous narrative with often uneven characterization, as Han explains in an oft-quoted passage translated by Stephen Cheng.

> Before one incident is over, another has begun; sometimes ten or more incidents are launched in succession. The narrative proceeds casually, frequently changing tack. No event is told in its entirety all at once, and

yet no thread is left out. Upon reading, one is aware of a 'text behind the text,' though it is not narrated explicitly, one can sense its presence.[21]

Han's explication of his discontinuous style suggests that the narrative is structured via the fluid and intricate social relations of the novel's world, especially as it follows the male clients who are (often capriciously or indecisively) moving between the women courtesans, men who are directed yet haplessly mystified by the wavering text of their desires. In regard to this hierarchically gendered and heteronormative narrative pattern, Starr observes a little sardonically that "the novel might more appropriately be entitled *Biographies of Shanghai Clients*, as it is their lives that provide the linkages between women."[22] Yet perhaps the opposite tack holds true as well: in its allusive attention to the empty disappointments and opaque stasis of feminine desire, it is then a little easier to recognize some of Chang's flickering modernity in Han's intermittent revelations—what David Der-wei Wang calls the novel's "new typology of desire" that sets desire in an understated tension with the tragic restraints of virtue.[23]

Though the use of the vernacular is far from Han's only literary achievement, the novel's unconventional (and unpopular) wielding of that language-politics is nevertheless its main legacy, for that made it an exemplary vessel of political and linguistic reform for Hu Shi's May Fourth Movement.[24] As I discussed in the first chapter, a key to this reform was to powerfully validate a move toward vernacular writing in literary production in order to reject the classical tradition of old. With Hu's affirmation as a forebear, Chang's Mandarin translation then sought to create, as Xiaojue Wang notes, "a uniform vernacular out of the original mix of the local (Wu dialect), the vernacular, and the classical."[25] Thus the mere act of this translation—as well as its publication in Taiwan, where Chang's loyal base of readers resided—is itself a gesture: such linguistic changes were bound up in decades of nationalizing and modernizing discourse about the state of the Chinese language and the vital importance of its reform, a conversation in which Hu played a central role.

Chang's extended attachment to the novel she translates twice—triangulated and indeed enabled by the advocacy of Hu himself—casts a different light on the ways in which *Shanghai Flowers* has been influential for her relationship to the several literary traditions and marketplaces in which she writes. In this light, it is not surprising that the published Mandarin translation is bookended by two contrapuntal voices: a preface by its champion Hu Shi and an afterword by its translator Eileen Chang, an arrangement seemingly inflected by their places in history and time. The echoes between the two in turn yield some telling insights into the contested, perhaps even contradictory modernity ascribed to this first translation. Where later critical attention has tended to focus on Hu's interest in the novel's Wu vernacular and its eventual association with the May Fourth Movement—indeed, Hu's preface underscores its status in the history of Chinese literature and the development of the Chinese nation as one of very few novels written in dialect—Chang's reading instead renders the comparatively minor moments offered elsewhere in his essay even more compelling. In her translator's response, the Wu is very seldom discussed despite being the primary reason for her translation; indeed, it is often treated as an aside up until one crucial final moment to which I will return. Instead, Chang's afterword orbits metatextual questions of structure, readership, and the historical contagion of narrative style, reflecting on the changes that she has made to the novel beyond the linguistic changes conventionally understood of translation.

And those very metatextual changes exert a gestural force beyond their immediate contexts, reaching toward yet another novel—this one not in need of critical recovery, being historically central to the Chinese tradition's imagination of literary textuality and a yardstick by which all later novels were to be judged. Perhaps the most striking point of convergence between the two writers' commentaries comes from a chiasmus of opinion structured by Chang herself.

> Hu Shi believed that *Shanghai Flowers* was published too early because in its time no one read *fiction, xiaoshuo,* as *literature, wenxue.* I instead feel that it was late by a hundred years. In 1791 *Dream of the Red Chamber* was printed, and a hundred and one years later *Shanghai Flowers* began its serial publication.[26] It was bad enough that *Dream* didn't get finished, but to have been continued by someone else for another forty chapters, only to return and revise the chapters that came before[, . . .] characters lost their multifaceted complexity.[27,28]

Where one of the principal authors of Chinese modernity positions *Shanghai Flowers* as a modern artifact before its time—whose project could only be completed in the future, and implicitly through its translation into modern Chinese as undertaken by Chang—Chang instead imagines the novel as inheriting, deepening, and ultimately completing a past tradition.

Importantly, the denotative subject of Chang's claim is not so much *her* translation as Han's original novel itself. By presenting *Shanghai Flowers* as the intertextual and transhistorical sequel to one of Chinese literature's most vital traditions, Chang makes the case for its importance in literary history, and by implication the need to translate it for a wider audience. Her complaint alludes to the complicated textual and editorial history surrounding *Dream*, whose primary author, Cao Xueqin, wrote its first forty chapters before his death. In its unfinished state, *Dream*'s first forty chapters contained clues to future plot points; based on these narrative clues and other notes from Cao, his contemporaries Gao E and Cheng Weiyuan wrote or reconstructed a further eighty chapters, thus—in this ambivalent way—finishing the text that is available today. In this moment, at least, Chang's interest is less the appellation of a historically-inflected modernity and much more a sense of modernist-aesthetic complexity and experimentalism that has been elided in the fractured completion of *Dream*—and which in her claim would be restored by Han's and Chang's *Shanghai Flowers*.

The analysis as put forth here is at least partially indebted to Hu, for whom there is also a strong resonance between *Dream* and *Shanghai Flowers* in their shared acts of literary experimentation, an aesthetic that renders them both modern in the political sense of forging a radical break from the traditions of the past. Indeed, as Hu notes, Han even goes so far as to style himself after the author of *Dream*, writing a *"wenxue shiyan, literary experiment"* that labors in descriptive realism and eschews the simplistic parallelisms or flatly allegorical characterizations prevalent in lesser vernacular fiction. The two authors, a century or so apart, are thus united by what Hu approvingly terms *youjihua de wenxue geming*, a *literary revolution guided by intention*.[29] Chang's commentary thus remains in a similar register when she consistently insists on the relationship between the incomplete text of *Dream* and the consummating sequel represented by *Shanghai Flowers*—even if her emphasis falls far more on the *incompletion* of a structurally and textually complicated project.

Yet the most intriguing aspect of Chang's afterword is a further claim that remains only tacit: that the incomplete nature of *Dream* has been—by means left subtle or undisclosed, a surreptitious textual substitution—transmitted to *Shanghai Flowers*. The point is made only by way of suggestion, through a loose epistrophe in her afterword: "*Water Margin* is truncated, *Plum in the Golden Vase* is censored, *Dream of the Red Chamber* is incomplete, and

Shanghai Flowers remains in oblivion."³⁰ In this regard, Chang's posited point of difference from Hu still harks to a deeper rapprochement: a shared interest in the readership of the novel—the one modern, the other belated. And, more than that in this narrative, Chang's translation into Mandarin Chinese is then positioned as a partial if weak attempt at completing a highly complex text, riven by narrative gaps and inconsistent characterizations through which translation emerges as a narrative *and* a metanarrative element.

There is little in the textual history of *Shanghai Flowers* to mark it as incomplete in any literal sense; perhaps the only ballast for this claim lies in the text's unpopularity among readers in both its own and later times—to which Hu Shi also alludes in the quote above. Unlike *Dream*, *Flowers* is incomplete to Chang's mind not because its author died but—in a more abstract way—because its readers or readership has died. At stake is how the taste of the reading public has been shaped and constituted: an important element in how critics have plotted the emergent contingencies of Chinese modernity via translation.

In Chang's account, the development of the Chinese novel—and more to her particular point, the failing readership of *Shanghai Flowers*—is intertwined with the late Qing and early Republican moment of intensified translational literary production; in this regard, the critical literature generally concurs with her argument.³¹ Indeed, a significant portion of her afterword is devoted to establishing this narrative, to the point that *Shanghai Flowers* is often elided in favor of discussing the ways in which *Dream* has been misread and miscompleted by its latter authors—a misreading that she analogizes or discusses in the same breath as the negative influence of the Western novel. What the final forty chapters of *Dream* has in common with the (perhaps overly simplified) Western novel is twofold: a simplicity of plot-driven narrative and a desire for heightened emotional expression that has come to form the middlebrow tastes of the reading public. These aspects of reading tellingly reflect what critics have elucidated as a distinctively teleological drive that sets Chinese modernity apart from previous historical change.³² As Chang writes with a hint of frustration, "The influence of the longer *Dream* [as completed after its original author's death] on fiction is inestimable. When *Shanghai Flowers* was published at the end of the nineteenth century, reading tastes were already formed. Their only standard was an extraordinary *qingjie*, plot and ordinary *xijie*, *detail*."³³ At other moments, she even cites and laments surveys in which readers are said to have only remembered plot points from the final forty chapters of *Dream*, in which much of its middlebrow action takes place, and criticizes the double standard that would not chastise Ingmar Bergman or Li Shangyin (standing in here as Western and premodern vessels of culture) for an "illusive, eliding, obscuring, abbreviated [*jianlüe*] style" but punishes *Flowers*—a modern experiment for China—for the very same.[34]

For Chang, if the tradition of the Chinese novel is immature, one has only the Chinese novel par excellence—or at least the fans of its latter forty chapters—to blame. The textual afterlives of *Dream* may thus even be read as an index for her skeptical or pessimistic attitudes toward the historical ruptures affirmed by revolutionary modernity: a triumphalism that masks something of a precipitous fall that was to come. Yet if so, then her pessimism is at least a qualified and attenuated one—one that is weak and allows for even the briefest and barest exceptions.

> [The tradition of the novel] was first interrupted when it reached the peak of *Dream*—only to have that peak crumble into a cliff. But to think that these *Flowers* should emerge a hundred years later. Twice having to live and be extinguished quietly by its own fire, a little part of this novel [*youdian shenme dongxi*, lit., *a bit of something or another, this or that*] has died.[35]

Unsustained and unsustainable by any readership in which it finds itself, Chang's beloved novel can only be the wick that at once conducts and consumes the flame of its own narrative existence—one in which an afterlife holds no promise and is far from guaranteed. That these hidden *Flowers* have emerged from the aesthetic rubble of an imperfect *Dream* may on the one hand point to the novel's surprising and even clichéd resilience—a wildflower blooming in the most adverse of circumstance—qua genre of the vernacular novel and its specific position within that history. Yet even as Chang notes—with equal satisfaction and pathos—its capacity for sustaining itself through this paradoxical sacrifice, she also connects that very capacity to its two events of publication and readership that precede her present translation work—those very self-consumptive events that precipitate its minimalist death. Neither a peak nor a cliff of the novelistic tradition, *Shanghai Flowers*, and its capacity to surprise, is instead something of a trope for that tradition itself: a syncopated history that wakes and sleeps in an unpredictable time that resists measure or rhythm—or a life that seems to die, at least twice, from which another insurrection may be derived.

More than that, this is not where the story ends. Indeed, in Chang's account, the story—properly speaking—*cannot* end. For in the same breath as she diagnoses the ways in which *Flowers* dies and dies again, she also goes on to end her own translator's afterword with an enigmatic couplet marking a third future death.

> Though all this [lack of readership for *Flowers*] cannot be completely blamed on the Wu dialogue, I have still translated it into Mandarin.[36] This is its third publication. I fear only that this book's story is still not complete; it is still missing a chapter, a chapter whose title reads:
> Five times Eileen Chang parses [*xiang*] the Dream of the Red Chamber
> Thrice do readers forsake the Biographies of Shanghai Flowers[37]

As a way to close what was indeed the third version of *Shanghai Flowers* in the public domain, what is most devastating in this final couplet is the way in which the readership's predicted three-time abandonment of the novel and its translation is framed by Chang's own acts of not-reading, too—an act of parsing *Dream* in its stead.[38] In a twist of the knife, Chang's translation will be yet another time for those *Flowers* to live and die by its own flame—a flame that is now shown to burn through the incendiary complicity of its translator. The dense syllogism—characteristically influenced by similarly structured titles that would have prefaced each installment in *Dream* and other late-Qing fiction—frames that complicity in two ways. First, as a parallelism or analogy: Chang's obsessive rereading of *Dream* is akin to—in a way that remains to be deduced—the readership's oblivious forgetting of *Shanghai Flowers*. On the other hand, and this time more teleologically perhaps, it may also be possible to understand the argument as a quasi-ironic meta-reference of cause and effect: *because* Eileen Chang is such a consummate exegete of *Dream*, as is done right here in her afterword, readers *therefore* have reason and occasion to forsake its heir yet again, distracted by Chang's own fatally divided attention that would substitute a description of *Dream* for a translation of *Flowers*—at once a bad reader and bad translator. The two readings are certainly not mutually exclusive: indeed, the existence of both broad interpretive possibilities intensifies the pathos that Chang codes as a "fear" for the uncertain future of her translation (a common enough topos for authors and translators). Less an agent of historical transmission and more simply a conduit to yet another abandonment, Chang's futile effort of translating *Shanghai Flowers* into what may seem like a more accessible language is—as she certainly registers—a largely Sisyphean task. Yet if we follow Chang's account in seeing *Dream*'s project belatedly accomplished by *Shanghai Flowers*, then the latter text can only be truly completed not by way of its own energies or Chang's translation but through her own incessant return to its prior text—a return of description, exegesis, and interpretation—with the corollary possibility that the past will still be sundered after all. Tautologically, the ultimate completion of *Dream* by *Shanghai Flowers* is to withhold its own completion, not in order to make possible an open future but simply to reenact a pessimistic, even fatalistic or melancholic repetition of past cruelties.[39]

Ending her account of her translated *Shanghai Flowers* not with death but the smaller cruelty of gradual and accumulated abandonments, Chang suggests that *her* work of translation is far from charged with the teleological pedagogy of May Fourth translation that sought to remake the modern Chinese reading public in the mode of its own plain speech. More than that, she intimates that *that* project has even been *too* successful. Rather, the strangeness of Chang's practice of translation is simply that it has no readers at all, least of all herself as translator: both its original and its target have been surreptitiously substituted for another text, so that translation may cleave only to the invisible casualties of the national reader qua social formation. To examine the implications of this for her life in both Wu and the English language, I turn now to earlier essays in which Chang engages in more direct reimaginations of language reform.

Unnecessary Distinctions: "A Few Small Observations on Modern Chinese"

Thus far, I have built a curious contextual frame that may help us read Chang's instances of sound translation: an anxiety over *interpretive* reading as it confers an instrumental value to translation, played out in a drama of literary tradition and inheritance in which translation even becomes an antonym to this mode of reading. And in Chang's "A Few Small Observations on Modern Chinese," a short and witty essay from 1978, she further offers an explicit thinking of translation as a strikingly futile apparatus that parses subjectivity and difference—and specifically sexual difference—through a translingual play on sound. First published in the Taiwanese newspaper *Zhongguo shibao* or *China*

Times, this previously unanthologized essay has only recently been collected and published.⁴⁰ Where her translator's prefaces often leave unexamined the question of equivalence and translatability, her observations and proposals in this newspaper essay precisely center on translation as a problematic obstacle, examining in particular some of the ingenious changes and untranslatable difficulties that arise within modern Chinese, especially as the language has constituted itself in the process of modernization. The prescriptive tone of the title and essay is suggestive, especially as Chang opens and closes her remarks by noting both the smallness and importance of the problems she names.

> In case this title startles, a hasty clarification: these "small observations" are not so named for being a rhetorical exercise in humble self-effacement but are actually themselves minute and insignificant. I too feel as if I am making a mountain out of a molehill, and so have never written about them despite always wanting to. But it's not all chicken feathers and garlic peel. It's easiest for the small burrs of fish bones and splintered chicken bones to get lodged in the throat, deep enough and it can be fatal.⁴¹ [. . .] Unnecessary distinctions and punctuation pile on and on, yet the necessary ones we don't have any of; this is a weakness of the Chinese language today.⁴²

The fish bones and chicken splinters are not rendered significant as instrumental elements of either a tasty dish (so to speak) or the body in which they accidentally end up; they merely exist in an irritating, distracting, yet possibly fatal relation to the body that attempts to ingest them. The details that marshal her attention are the surprisingly generative "unnecessary distinctions and punctuation" that crop up as the Chinese language encounters the difference of the other—held as different from the "necessary" distinctions that aid in clarifying meaning in reading. In a nuance on the Saussurean view of language—and in a subtle revision of my argument as discussed in the introduction—Chang points toward the modern Chinese language as a system of differences with no positive terms, whose differences intersect with another system of differences, also and similarly with no positive terms: a linguistic value that does not, after all, make any meaning at all.

The argument then recalls and generalizes Haun Saussy's observation that Chinese becomes described as a "language founded on an absence" of grammar only when it was the object of Western philologists and interacting with their assumptions and epistemological priorities: the paradigm of loss and lack (rendered most clearly in English-language critical discussions of Chinese "lacking pronouns, grammar," as Saussy describes, and "lacking time," as discussed in chapter 4) is only relative to the presumed positivity invisibly supplied by the Western observer.[43] Through this muddied lens, Saussy argues, the Western translator misses the complex idiosyncrasies at work within Chinese: what begins as an interval of difference between two (or more) languages is then epistemologically and descriptively flattened into a unilateral lack. It thus seems as if Chang inherits a related narrative: a similar absence is at work when the Chinese translator encounters a Western text and reflexively locates the loss within the Chinese language. Yet as Chang also notices in the inventive and gratuitous proliferations of new words and punctuation, the so-called absences of the Chinese language become themselves quasi-generative—though stopping short of being useful or even signifying—in part through a consciousness of lack.[44]

To demonstrate: one of the major examples in Chang's essay is a long discussion on pronouns in both the Chinese and English languages. In a chapter extensively discussing the first-person deictic, *wo*, in modern Chinese (without discussing Chang directly), Lydia Liu is particularly interested in its status as a literary trope around which deictic relations are drawn, yet these coalesce around something that is properly and absolutely translatable.

> What is the deictic status of the first-person pronoun in modern vernacular Chinese fiction? Without risking too much generalization, let us briefly recall that, in the texts of Guo Moruo, Shi Zhecun, and Yu Dafu discussed in the preceding chapter, the first-person narrator always finds himself embedded in an interlocking set of symbolic correlatives: I/she (gender), the real/the fantastic (psychological), now/then (temporal), here/there (spatial), the living/the dead (metaphysical), Chinese/foreign (national/linguistic), the modern/the traditional (historical), and the like, each being organized around the desire of the male narrator *wo*. It is important to bear in mind that these deictic constructions no longer reflect a purely linguistic reality that Benveniste identifies in inflected languages, but offer themselves up as literary tropes that cut across linguistic boundaries. They are deictic tropes, so to speak, of gender, subjectivity, time, and space that are constructed as such to represent the

Chinese experience of the modern while never ceasing to make reference to non-Chinese languages and literatures. *Wo* in modern vernacular texts signifies at least two things: it acts as a first-person singular in the language, and it carries the signified of translated deixis. It is, therefore, a perfectly translatable pronoun.⁴⁵

As a pronoun, the modern vernacular *wo* is "perfectly translatable" for Liu because it provides the deictic grounding upon which the textual tropological system will arrange and rearrange itself when the two language systems quietly encounter and refer to one another. What interests Liu here is the explicit and empirically verifiable crossing of the first-person singular from the non-Chinese languages into the modern Chinese language, precisely as a carrier and index of its modernity.

Yet Chang is asking if the first-person "translated deixis" was so translatable in the first place—especially given the structures of signification that are built on its back. For this reason, she seeks to offer a helpful alternative to that *wo*, semihumorously writing that

> I have always most admired the so-called "bald-headed sentences"⁴⁶ in the Chinese language—just as frequently for the old [classical] poetry as in colloquialisms, translators of poetry have routinely had to supply the "I" [*wo*]. The third-person "one" [Chang's text interpolates this in English] is closer to the original meaning. This type of *qingling piaoyi, sprightly drift*, is a special feature of the Chinese language.⁴⁷

For Chang, the perennial difficulty of translating Chinese lies not simply in supplying the *I* in an invisible and routine way, but, further, in even knowing which pronoun to use in the first place. Instead of the *I*, she offers another English alternative for translating the subjective deixis of classical Chinese verse and vernacular writing: the third-person impersonal pronoun *one*. The effect of such a translation might be twofold: it evades the direct interpolation of a first-person *I*, and it further defers the stabilizing potential of this gesture, such that "one" cannot find a stable resting ground for the subject of enunciation. In this case, what I with Chang have so far been calling the "third-person pronoun" cannot even go by this name in a strict sense: rather, it is a kind of multiplied enunciation, in which there is more than one possible subject position without any priority of origin or interpretation.

This argument is rendered even more complex when Chang endeavors to move past the consideration of the first-person pronoun and into a consideration of the second- and third-person pronouns, which are deictically premised on the first person but have had to be inflected with sexual difference when translated from Western languages. In comparison to these second- and third-person pronouns, the *I* is not only perfectly translatable; it is also perfectly sexless, neutral, a "one" that is precisely not one because it is universally without difference. (This is not to say, however, that the many senses of Chinese selfhood are ungendered, only that selfhood is gendered through means other than the differentiating effects of the pronominal.) This property of the first-person pronoun cannot be applied to the second and third persons. As Chang writes, in a remarkable passage only translatable in exposition and commentary:

> 最初提倡白話的時候，第三人稱只有一個"他"。創造"她"字該是為了翻譯上實際的需要，否則有時候無法譯。西方各國"他""她"二字不同音，無論載對白或敘事中，一聽一望而知是指誰。都譯為"他"，會使人入贅五里霧中。此後更進一步，又造了個"妳"字，只有少數人採用，近二十年來才流行。偶有男女大段對白，而不說明是誰說什麼，男方口中的"妳"可以藉此認出發言人是誰，聯貫的上下幾次的人都清楚了。不過難得遇到這種場面，而"你"字又常誤植為"妳"，更把人鬧糊塗了。——"妳"字倒从來不誤作"你"。。。
> 　　美國新女權運動的一個笑話，是把"且門"（主席）改為"且泊森""賽爾斯門"（推銷員或店員）改為"賽爾斯泊森"，因為"門"的意思是"男子"，難道女主席女店員就不算？
> "泊森"是無性別的人。——其實"門"的另一義也是"人"，兩性都在內。——與"妳"剛巧相反，一個是要把女人包括進去，一個是要把女人分出來——男女有別。中國人之間的女權論者也很活躍，倒沒有人反對"妳"字。[48]

What frustrates the English translator in this sequence lies in a twofold problem: the graphic radicals that compose Chinese characters and the fact that there are several homophones and harmophones at work here. Chang is playing on instances of script reform in the modernization of Chinese writing, in which radicals in already established words might be substituted to form new words with new implications; the resultant two words would be sounded in the same way but are only *visually* differentiable.

The specific creations to which she alludes are the feminine and masculine pronouns 她 and 他 or *she* and *he*, both spoken as *ta*, as well as the feminine and masculine second-person 妳 and 你 or *you*, both spoken as *ni*. Both *ta* and *ni* began life with the radical for "human," as seen in 他 and 你, and were at first tacitly understood as universal. The shift first began, Chang explains, when translating Western texts into Chinese: as many Western texts have two different words for a feminine *she* and a masculine *he*, Chinese translators sought also to create an equivalent differentiation, therefore masculinizing the existing term and creating a neologism by swopping out the "human" radical for one meaning "woman, female," thus creating the feminized *ta* 她.⁴⁹ By beginning with the need to translate the she/he distinction, they imported a nuance where none existed before: the words for a previously universal *he* 他 and newly particularized *she* 她 would be visually and graphically differentiated even while sounding the same.

Yet what began as a presumed need for equivalence in this translingual contact with Western texts became more enigmatic or even gratuitous when the very same gesture was repeated in the similar Chinese word for *you*, the second-person pronoun, which as Chang implies (and to my knowledge) does not require a gender distinction in any Western language. Indeed, as Chang notes, the feminine *you* was not popular in China until the past twenty years. Somewhat sarcastically, she explains that it might have been helpful to differentiate second-person pronouns through gender, especially in large swaths of dialogue between a man and a woman in which it can sometimes be difficult to interpretively follow who is speaking at any given time: if a man—as previously marked—was speaking to a feminized *you*, then that would help clarify his own subject position as a man.⁵⁰ Yet this is a fairly uncommon scenario, as Chang notes; further, the masculinized *you* frequently gets mistranscribed as the feminine *you*, not vice versa (though Chang does not name any examples that she might have in mind in making this claim), causing even more confusion in the misattribution of gender.

Such a striking gesture finds an interestingly dissociative counterpoint in the same passage via a reading of the feminist movement in the United States, in which discursive conventions have instead sought to *include* women within a newly formed gender-neutral and universalizing category. Her examples are the difference between the English words *chairman/chairperson* and *salesman/salesperson*. Here, the analytical movement from *man* to the gender-neutral *person* is charted as beginning with man-qua-male, moving to personhood, before briefly and passingly recalling that man-qua-human could historically also be a universal concept that includes both sexes and gender. Yet Chang frames her account of this inclusionary and universalizing gesture in the US context as a joke: in her writing, English words like *chairman* have been transliterated into Chinese words that sound just like their English pronunciations, with no regard for what those Chinese words might mean. Thus *chairman* has been rendered as *qiemen* or 且門: dissociatively, the transliterated word for *man* is *men*, meaning *door* in Chinese. More than that, Chang carries the joke on transliteration to its full metaphorical and semantic potential, continuing to use the word for *door* in her discussion of *man*. The visual joke that she makes clear is that the character for *door* ends up meaning both *man* and *Man* when run through the circuit of translation: from the sound of the English into the sound of the Chinese and then into the semantics of the Chinese.

While it is not my intention to make too much out of this revolving door, what seems clear in a final analysis of these translingual differences is how they lead as if inexorably to another kind of sameness: the modern vernacular *I* may not in fact be so perfectly translatable and neutral—especially insofar as its deixis is compromised by its tropological relations with the second and third persons—and yet crucially gives life to a series of seemingly uncontrollable and nonsignifying substitutions. If Chang's commentary on the second- and third-person pronouns holds—and if the deixis of the *I* is tropologically figured in relation to these pronouns—then by implication the first-person pronoun is also riven and shot through with the sexual difference manufactured by the mechanisms of translation. Even the *I* that is routinely supplied in both English and Chinese writing might well turn out to be closer to the *one* (as pronoun) previously described, in which more than one subjectivity might be at play simultaneously: here, however, the more-than-one structure directly addresses and implicates a you, a him, a she, and yet others. By tracing the untranslatable formation of a floating subjectivity, Chang lights upon an equivalence rooted in the interpretive *excess* of those distinctions that never had to be made after all.

A Philology of Error: *Malentendus* from the Wu

Written some ten years later, close to the end of Chang's life, a pair of pseudophilological essays on the unstable movement of archaic words from the Wu into both its regional kins and Mandarin may well shed some surprising light on her earlier commentary for *Shanghai Flowers* and the recent predicaments of modern Chinese language reform.⁵¹ Written in 1989 and 1990, respectively—when she may well have been working on the English translation *Sing-song Girls*—the short essays are titled after two humorous and ultimately instructive *malentendus* from the Wu and are thus best rendered in transliteration and transcription. Each is framed as a way of triggering a mental investigation into some words of old: the first is titled "Caolubing" (1989), and the second is titled after an utterance particle from the Wu as it has been rendered in an archaic character "嗄" (1990), roughly sounding like *sha*.

The essays' trains of thought are based on the many homophones in and across the vernacular languages of China. To complicate matters further, vernacular speech often had no directly corresponding script character in writing—a linguistic property generally known as *youyinwuzi* or *speech without writing*. Thus, any given written character may well be said and pronounced in myriad ways across the regions of China; in another context, such regional variation may be less meaningful and simply inconvenient, but in a context in which the relationship between speech and writing is so complex, a small difference in pronunciation can often produce a significant difference in meaning (an example in English might be "grass/crass") that may lead to humor or absurdity.⁵²

Each essay traces the translingual pragmatics and afterlives of a word heard one way in Wu and another way by a neighbor or kin to the Wu and thereafter transcribed in writing in often unstable ways: in recuperating the modern stigma of a language whose orality exceeds the capacity of its writing to flexibly signify, Chang reads phonemes with no direct correlate in writing as vagrant, drifting, and disembodied scraps of language—finding in them contingent points of translingual and orthographic transfer between three different languages. Through the typically loose and essayistic structure of Chang's writing, this philology of everyday and vernacular error—with all its contingencies—then shines a different light on Chang's relationship to the canons of translated modernity, further revealing the political possibilities dormant within her pseudo-paleographic approach to language reform.

"Caolubing" was published in 1989 in a Taiwanese periodical, *Lianhe bao*. It begins with a memory brought on by reading a novel from the mainland, in which a protagonist eats a mysterious oilless flatbread typically known as *chaolubing* 炒爐餅, literally, *fried flatbread*. This trope of an unfamiliar flatbread—unfamiliar to her because it was largely a food for the laboring class, as Chang would later inform us—then brings her to an early girlhood memory of listening to the cries of a street vendor in Shanghai selling some type of flatbread with what sounds like a cry of *caolubing* 草爐餅 (the essay's title), here translated literally as the non sequitur *grass flatbread*. It is only then that she belatedly realizes, as if in the time and scene of writing, that the oddly named *caolubing* must have had the same referent as the more logically named *chaolubing*—only it is pronounced differently in Shanghai and particularly by the vendor whose voice had become, by the end of the essay, "the refrain of Shanghai." What begins as a banal *malentendu* then catalyzes a memoiristic reflection on wartime Shanghai, written from a much later time in her life, in which the puzzle of the flatbread slowly becomes displaced by—and is almost fungible with—the puzzle of the laboring man who hawks the flatbread as a ware.

The agent of this substitution is, as it turns out, simply the *voice* of the man—a voice that is markedly parsed from the body of its speaker. For the next memory that follows the one from girlhood has Chang's speaker stumbling upon what must be the same man selling the same flatbread much later in life. In remembering the brief encounter, Chang speculates that he is a Shanghai-born native (few people living in Shanghai were born there, and the distinction between natives and Han newcomers was typically also classed) based in particular on the darkness of his skin, likening him to the putative darkness of Indigenous Pacific Islanders.[53] What begins as a moment of casual and troubling racialization—and indeed a small seismic twist of Shanghainese identity under modernity as it is often generalized qua ethnic *Han* identity—then takes on further dimension when she goes on to speculate almost fancifully about the man's personal history and deduces aspects of his everyday life via the minute details of his clothes, appearance, the various apparatuses that help him hawk his wares, and so on. Yet she invents this act of remembrance of the prosaic and material details of his embodied life—rendered in the realm of the ideal—only in order to eclipse them with the disembodied sound of his voice, which stutters and wafts across the essay like a crackling radio.

I remember all this [the particularities of this man and the encounter] only now as I write; at the time it just seemed like a bit of a shock [*hairan*]. And it was only for that instant, just for a moment: afterwards, whenever I hear the cry of "ma . . . caolubing," it remains a pure euphony, and I completely forget this man who had been made strange by his emaciated darkness. At least for me, his street cry was the real *Sound of Shanghai* for those times—the pop songs of Zhou Xuan and Yao Lee are only white noise from the neighbor's radio, background music and not the theme song.⁵⁴

By the end of this short narrative, one gradually realizes that titling the essay "Caolubing" is less a tribute to any particular flatbread and more a reference to a found utterance—a denial of its speaker and referent—set into a tropological motion that is at once translingual and transhistorical, marking a way and manner of saying that is at once lost and yet still floats on, buoyed by these new waves that are beyond control. For in this moment, Chang implies that her remembered sound, so distinctive to her old Shanghai and the fodder it gives for her nostalgia, still happens through a necessary and imaginary loss of the racial outsider who has not only been the *instrument* that transmits this sound but also its *origin*: a medium that becomes radically disconnected from its message. Thus what begins as a linguistic puzzle written from the nostalgia of exile reveals a far more astringent political work: in reconstructing the life of another—staged through a scene and act of writing but only in order to forget it once more—Chang forges an allegory of what it means to have a speech without writing and the abstracting lengths it would take to create a writing from those ruins.

Such a relationship to a mediated past becomes inflected in an even more complex way in an essay titled "嘎" (1990) written only one year after "Caolubing" (and nine years after the Mandarin publication of *Shanghai Flowers*). Importantly, the word 嘎 may be pronounced two ways: *sha* or *ah*, where the latter is akin to an exclamation. The essay's confessedly tiny drama is to ask how we move from the first way of saying to the second. Its titular utterance is explained in the essay's opening: in her account, Chang was revisiting her written screenplay *Taitai wansui* (a film with a contemporary setting written during Chang's earlier career in mainland China, produced and released in 1947) when it was reprinted in the periodical *Lianhe bao*. Yet more than forty years after the film was written and produced, she had found that the film company's scribes had silently substituted that unusual archaism for her original choices as they were transcribing or reproducing her work.⁵⁵ The discovery then sends her down a paleonymical and philological rabbit hole of research into this word that is (coincidentally or not) prominent in Wu vernacular writing like *Shanghai Flowers*—and in particular the processes of signification and substitution that have simplified and therefore erased the term in more recent years. *Speech without writing* thus presents a problem of orthography insofar as the lack of a direct correlate in writing paradoxically proliferates the number of possibilities in the process of transcription, such that the apparently mechanistic work of "copying" becomes also (albeit unintentionally) a philological and translational one that generates hitherto unforeseen possibilities of equivalence.

Most salient for present purposes is Chang's long discussion of 嗄 as it appears in the very first version of *Shanghai Flowers*. The central work of the essay traces the movements and transformations of its various homophonic relatives as they are heard and written across Shanghai, Suzhou, and Yangzhou—that is, the essay dwells and tarries with the apparently minor differences in enunciation across regions close to one another—as well as how they become stabilized in the imminently standardized Mandarin. What this means is that a word easily understood in Shanghai, for example, may not be so easily understood only sixty-five miles away in Suzhou; since readers in each place may hear the same written word differently, they may not infer from it the same idea or function, because how it is heard regionally also has implications for its signifying function within the text. This general problem of the languages across China is what Chang has in mind. And in seeking to solve the typographical puzzle of how her own fairly common word was substituted for this comparatively archaic linguistic antecedent, Chang not so coincidentally turns to an author whose work she knows extremely well, for he too has also engaged in a similar act of substitution.

> *Shanghai Flowers* was written for Wu-speaking readers. If its author Han Ziyun [courtesy name of Han Bangqing, often used interchangeably in literary contexts] pioneered the use of 嗄 to represent 贾, not only do 夏 and 贾 not even sound the same, but he should also have realized that readers may be confused, uncertain if 夏 follows their own pronunciation (*dufa*) or if it follows Mandarin (*guanhua*). Whenever there is someone already using 嗄, Han has borrowed [the word].⁵⁶

Yet what for Chang had been a typographical *error*, apparently contingent on the text's conditions of production, is for her predecessor Han something of a linguistic or literary *innovation* that may nevertheless have unintentionally confounded his readers. Yet this innovation is not a neologism per se but rather a novel borrowing and relocation of a term in a new linguistic context, partly akin to a foreignization as understood in translation studies. However, it still begs the question, from *where* has he borrowed it? Chang partially addresses the question when, shortly after the same moment in the essay, she inflects her original interpretation in another direction.

> The Yangzhou language (*hua*) is in contact with the trends (*zhuliu*) of putonghua, but the 嗇 that ends questions in contemporary fiction is unique to the north of Suzhou. 嗇 may be spoken as 沙 or 舍, and probably was originally 嗄 before the accent gradually slipped (*nian zou le qiang*) and it became 沙 or 舍 because it was easier to say [lit., *a matter of saving some energy for the lips and tongue*].
>
> 嗇 has a connotation of anger and irritation, similar to the 嗄 in *Shanghai Flowers*. Thus Han may not be said to have borrowed 嗄 ; rather, it has always existed as a word, only pronounced with slight differences (*shaoyi*) in Suzhou and Yangzhou.⁵⁷

In an instant, what had appeared to be a debt or misappropriation—a flouting of linguistic property and propriety across the regional territories—is transformed into a question of mere linguistic variation: it is not that Han has taken something from somewhere; it is rather that he has used it so that it is to be said *differently*. Indeed, what is also striking in this moment is Chang's own careful differentiation of, on the one hand, linguistic borrowing and, on the other, having "always existed as a word, only pronounced with slight differences" (all the words above are spoken on a spectrum from *sha* to *xia* to *she*). While not necessarily posited as binary opposites, the two are presented as distinct modes of relation and indeed substitution.

Yet the story of how 嗄 came to be spoken as *ah* has a final act in Chang's narrative, this time through a specifically *typographical* rather than spoken slippage. Such a twist happens precisely when the titular 嗄 enters written dialogue—which is to say, the writing of speech that is partially drawn or transcribed from speech but that also eventually directs the way such written speech is spoken—and initiates something of a trend in the region.

> *The Plum in the Golden Vase* [*Jinpingmei*] has the word 嗄 without using it in this way [as an utterance particle], but later talking scripts may have done so. Once 嗄 entered the stage or scripted dialogue, it must have been simplified to 吓. With fewer strokes for writing, it must have been more expedient for the writers and their scribes, making it trendier than 嗄. The trend reached the outer limits of northern Suzhou, and without the 嗄 at the end of sentences in Yangzhou, people there did not know what to make of it, and thought that it might have been the most common exclamation at the end of sentences 呀. At that time Suzhou did not yet have Han [Bangqing, author of *Shanghai Flowers*] and had not yet experienced his discovery that 嗄 was merely 贾 but pronounced with a slight difference in the Suzhou vernacular. And so they did not recognize that 嗄 had been simplified (*suoxie*—lit., *shrunken writing*) as 吓, and followed everyone in using it as they would 呀.[58]

The passage traces the gradual twofold typographical simplification of 嗄 *sha* to 吓 *xia* and then to its lookalike 呀 *ya*—and finally, as the reader is to infer, to where it ends up in Chang's transcribed dialogue as *ah*. While 嗄 had been transcribed as 吓 due to similarities in pronunciation and a comparatively simpler written character, 吓 *xia* becomes 呀 *ya* only through the sheer ignorance and even wild assumptions attributed to the poor readers of Suzhou, who found those two words not so different after all. Bracketing the reliability of Chang's quasi-philological fiction (impossible to verify or adjudicate), what emerges through this winding path of malapropism is a simpler observation: *these* malapropisms have ensued not through the slippage between regional dialects but through a readerly laissez-faire of the sort that had opened Chang's essay—as well as my chapter—to begin with.

3   Concrete Translation
Theresa Hak Kyung Cha

The Activator of the Pieces

Dictée by Theresa Cha is not a text for laissez-faire reading. The first page establishes its conceit and central theme: a French dictation exercise that requires one to transcribe any given speech into writing, followed immediately by translating the transcribed French paragraph into English. Transcription and translation live in the same space, on the same page, but the paragraph of French appears on top of the English as if as a frame, with only a narrow gutter lying between the two blocks of text. It takes a little beat, just a quick moment, even to realize that the two paragraphs are sisters, especially if one was not especially familiar with the French that opens the book: at first glance, one notices that they are of roughly the same length, then that every word or phrase is separated from the next by an unusually wide space, making it easier to identify a French word or phrase with its English sister. Only after making this connection does one realize that there is something peculiar about the transcription: in a fashion that may be passive or impish or both or none, the scribe seems to have written down even the words dictating the necessary typography and punctuation: *Aller à la ligne* reads the first line, corresponding to *Open paragraph* in the English paragraph; *point* reads the French, and *period* reads the English.[1] Odd fidelity if it can even be called that: on this goes neatly for a line or so until they start to become difficult to match up, either because the French phrases tend to be longer in length than the English ones and thus occupy more of the line or—as the reader may detect when they slowly compare the two in order to find their meanings in identification—the slightest inconsistencies are slowly being introduced between transcription and translation: *loin* translates to *from   a far*, the English phrase fractured by distance and redolent with the effort of breath. At least one set of *ouvre les guillemets* and *ferme les guillemets* (*open quotation marks* and *close quotation marks*) seems to be missing from the English, the reader notes with confusion and perhaps even a bit of relief, for their presence was starting to make the reading all the more difficult. In trying to form identifications between these two apparently equivalent textual entities arranged just so, one finds only the smallest differences from which one's reading must begin.[2] Translation, learned slowly and surely in this laborious reading, is at once too enduring and too filled with holes; transcription hides the imperatives of convention by subsuming its dictates into the arrangements of textual space. And even when its secret arrangements have been revealed, it is only too easy to lose sight of them once again.

The very premise of *Dictée* is a conceptual torsion for the previous chapter's argument. Writing about Eileen Chang's transpacific late work, I traced the minimal equivalences of sound translation—rooted within the fiction of transcribing the vernacular—as an anti-interpretive gesture of translation. In this chapter, I build on the implications of that argument, searching the political limits of an anti-interpretive mode of reading in order to bring forward the *spatial* codes of equivalence built into Cha's phenomenology of duration and politics of unintelligibility. By the time one encounters these sister processes of transcription and translation on the first page of this curious book named *Dictée*, they have already been completed and sit static on a page. Yet there is a potent friction between the two, animated by an eye and mind of reading that seeks meaning in that oscillation only to encounter its withholding.[3] The place of the audience or reader in Cha's art is consistently a pronounced one: "S/he is the receptor as well as the activator of the pieces," reads an early statement of her aesthetic intent to which both Cha and her commentators persistently return.[4] For Cha and her life in performance and media art, translation is not so much a meaningful traffic between different languages as a strenuous linguistic negotiation of human and textual bodies with those spaces and times that threaten to overwhelm them. Reading Cha's translation can never simply be an exercise in interpretation, hers or ours; rather, it is to *participate* in those broken processes of language and subject formation within which the space of difference becomes a vanishing target that invites a collective experience, a "space where the audience are left free to imagine, to remember their own memories."[5]

In this staging of *Dictée*, I am indebted to an extensive critical tradition for whom Cha is an especially unlikely source for any affirmative claims about equivalence. An avant-garde performance artist and writer, as well as a practitioner and scholar in the field of apparatus theory, Cha was primarily active in the Bay Area in the 1970s and left behind an intimate corpus of art and writing after her untimely death in 1982. Born in Busan, Korea, and migrating to the United States at the age of thirteen after the Korean War, her category-defying work has drawn readers deeply invested in third world feminism, American literature, Asian American literature, diasporic writing, and postcolonial translation. Critical readings in these veins have clustered around her sprawling and intractable epic *Dictée*, a text that works through compositional principles of assemblage, filled with invented citations and untraceable borrowings from somewhere else, in purporting to tell the interrelated stories of several women across the history and terrain of the world, ranging from Joan of Arc to Cha's own mother, who left Korea to seek refuge in northern China during the period of Japanese rule in Korea (1910–45). Throughout, there is no consistent diegetic voice in evidence, only crosscurrents of resonance between the multiple voices of the text that can be difficult to hear. Translation—qua formal practice, theme, and metaphor—is central to the metatextual framing of the quasi-historiographical project, its disobedience to history taking indirect and even passive forms in pseudomimicry and the very slightest elisions.[6] Thus Naoki Sakai notes that the dictation exercises serving as its guiding conceit turn out to mime the fractured impossibilities of representation, exposing the sheer labor—and provisionality of meaning—of moving from one language to another in their disjunctures.[7] In that process called translation, and in instituting a stuttering distance between original and target (paralleling the distance between speech and writing), *Dictée* frustrates the developmental narratives of racial formation and integrative immigration to bear witness to their lacunae.[8]

Hinging on the ethics of an relatively legible difference emerging in translation, the very same factors that made *Dictée* an insurgent classic of third world feminism and Asian American writing recovered in the early nineties then also make it an important case *against* claims of equivalence for critics influenced by the postcolonial theory of the same historical moment. In this context, the critique of equivalence takes two related forms. First, any false equivalence will always fall short of an origin dictated to the displaced migrant and racialized subject, for whom alienation will always be a social fact. Second, refusing equivalence also expresses a concomitant need to refuse the solicitation toward the nation-state and other institutionalized collectives in which one may experience the comforts or pleasure of identification, yet thereby become open to exploitation by those modes of power. In this context, Lisa Lowe observes that "it is precisely at the junctures of proposed equivalence that ideology may be interrupted and challenged and that specularity, homology, and identification are each vulnerable from the standpoint of differentiated social and material relations," highlighting the political stakes of insisting on an anxious irresolution—melancholia—that must be endemic to any reconciliation offered through the promise of equivalence.[9] And as Shelley Sunn Wong further notes, building on the postcolonial theorist Homi Bhabha's critique, "The translation exercises in the text of *Dictée* open up the possibility of thwarting operations of equivalence and commensurability at the same time that they allow the dictated subject to claim her own ability to signify."[10] For critical projects seeking an oppositional politics from Cha's abstract work, at stake in *Dictée*'s vexed translations is the critical self-positioning of the subject and her unplaceable, heterogeneous position in history—which is to say, a nonequivalent translation is that subject's means of anticolonial struggle. Without identity of origin, and against the contradictory forces of overdetermination and interpellation, equivalence is not the goal but only that subject's false and coercive premise.

For the field of translation studies, the analysis of a vanishing yet forcefully critical subjectivity (as exemplified by Lowe and Wong above) bears powerful consequences for conceptualizing the interventions of translation.[11] For even as both fields have in common a general insistence on attending to forms of agency within structures of differentiation, they have done so with separate ambits: where the field of translation studies is centered on reclaiming and asserting the differentiating interventions of a translator over and against the question of originality (because the translator has hitherto been understood as secondary to an author invested with the authority of the original), the early moments of Asian American studies have been more concerned with the production of difference as a *mandatory* space. Where the translator has been required to be *invisible*, the Asian American subject has been required to be *different* in that they are subject to the workings of social differentiation rooted in the inhospitable parameters of US state and imperial violence—including the softer coercions of a multicultural or "postracial" framework within which a lived difference is subsumed into the larger political commons. From that shared tension, I would suggest, emerges a need to reimagine the agency of the translator—a task to which Cha dedicates herself across her writing and an indispensable argumentative move for this book. For even as *Dictée* called upon earlier scholars of Asian American studies to translate its unfinished subject into the sociopolitical claims that have always haunted its pages, it also invites translation studies to denaturalize—or render into a concept, a figure, a matrix—the systemic grief that may attend the claims of the translator herself.

Thus I propose an unexpected return to equivalence as a way to affirm the agency of the translator without forgetting the machines of social and biopolitical differentiation that make her who she is: an aesthetic strategy of arrangement that I call "concrete translation" peppered across Cha's work.[12] For insofar as the translation exercises of *Dictée* seek to return agency to its subject through a politics of unintelligibility, its task still relies on a self-identifying reader whose protocols of reading were staged in the opening of this chapter: a reader who must fail in their interpretation in precisely the same way the subject of *Dictée* fails in hers, in order for the critique to succeed in that transferential relationship. "The artist becoming object for the viewer, the viewer as subject, the artist as subject, and viewer as object"[13]—in the aesthetic covenant that Cha forms in even the earliest moments of her work, nothing succeeds like failure: realizing the political project of *Dictée* requires one to posit translation—a vector of racializing power via language—within a hermeneutic and epistemological frame, so that it is only by falling short in those capacities—finding that one cannot be equivalent—that the text generates its critical dissonance, confounding protocols for reading by requiring another one. May the text's ethical allegiances to a subjectless existence[14] be more fully realized if the frame of translation extended beyond even the claims of my and another's reading and knowing—reduced to a (no less colonizing, no less racialized) register of space and time that "plays up the arbitrary relation between the sound of a word, its visual spelling, its multiple referents, and its foreign mate in translation"?[15] Asking this question, I argue, brings into view the critical interventions of Cha's translation in often undetectable *forms* on the page or screen. Concrete translation names the *arrangement* of many moving parts to compose a translation—and only after that, a subject of translation, a translator—so as to offer shelter from the violences of recognition, amplify the scope of critique, and ignite radiant alternatives to those logics and organizations of racial and geopolitical space that render translation necessary to begin with.

To develop this argument on spatially arranged modes of equivalence, I look beyond *Dictée*, arguing that Cha's rigorous parsing of translation in her minor works transforms her melancholic—and stridently negative—"anti-documentary desire" into an insistent and abstract flexibility.[16] Of the many experimental strategies Cha deploys in her minor works, one in particular stands out in its consistent use for translation: superimposition, a technique of layering one image or sound over another with the effect of distorting or occluding the multiple layers—even as it also generates a seemingly simultaneous co-incidence of distinct layers, thus spatially laying claim to a palimpsestic organization of time through which past, present, and future may be constellated into nonlinear relation.[17] The technique extends beyond its roots in photography and film, appearing in coded ways in her writing too. Taking seriously this formal technique as a performative instrument of Cha's political and theoretical claims, I argue that Cha's critical translations are embedded in the discontents of concrete form, describing translation as a "tension of things-words in space-time" with elements that are at once "verbivocovisual."[18] Layering scenes, bodies, and words upon one another—each unreadable because of the others crowded into the same space—excavates the critical potential of abstraction and a sameness between vanished objects that cannot be named or distinguished from one another: in Cha's words, that promise is "the search the words of equivalence to that of her feeling. Or the absence of it."[19] In her erratic manipulating of her translations in their spatial dimensions, concrete translation is a means to seek shape and shelter from the material violence of nonequivalence. It is precisely when translation is reduced in extremis in Cha's work that I imagine another equivalence, saturated by an ambivalent impulse toward regulation. By focusing on the self-concealing work of arrangement—most often exemplified in the logic of superimposition—I trace how Cha's critical translations modulate one life, time, and home with all of her others, reconstituting the startling power of reduction in an age of transpacific abstraction.

In the four sections that follow, I first examine an enigmatic play of time that traverses the space of the Pacific, the result of Cha's first return to Korea after seventeen years and recorded in the poetry of *Temps Morts*. I then turn to her notes and sketches for the unfinished documentary that occasioned the return to Korea, *White Dust from Mongolia*, which reads as something of an early *Dictée* and which she imagined as a cultural translation for a US audience: for this documentary, Cha had envisioned translational voices as crucial aspects both within and outside the film's diegesis, yet these are figured with subtle shifts in representation and tonality. Last, I return to *Dictée* in light of these other texts, examining a metatextual allegory stemming from an enigmatic *delay* of translation between the Chinese and the English and uncovering its consistencies with and divergences from the critical consensus: like Fenollosa, Cha did not know Chinese and very likely cribbed or photocopied this translation (from a source that I have not been able to identify). And like Fenollosa, the formal possibilities of Chinese writing were of special interest to her. Yet *Dictée*'s preoccupations at once demolish and reconstruct Fenollosa's gestures, animating them with the force of memory and time and, I contend, bringing them full circle for my argument. Cha's arrangements break down distinctions and theorize the condition of transpacific translation as one of dynamic regulation against the organizations of space and time. At stake in this collapsed and flattening regulation—what the first chapter presented as a form of abstraction—is what she calls the "trans-immigration of image and memory" traced across the pages that follow.[20]

Against Space: Translating Time Difference in *Temps Morts*

In 1979 and then 1980, Cha and her younger brother and cinematographer James made two trips to Seoul, South Korea. For both, these visits were the first return to Korea since moving to the United States and as such seem to have assumed a great importance in Cha's mind. The second trip was to gather material for her work on a new documentary envisioned as both a film and a historical novel, *White Dust from Mongolia*, as well as other shorter pieces of video art. For *White Dust* Cha had received a small grant of $3,000 from the National Endowment for the Arts (NEA) and a Chancellor's Postdoctoral Fellowship of $15,000 from the University of California, Berkeley: the grant application's "Statement of Plans" indicates that she had pitched it as a work of cultural translation of Korea for an American audience for whom the Korean War was the only point of understanding or entry.[21] Her notes for *White Dust* (which I examine in the next section) indicate that she took this aspect of her promise seriously, going so far as to plan in detail how various translating narrators would function within and without the documentary's diegetic world. Yet the work on the film was ill-fated and, being unusually difficult to make, never finished. During their visit in May–July 1980, a series of political exigencies got in the way of their work, leaving them adrift in a newly inhospitable home: South Korea was in the midst of political tumult following the October 1979 assassination of then-president Park Chung-Hee by his security chief and director of the Korean Central Intelligence Agency.

With rumors flying across the country and heightened unrest in Busan (the hometown that the Cha siblings shared with the assassin, Kim Jae-Kyu), two young people carrying a large camera—and who spoke limited Korean by that time—had a difficult time earning the trust of the locals and getting the footage that Cha had wanted and planned. Cha did not adapt her private intentions to suit the rather more dramatic political situation in which she had accidentally found herself. Instead, her reaction was to abandon the film altogether and rework *White Dust* as a historical novel instead—possibly what would eventually grow into the much wider scope of *Dictée*. All that now exists of *White Dust* is thirty minutes of raw footage and the planning notes in her papers and journals.

Before turning to her work on *White Dust*, I want to contextualize it through a muted logic of superimposition—presented through a heightened spatial awareness—in Cha's poetic writing, unexpectedly taking place through an abstraction of global modernity most commonly known as standard universal time. Upon returning to the United States after her first trip in 1979, Cha repeatedly returned to the motif of a sixteen-hour time difference and recorded those thoughts in her poetry collection, *Temps Morts* (1980). Sixteen hours is the difference between the Pacific Standard Time of Cha's base in San Francisco and Korea Standard Time, the two time zones most prominent in her life. Yet in her poetic writing, that apparently simple explanation takes an unusual form and indeed does not ever get named as such. In this mode of translation, prose yields to number, recording a tally that does not add up.

> she tells me it's always the woman operator
> she tells me it is sixteen hours
> sixteen hours from here   a head
> ahead of this time she says, if it is four thirty
> p.m. here, it is eight thirty a.m. there.
> the next day.
> if it is twelve midnight here, it is four a.m.
> there the next day.
> if it is seven a.m. here it is eleven p.m. there
> the next day seven or seven thirty
>
>   eight thirty   -1
>   nine thirty   -2
>   ten thirty   -3

           eleven thirty   -4
           twelve thirty   -5
           one thirty   -6
           two thirty   -7
           three thirty   -8
           four thirty   -9
           five thirty   -10
           six thirty   -11
           seven thirty   -12
           eight thirty   -13
           nine thirty   -14
           ten thirty   -15
           eleven thirty   -16
that would be the right time precisely just right
it's ringing at the other end all these months
she tells me it's sixteen hours ahead then the
other night she tells me it's seventeen
    midnight there   the next day   always[22]

Translation is the purview of the patient and reliable "woman operator," whose job is to translate one time into another across the implied space of the Pacific. Tellingly, the simple conditional is attached to "here" rather than "there," suggesting that it is "here" that is ultimately fragile and provisional. The time difference between "here" and "there"—those spaces contoured by the movement across the Pacific—insistently position Korea in the place of the future, "the next day," sixteen hours ahead. Reading this particular moment, Ed Park notes with some pathos that despite Korea being aligned with the future, "the irony is that for Cha, Korea is the past, *her* past."[23] But even as that awareness dominates, Cha still writes in a simple present tense—a superimposition of the future onto the present. Korea is not a past to which one will return, or a future to which one strives: it is, quite simply, a future that quietly inhabits the now. This space of the future is thus neither a nostalgic projection nor a utopian promise. Instead, the temporal relation between Seoul and San Francisco is transcribed as an idiomatic difference that is asserted in the realm of the given—to put this as a tautology, it is what *is*—but that cannot quite be collapsed into the American and self-situated "now." For Cha, "here" and "now" come apart and cannot be put together—the condition of exile irrevocably severs space from time—because between the competing abstractions of standard time, on the one hand, and the concept of the present, on the other, "now" may now be stretched across so many parts of the world, yet reconstructed and layered in one. The accounting of that difference from within the vast terrain of the present is precise, yet mathematically difficult to grasp: not only does it expose the artificial interpellations of time as an apparatus, but it furthermore presents the future to us as *already* a part of the effect of the given world.

And in the arrangements of poetic form, the relation between the time of "here" and the time of "there" is deeply unstable and not always reliable. When these deictics first appear, they appear in the same line: "if it is four thirty / p.m. here, it is eight thirty a.m. there. / the next day." Following the denotative meaning of the passage, one may wonder why the line breaks where it does and why "there" closes out the line with a period. A more precise (or pedantic) mathematical reading would require an enjambment to the next line: after all, it is supposed to be eight thirty a.m. *the next day*. Indeed, a similar enjambment does happen in the second appearance of this paired deixis, albeit with another curious break in the line: "if it is twelve midnight here, it is four a.m. / there the next day." With the Korean time dangling so close to "here," it is only the poetic motion of enjambment that brings us "there" and to a time of "the next day." It is then the trope of the next day that becomes the crux in the final pair of "here" and "there," where one learns that "if it is seven a.m. here it is eleven p.m. there / the next day seven or seven thirty" with no punctuation this time and only a line break to mediate the several clauses in the two lines. For even as "here" and "there" are once again restored on the same line, a closer inspection and calculation reveals that a sixteen-hour time difference would not bring us from seven a.m. to eleven p.m. the *next* day; instead, those two times would remain in the *same* day (at least according to the temporal conventions with which the text is playing). Enigmatically—and in striking contrast to its first appearance where it was set off and defined by both an ungrammatical period and a line break to be enjambed—this instance of "the next day" is grammatically unmoored and contextually meaningless even as it is formally integrated into the line: more than careless math, its catachresis marks a future that belongs only in the realm of form but not in the grammar of time and the space it traverses.

What is more, even the convention of standardization is forced awry when the sixteen-hour difference becomes seventeen. The simplest explanation is a banal one: South Korea does not practice daylight savings time, and so when Pacific time falls back by one hour, it leaves Korea another hour ahead. Yet this fact does not answer anything about the poem: Cha's poem does not register this banality, nor does it mention the fact that seventeen will return to sixteen in the spring in a cyclical rather than linear mode of time. Instead, the poem burrows deep into the pathos of a future that would seem to be constantly recalibrating itself, unreachable: a moving and even unrecognizable target of translation.

What frames and brings us to the unstable future is a pronouncement with no clear antecedent: "that would be the right time precisely just right"—an uncanny equivalence between "there" and "now" spoken by and promised to no one in particular, and only in the subjunctive mood, asserted against the instability that came before. By which logic of regulation could these incalculable and imprecise times possibly be "right"? By the end of an exhaustively measured and assiduously reduced journey from the now of the *here* and the now of the *there*, any possible arrival can only be measured by an absence—the word *here* no longer makes an appearance. Instead it is only "midnight there the next day always" —from the temporal threshold of midnight there, it becomes possible to reach across a textual gulf toward the next day, and the spatial distance on the page between those two deictics is only equivalent to the distance between the next day and "always." Superimposing "here" onto "always" may well be one of the consistent gestures of Cha's work; in the process, this quietly multiplied "always" becomes the home of a translated time.

Furthermore, the layered translations of standard time get inscribed onto another abstraction, the body, developing the leitmotif of the sixteen or seventeen hours in the next poem of *Temps Morts*. Where the previous poem is an account of making a long-distance phone call, the same figure of temporal difference becomes improbably threaded into a *spatial* account of gradually walking into the sea with a rope and a stone. Yet despite its very different register, the figural specificity of a malleable, inchoate time difference—and even of a "ringing at the other end"—remains intact amid the drift.

> walking into the water into the tides wearing
> it's in black and white the waves tides come

> still walking into water knee deep into waist
> deep into chest deep for to meet with to make
> invincible compress seventeen hours what used to
> be sixteen it's this ringing at the other end
> station to station neck deep it's in black and white
> sheen of white foam the iridescent grey foam
> silver pearline
> at the edge of this tip water rope and stone tied
> at the end keep throwing it might land at the
> other edge seventeen hours ahead tomorrow there
> what used to be sixteen[24]

It is difficult to say definitively that this is a scene of suicide, for even as it pits a vulnerable body against a forceful ocean, the sure destruction of that body is far from its central drama. Instead, in a series of syntactically jagged lines, the poem meticulously calls attention to how that body continues to *measure* even as it wades into that ocean, what its hands seem to continue doing, and indeed where it may yet go with and against the forces of tide and wave. Such difficulty may well be the crux of the tensions only quietly disclosed in this poem. Like the calculation of time difference it is at once a scene of loss and a scene of progress (in which the latter does not cannibalize the former), the objects and goals of which are impossible to name and track other than through numbers there and bodies here: first "into the water into the tides," then "knee deep into waist / deep into chest deep" before, several words later, becoming "neck deep." Between chest and neck is the meeting and making of an "invincible compress" intransitively aligned with "seventeen hours what used to / be sixteen it's this ringing at the other end"—which, in yet another moment that may or may not be transitive, is enjambed toward "station to station." Between those stations (perhaps) a ringing may or may not be taking place: the borrowed figure from the previous poem suggests that it may be the ringing of a telephone, yet here such a ringing may well also imply a different form of resonance between two spaces—even times, futures—yet to be specified.

The enigmatic ringing is further developed in the second half of the stanza, in which the image of the sea intensifies in the vivid black, white, silver, and "iridescent grey foam" grains of photographic forms even as the protagonist of the poem is told by the speaker to "keep throwing it might land at the /

other edge" of something else also unspecified. To these relational and spatial figures that point without pointing *to* an object, the only possible answer is an old refrain: "other edge seventeen hours ahead tomorrow there / what used to be sixteen." What distinguishes this appearance of the future from its previous instance in the same poem is not only where the line breaks but also an addition of "ahead tomorrow there"—an edge of the future encoded there where the line breaks between the seventeen hours and what it used to be. For if the poem can be read as a dance with the future, or an attempt to traverse the ocean standing between present and future, then its dance also seems to poetically slide from a ringing "at the other end" to what might be a landing "at the / other edge." From "end" to "edge" the figuration through which we get to that elsewhere yields and softens from an "invincible compress" into a foam that is "pearline," from the definitive end of a story to simply a sharp and elongated border beyond which something else still lies, shimmering, iridescent, opaque, yet not without menace.

If nothing else, this is a scene of translation as a zone of formal accommodation, even incremental adjustment, amid the body's annihilation—a dangerous intimacy with the "invincible compress" of the ocean and of time. Like water, this compress is thoroughly and forcefully dynamic, and its force, ultimately unreadable: we cannot tell if it pushes the body forward or holds it back or indeed which of those options might be better or worse, desired or not. Yet it is a movable force, as *Temps Morts* takes pains to remind us, first plangently and then persistently. At stake in this insistent elegy not just for a now that is sixteen or seventeen hours in the future, but even more precisely for that very time difference that "used to be sixteen," is the way in which the small adjustments of standard time—and the grammar of its arrangement—become a way to regulate and even compress the distance between here and there. For the object of melancholia can no longer be taken as Korea itself but rather a time that Korea *used* to be and is no longer; or perhaps a distance that has recalibrated itself and recedes ever further into a temporal future—a moving target written on a moving body. Cha's motifs of transpacific time difference finally show us what happens when translation takes the form of a spatial phenomenon—and it is the subtle subterfuges of this world that brings us to *White Dust from Mongolia*.

A Theory of Superimposition: The Complete Transference

Despite the fact that it was never finished, there remain several accounts available of what *White Dust* could have become, scattered among Cha's archive at the Berkeley Art Museum and Pacific Film Archive (BAMPFA). The implied reader seems to have been Cha herself, and perhaps a very small group of trusted collaborators like her brother who would have helped to make the film. Read together, these traces hint at a fervid creative process, a wild self-analysis of methodological reflection and passionate speculation in which Cha seems to be writing in order to find out what she has to see and say. Single thoughts are expressed through myriad impressions, the sum of their variations amounting to a film that would ultimately have been impossible to make but possible only in writing or on the page. Yet the question that insistently haunts the notebooks and sketches of *White Dust* is not an impossible film per se but the sheer proliferation of possible ones. In those archives and collections, all of Cha's imagined narratives are—to use her favored technique as a metaphor—*superimposed* on one another in order that they may exist synchronously: so profligate as to then be ultimately next to impossible.

In the methodologically rigorous world of Cha's work, such strenuous making and careful imagination may well be the decisive plot itself: to craft a film so abstract as to be absolutely true to the illegible experience of exile and thus to explore the limits of expression itself. Yet this unfinished project also has a more conventional sense of plot, as Cha writes summarily in her "Statement of Plans" seeking funding for writing *White Dust* as a historical novel.

> The main character in the story is a young woman, Korean by birth and living in China. An unforeseen experience occurs during her young adulthood which causes her to lose all memory, and lose at the same time her capacity for speech. . . . Having been forced to leave her native country as an immigrant to China, where again the Japanese had, by their law, enforced their language, she is doubly displaced. She is not permitted to speak her language to begin with, then finally, she ceases to speak at all.[25]

Its similarity to *Dictée*'s central narrative is strong, yet the means of writing or rendering this narrative are strikingly different in this moment. For the film version of *White Dust*, Cha provides a more technically challenging description of how the very same plot is to come together and what its central compositional principles might be.

> The film is a simultaneous account of a narrative, beginning at two separate points in Time. The two points function almost as two distinct narratives, the "Times" overlap during the diagesis [sic] of the film, and a final conversion of the two points is achieved to one complete superimposition, to one point in time.[26]

Strikingly, the two separate points in time must undergo "conversion" in order to finally be superimposed, recalling the time differences discussed in the previous section of this chapter. This description is provided at the beginning of Cha's "Project Description" for *White Dust*, as if to provide a kind of road map for the film it describes. When the narrative begins, there are two separate threads that are to intersect, overlap, and ultimately converge. Reading on, one learns that the first narrative is located in a forgotten past, wherein "she [the protagonist] is without a Past, her past is speculative, fictitious, or imagined."[27] The second is located in the narrative present, positioned "at the moment of the return. . . . The return re-marks the locations, points in memory, re-peats the Past sequences" as an uncanny echo of the first.[28] Cha ascribes two different voices or characters to each of these narratives, although the loose understanding seems to be that these are two doubled expressions of the protagonist, for whom displacement takes textual form as a compositional principle and thus cannot simply be univocal. The central drama, then, is not exactly the recovery of memory and speech—although it is at moments cast in those terms—but more accurately, a simpler desire for the fictitious past and present selves to converge in *one* time, through which they may find a means to reconstitute an echo chamber. These very echoes are the only resources made available by the material of history; still, their recovery cannot thereby be assured.

The medium of that narrative convergence is mysterious in both conceptualization and planned execution. On the one hand, it may seem that it is only and especially in the medium specificity of film that something like "one complete superimposition" can be achieved as an aesthetic restoration of a lost speech, memory, and identity—and whose longed-for result can only be distinctive layers of cacophony. Yet on the other hand, Cha's own conceptualization, sinuous and contradictory as it is, offers a further possibility for that cacophony of historiography beyond the medium specificity of film. More than a superimposition, there also, in the first narrative,

> exists a "Hole" in Time, a break in the linearity of Time and Space, and that empty space, the Absence, becomes the fixation, the marking that is the object of retrieval, a constant point of reference, identification, naming, the point of convergence for the narratives, the point of rupture, which gives, considers the multiplicity of the narrative, multiplicity of chronology.[29]

In this moment, Cha moves from the medium of film to the medium of thought, in which absence and nothingness nevertheless still allow for mediation. Convergence is possible only by breaking linear time itself and moreover rendering that space of rupture as a radically capacious nothing in which any and all multiplicity may in turn seek shelter. Many personal histories, it seems, seek to become one in the fantasy of univocality. Yet instead of the ontological fantasy that may be suggested by a total superimposition, this point of reference is simply a rupture in time itself, providing a space of exception "which gives." The sense of "give" here is unsure, on the one hand, pointing to a sense of generosity in playing host to a "multiplicity of chronology" within one narrative and, on the other, hinting at a collapse amid rupture, which in turn yields the ground to these multiple narratives.

And even as this point of convergence is a narrative destination, its status as absence also "becomes the fixation," as well as "the object of retrieval"—an unusual formulation to describe an absence. To suggest that an empty space is an object is already enigmatic; to suggest that it should be retrieved or recovered then suggests that such an absence was formerly a part of something larger than itself and from which it has been lost. One relatively familiar explanation for this may be Cha's long-standing affinity with poststructuralist theory—via film and performance theory—and her perpetual interest in understanding linguistic and bodily expressions via the structures that subtend and constrain them. In that vein, the absence that is lost and to be retrieved may be understood as a structuring absence central to the constitution of language and meaning-making. When that absence is lost, so too is the possibility of making any meaning at all, so that it is then precisely the origin and the end of language itself.

Yet these theoretical mainstays cannot quite explain the ways in which such an absence takes on a volatile life of its own throughout Cha's work:

even within the material associated with *White Dust*, absence and other core elements of the work are subject to constant revision and reiteration. Such is the case in another rewriting in her "Statement of Plans" for *White Dust*, this time rewriting absence—that space of convergence—as instead a space of memory. But here the space of memory, where all things meet, is indeed closer to an object that will be charged with "almost" ontological possibility.

> All the elements I have outlined [about the historical and cultural aspects of *White Dust*] are encompassed in the larger context of MEMORY which I would develop in this book as a collective source, as almost having physical and organic dimensions, where space and time superimpose within it. It represents a body of time, units in time inside the time mass that is eternal and immeasurable, within which our existence is marked like a wound.[30]

Unlike the previous account—in which two different narrative times and spaces come to be superimposed on one another and are indeed far from immeasurable—the two things being superimposed here are even more abstract: time and space writ large. The result is what Cha theorizes as memory, her central theme in *White Dust* (and arguably in *Dictée* as well). Crucially, memory is a "collective source," a repository through which that superimposition can take place, perhaps akin to that previous space of absence in which many narratives may repose equally. And in what is perhaps the most startling figuration of that abstract space of convergence, Cha writes that this repository, memory, "almost ha[s] physical and organic dimensions," insofar as it is itself a representation of "a body of time" (that too is a metaphor, reminiscent of the body that wades into the waves in *Temps Morts*)—a universal and transhistorical "time mass" that is "wounded" by the finitude of human existence. In this moment, Cha's powerful abstractions that cut across linear history also live alongside a potent sense of time as a massive physicality, within which our wounding finitude mark only "units of time"—and even then quite futilely so, for memory in all its vastness is ultimately "immeasurable."

If there was one place to look for this physics of memory, and at how Cha had hoped to render these difficult formulations into praxis, it would be in her detailed descriptions for the performances and movements demanded by *White Dust*. In these storyboards, Cha sketched out some visual plans for the footage collected in Korea and even planned (in writing) a series of around twenty-three scenes for the film. It is not clear if she considered this stage of the planning process complete: despite the amount of technical detail they provide, there are also moments that are difficult to imagine in practice, often shading toward a kind of private or poetic language even if mobilized in technical vocabulary. In one particular moment that may serve as a case in point, the trope of memory and technique of superimposition come together in a crucial scene for the film.

> 14. As two women continue their exchange (the partition of gauze curtain removed?) and the shadow projection is changed: the figures are seen without the silhouettes, there is no camouflaging. Images begin to appear behind the two figures, and gradually the women fade out and only the images are left.
> the image becomes larger (CLS to the image projected)
> larger still until the image takes over the whole room—Memory, projection takes over completely, the complete transference—trans-immigration of image and memory
> portraits in studio windows—Busan
> airplane
> railroad tracks
> inside the train
> family photo genealogy
> in/out of white of single images until two images simultaneously superimpose and become one image[31]

Memory "takes over completely, the complete transference": at this point in the narrative, such an absolute fullness is something of a relative, even uncharacteristic triumph, because memory had begun the film (in scene 1, thirteen scenes ago) visible in its "decaying sense" through "faint images, resemblance of images" that fade in and out of the film.[32] In striking contrast, the images here grow toward a deeply counterintuitive strength: Cha's thinking is not one in which the notion of completeness is easily invoked. What differs from the earlier scene is the diegetic presence of the two women or figures (whose characterization I return to shortly): as we saw in her previous notes and as we will see in *Dictée*, their narrative convergence—and simple physical encounter in performative terms—is the beating heart of *White Dust*. When the women fade out and the images come to dominate, the images lend a power to what they have displaced, performing an anthropomorphic work through what Cha calls their "trans-immigration." Yet of course memory has always only been rendered in images; the "transference" or "trans-immigration of image and memory"—if understood in these largely abstract terms—is then a conceptual sleight of hand that can only take place within the realm of the insensible.

Yet it may well matter which images are mere images and which may be "memory"—even if their indistinguishability is central to the film's project. After all, imagine a projected image taking over an entire room: *what* it shows is magnified and is at least as important as *how* it shows. Notably, then, when it comes time for the various images to converge and be superimposed, Cha does not specify which two images should be superimposed. It is unclear if she simply never got around to doing so—since the entry for scene 14 ends there—or if she perhaps wished to leave open an element of chance. Perhaps too it was the final two images that were meant to merge: a scene inside a train (which refugees like Cha's mother would have used to leave Korea for China) with a family photo genealogy. If so, the result would be a palimpsest writing over a state history that could be anywhere and for anyone, family photos that superimpose people onto an empty train: a belated, almost willful deixis. This then is how to make a memory in Cha's world: without instruction, without specificity, and with only bare speculation for the bare means that remain.

In scene 21 a version of my speculative reading does take shape: one of the woman performers reappears, and she "physically enters the image" of train tracks taken from the trip to Korea (presumably an image projected onto a screen by a projector) before the scene fades to white.[33] This too is a superimposition of a sort even if it does not go strictly by that name. That her physicality even needs to be specified is itself telling of the extent to which the physical world has been transmuted into the ether of image, perhaps recalling the "almost" physical dimensions of memory that Cha has theorized for herself. In the collision of flesh and figure with image—a diaphanous opacity—and still mediated by filmic technique, it becomes even more difficult to read the "complete" dominance of memory-via-image in this last half of *White Dust*. This will be the last seen of the women and also the final diegetic scene in the film: the protagonist—her two voices now reconciled, fully or not one cannot know—steps into an image-memory of train tracks that can only promise to bear her away.

With Slight Delay: The Translating Voice in *White Dust from Mongolia*

Superimposition rearranges the metaphysics of memory, and the fruits of that theorization are brought fully to bear on Cha's imaginary translator in *White Dust*. The final description of the film, however, points to yet more elliptical ways of arranging the work of translation in the future film. Even as *two* narrative threads were to structure the film, *three* intersecting voices were ultimately imagined for it, each of which were to bear an evolving relation to the narratives they serve. Each was to also carry a particular affective tone appropriate to its role: "#1" is an amnesiac and aphasic woman protagonist; "#2," one who gives memory and teaches language to the first; yet despite Cha's care in parsing one voice from the other, she insists too on their sameness in the final analysis. Both narrative voices inhere within a singular protagonist whose identity remains always indeterminate, subject to struggle and the threat of failure.

To this coupling Cha added a third voice. The third voice has a distinct status because it was not assigned a number like the other two; instead, it is simply marked "#A." #A was to be a voice of a translator: largely diegetic in its position, indifferent in tone and inflection, this translator took shape slowly in Cha's imagination, its characterization traceable from her journal notes to what became its finalized description. The narrative voice of the film was thus to be something of a Greek chorus—an assembly of tonalities more dissonant than harmonious, even if they were in the end dissonant expressions of the same. By the time Cha begins work in earnest on the film, the themes of her later work in *Dictée*—the laws and violences that inaugurate identity, the ways in which voices are made through interrogation and resistance, the forceful and glancing blows of linguistic repetition—have already been concentrated in this narrative "documentary voice, indifferent voice of announcer," which tellingly speaks first in Korean and then as a translator into English. This figure of a translator is formulated in a rather striking way in Cha's finalized description for the film.

#A Documentary voice, indifferent voice of announcer, as marking as punctuation to the film—within the diagesis [*sic*] of film
 a Korean voice
 b Translator into English

> c   Voice giving identity: voice of interrogation
> enforcement of identity
> repeating same material as the voice that teaches, gives speech and memory[34]

Intriguingly, Cha notes that this "documentary voice" should be "within the diagesis" of the film; that is to say, it should be internal to *and* coherent with the established plot. In this requirement, Cha subverts the conventions of a documentary in which the guiding narrative voice is typically extra-diegetic, intended to construct—without participating in—the narrative world of the film. Speaking from a fluid narrative position wherein world building and world inhabiting coincide, this voice is then intended to function as something of an insider guide, perhaps even a native informant in the estranging landscape that is the film. Yet given Cha's interest in the distant unpredictability of addressee and audience, one may well wonder if the proscription of diegetic from extra-diegetic is meant to be defied. Coming from a writer and artist whose recourse to meta-reflection is strong, a translator-character who remains behind the fourth wall comes almost as a breath of fresh air.

Poised as an intermediary between the two other voices of the film's protagonist or main subject, the "indifferent voice of announcer" #A is not *primarily* a translator, but rather a narrative strategy by which to establish the law of the film's world. It is then a particularly striking choice to begin with a "Korean voice" to be translated, especially as Cha elsewhere claimed that the film's audience was one ignorant of Korea beyond its Cold War presence in the American imagination. Yet to call it a third-person narrator as required by narratological convention would be inadequate or indeed inaccurate, for inasmuch as it is an impersonal, mechanical persona of law, it is also responsible for "repeating same material as the voice that teaches." That is to say, this tonally "indifferent" voice #A is bound to repeat voice #2 as something of a forceful echo; the fact that it is to give and enforce the identity of the protagonist then suggests that it carries a haunting threat.

Without any scripted dialogue, it is difficult to speculate on the effect of #A simply repeating the words of #2. As Cha writes it, voice #2 is, more precisely,

> #2   In the first person only (?)
> In the present tense only
> Voice giving Memory Voice teaching Language[35]

Each reinforces the other through repetition, and it is only the simplest forms of language and thought that are subject to such treatment. Yet these elemental forms and bare syntax—the first person, the present tense—are precisely those things that pose a limit of thinking for the text, in which speech cannot be inhabited by first persons and the narrative incessantly pulls away from the present in order to find the past. Indeed, Cha herself seemed to have wondered at the choice of the first-person subject position, marking it with a tentative "?" in parentheses; certainly, a second-person voice, or even a third-person narrator, would have been intriguing (and perhaps more consistent) complements for her concerns elsewhere in this text. #A's repetition of #2's speech may then allow for only the effect of a tonal difference: from an unspecified tonality—perhaps left to the performer, perhaps left to the future—to one that is avowedly "indifferent," functioning as an "announcer" whose audience can only be the person/s *within* the diegetic world of the film, but who is of course an announcer and translator for the film's own audience as well.

However, there remains one crucial difference in that repetition: #A is an interpreter and translator who thereby doubles the repetition—first in a "Korean voice" and only thereafter as a "Translator into English." The former is itself an interesting construction suggesting that a voice may be ethnically, nationally, and metonymically marked in its "Koreanness" rather than being linguistically determined as *speaking* Korean, which one may expect from the context; it is made even more striking by the latter "English," positioned as a language rather than a property of the voice. Further, this bilingual specter is given the task of "marking / as punctuation to the film": a task not assigned to the voice #2 that it mimics and repeats. In these ways the third voice "#A" establishes, controls, and interrogates both a law of bilingual language and a law of time: "punctuation" moves beyond its graphological, linguistic, and syntactic sense—with which Cha is deeply obsessed in other moments in her work—toward a form of temporality that, as seen previously, punctures a hole in time at which all narratives may converge—an infinite mass wounded first by our finitude and here by an announcer and translator whose voice is neutered amid that multiplied chaos. To speak in translation is to punctuate—but also to gather, to violently *concentrate*—a new rhythm of space and time.

Yet the coincidence of translation with temporality had not always taken this precise form in Cha's notes and sketches for *White Dust*. Time finds different centers of gravity every time Cha writes about it—sometimes falling on the notion of finitude, other times affirming the monotonous labor of duration. And in an earlier journal entry—a much more provisional and unguarded iteration of this work—Cha's scattered thoughts anticipate some of the strategies that she would amplify in the relatively complete version of the work. Here, the narrator-translator, coded #2 (no apparent relation to #2 of the previous discussion other than by number), is first one voice, then two, then one again.

> narrator #2—in diff/voice documentary voice (no relation to amnesiac—) one voice in korean reading the article—the other voice translating into english—superimposed two voices with slight delay.
> background history—the person—anonymous female
> the context—disappearance/event, the "story"[36]

This earlier formulation of the film's translator only partially anticipates ideas from its later iteration: both versions call for Korean as a source language and English as a target, with each language being associated with a different voice; both versions explicitly cast this narrator as a "documentary voice." However, they differ considerably on how that documentary voice is to be presented and situated vis-à-vis the narrative of the film. It is worth noting, for instance, that unlike the previous "#A," this narrator's number, #2, tacitly indicates that it is to be of the same category as the other speaking characters in the film, all of which are named numerically #1, #2, and #3. This difference in classification is one of two hints we get about the diegetic place of the narrator in this earlier version; the other hint lies in the final two lines in which the narrator is associated with an enigmatic list of narrative functions, in which it is to be responsible for discussing "background history—the person—anonymous female / the context—disappearance/event, the 'story.'" What connective logic resides *between* these nouns is perhaps the real narrative drama driving this poetic list, but it is safe to say that this is a narrative and a narrator who begins with "background history" and ends with a "story" curiously inflected with what seem like scare quotes as if to suggest the disappearance of the story itself, a linguistic means of questioning its ontological status after having traversed person, anonymous female, context, disappearance, event. Even more telling are the elements that do not appear anymore in the later version and that come to be replaced by Cha's stronger themes: identity, enforcement, pedagogy, memory. These ideas began life here in a mode of bare thought; perhaps they simply fell out of Cha's thinking and work, leaving only their traces behind and existing as a clutch of possible techniques and impossible lacunae.

Perhaps the difference most closely associated with the previous close readings in this chapter is Cha's formal description of how the Korean and translated English voices are to be constellated. In this earliest version of her thinking, she writes that in production there should be "superimposed two voices with slight delay." Like elsewhere in her notes, she does not specify the length or duration of this delay, but its slightness, coupled with the insistence on the technique of superimposition, suggests that the layering of Korean and English can only result in an almost incomprehensible babble, foregrounding technological *and* linguistic mediation as an artificial interference. Instead of an authoritative, law-giving voice that punctuates the narrative (which is where she eventually ends up), this early version offers, in sharp contrast, a manufactured chaos and semantic crisis arranged by the cinematic technique of superimposition and the formal-temporal logic of delay. And in a further contrast to what would be her later recourse to *simultaneous* superimposition of images, the voices and languages here are *not* simultaneously superimposed; they do not become one even as they *slightly* converge within the media of sound. Delay in this instance—even at its slightest and least effectual—puts both time and space between the Korean and English voices, source and target, maintaining their particularities and putting the translator-narrator between the inevitable gravitational pulls—of coloniality, pedagogy, memory, history, generational trauma—that will still always hold the film's three voices together.

Moreover, this early narrator is described as reading—repeating—an article in Korean (to be translated into English for the Anglophone viewer)—a source text and intertextual narrative technique nowhere to be found in the later version of the work. It is not clear to what article this refers and who its author might be: perhaps it was Cha, perhaps it was something she was reading in preparation at the time. One possible inference lies with the "documentary voice" and the "background history," and so on, discussed above. Such a form of repetition is also a significant difference from the later translator's task of "repeating same material as the voice that teaches." In this way, we gather that the mysterious article eventually becomes displaced by another narrative voice as the origin of the translating narrator.

The early relation between the translating narrator and the other voices in the film is one of the main difficulties animating my argument. Cha writes from the beginning, in no uncertain terms, that her translating narrator is to have "(no relation to amnesiac—)," the first voice in her narrative setup. This is surprising given the many recursive convergences she imagines for *White Dust*. Why does Cha so carefully parse the translator from the amnesiac here? Does the translator get subsumed into the ether of the other voices? And how do they later come to be one and the same? For even if the ultimate project of *White Dust*—and, as we shall soon see, *Dictée* as well—is to braid its three or multiple impersonating narrators together into one built or formed subject, Cha takes extra care to define this translator through a negative distinction, an analytical gesture that is unique throughout her sketches for these voices and a notable departure from the didactic imperatives that characterize her style in these artist's notes to herself. Analytically distinct from her other bare voices that are recovering their memories, speaking to themselves, fretful and forgetting in the first person, Cha's translating narrator in *White Dust* is perhaps only one of her many unfinished tasks in this film. And it is also what finally brings me to her work in *Dictée*.

Concretizing Translation in *Dictée*

I return to *Dictée* as the final move in my chapter for two related reasons: first, to reevaluate its critique of translation in light of my readings of *White Dust* and *Temps Mort* thus far; second, and fortuitously, to examine an imperceptible arrangement of delay in *Dictée* tied to an instance of Chinese-English translation. Though Cha did not herself know Chinese, its presence in her work very likely bridges political history with personal memory: her mother, like many Korean refugees of her time, had sought refuge in China from the Japanese occupation—an experience referenced in *Dictée* and her notes for *White Dust*. The Chinese and Korean languages have close ties from a long history of geopolitical and cultural proximity, as well as semicolonial Chinese occupation. Furthermore, working as she did in the artistic milieu of the Bay Area in the seventies, Chinese script may have arrived to her via the experimental American poetics of the time. At once an index of a colonized relation to an almost lost Korean self and occupying an uncertain place in her intellectual work, Chinese script thus represents a particular point of difficulty for thinking about Cha's approach to language politics and translation. For in *Dictée* and elsewhere, her translations tend to move between the English, French, and Latin, colonial languages that she had acquired in her Catholic education after moving to the United States, vessels of colonial pedagogy in Korea, and languages in which she was fluent; those translations are more likely to have been written by her. In addition, Cha heavily invests the *hangul* or Korean alphabet of her distant childhood with the pathos of strained articulacy and even an untranslatable aphasia. It is this linguistic complex— English, French, Latin, and *hangul*—that generally leads critics to consider Cha a multilingual writer of migration and displacement.[37] Conversely, her relationship to Chinese script—which appears once as writing and another time as an acupuncturist's anatomical diagram in *Dictée*—is far less legible or even semantically weighted, perhaps because of its somewhat casual and passing presence in the text itself and perhaps because it is unlikely to be of Cha's own hand. Yet in that brevity it presents a greater enigma, made all the stranger for the text's relentless probing of translation. Where I have previously argued that translation was a slow reduction of distance encapsulated in the technique of superimposition, here I consider the final limit of that claim: a translation arranged to make the work—and meaning-making—of translation disappear.

 The first clue is that its source and target are nineteen pages apart—already a striking departure from the other moments of translation that are textually and legibly staged as such, most often between the French and the English. Near the end of *Dictée*, on page 154, there is an instance of Chinese calligraphy, a presentation of a Daoist cosmological principle. The gesture is initially enigmatic even to one for whom the Chinese language is available. It appears with no related gloss or accompanying translation and initially at least seems like yet another gesture of heterolingual opacity in which the relation between texts is withdrawn and awaits interpretation. Only nineteen pages later, on page 173, do we get an approximate transliteration (via Cantonese) and translation of this diagram. The content of this translation is unremarkable and reads as a simple annotation for English-speaking people unable to read Chinese. It too appears with no explanation and is in fact located in an entirely different section, such that any reader is likely to miss the relationship between the two textual moments. (Indeed, on my first reading of *Dictée*, I did too, despite being able to read Chinese.) Both have likely been copied from an English-language source text about Daoism, although I have as yet not identified her source.[38] In a text so resistant to linguistic and cultural translation as an ideological apparatus—and which derives its modes of signification through that voided resistance—it is striking to note that this translation, though no doubt a seam in a text, also blends in and becomes one seam of many. Translation almost becomes poetry not via an epistemological passage but only via the special arrangement of a delay in narratological space, rendered *almost* illegible as a result: the movement from page 154 to page 173 parallels—if not *is*—the movement of that translation.

Jonathan Stalling writes helpfully about this same textual moment in *Dictée*, explaining that the diagram is a Daoist account of the self-emptying origins of the universe. By addressing the cultural and semantic content of this diagram, Stalling theorizes that Cha's engagement with Daoism—which he qualifies as a heterogeneous set of practices exemplary of an imagined transpacific, most evident in a resurgent interest among twentieth-century American poets in "Eastern aesthetics"—leads her toward a charged and signifying sense of nothingness and the void, as well as a systematic exploration of self-emptying and divestment. For Stalling, Cha's conceptual investment in the void is not so much the violent loss born of coloniality as it is the generative origin of Daoism, "becom[ing] not another ideological refuge, but a refuge from ideology."[39] Yet in a text that so persistently returns to aphasia and the broken processes of translation, I would argue, Cha's work is dominated by the dialectic between the two, an awareness that such a refuge does not and cannot exist even as she takes nothingness as the material by which to imagine such a refuge. Thus I build on Stalling's reading of her work with Daoism and related Asian practices, taking it seriously as a critical *translation*.

What rests in the space between source and target is also what connects it to my discussions of concrete translation as an arrangement of bodies and letters against the organizations of space. Nineteen pages apart, they bookend two narrative sections, the eighth and ninth (final) sections of *Dictée*, respectively: one is titled "Terpsichore/Choral Dance," addressing, in a series of recursive imperatives and declarations about time, matter, mass, and the body, a "you" who "having bartered away your form, now you are formless"—a formlessness that nevertheless culminates in "water, teinture, blood" oozing from and staining a stone.⁴⁰ The other, *Dictée*'s final section, is titled "Polymnia/Sacred Poetry" and depicts—in a relatively conventional narrative—a young girl who meets a mysterious young woman at a well in a barren desert. The girl is given a bundle of medicine and remedies to bring home to her mother, and as she returns from her encounter in the desert, "she became aware of the weight of the bundles and the warmth in her palms where she had held them. Through the paper screen door, dusk had entered and the shadow of a small candle was flickering."⁴¹ These battered gestures toward reparation—even if only in stains and glimmers—have led critics such as Timothy Yu to read the neglected latter section as a textual crux presenting a possible movement through writing, beyond the historical stasis or even "paralysis" that has preoccupied the text thus far.⁴² Cha's strange and surely deliberate arrangement of her borrowed Chinese and its translation suggests that it has a role to play in the movement Yu charts; indeed, another name for that movement may well be translation. Yet why then depart from the textual principles of translation throughout *Dictée* by presenting *this* translation as a pair of severed bookends rather than an integrated text? Building on Yu's argument, I argue that *Dictée*'s delayed translation gets taken up as a formal and imagistic principle for this final section of the text and by extension is suggestive of the text's final reckoning with the fragments of translation staged from its outset. Taken together with the meditations on translation and the strained personhood of the translator in *White Dust* and *Temps Mort*, the stories of inheritance and futurity that emerge in *Dictée*'s final section then also invite a reading of the enigma of a translation, concealed by the logic of narrative space and time, as a metatextual allegory for translation itself.

A closer look at those translations and transliterations brings into view something even more pressing. The Daoist cosmology presented is a series of ten structures or forms of organizing and reading the world.

> First, the universe.
> Second, Ying and Yang.
> Third, Heaven, Earth and Humans.
> Fourth, the Cardinals, North, South, East, West.
> Fifth, the five elements, Metal, Wood, Water, Fire, Earth.
> Sixth, Four cardinals and the Zenith and Nadir.
> Seventh, seven stars, the Big Dipper.
> Eight, the Eight Diagrams.

Ninth, Unending series of nines, or nine points linked together.
Tenth, a circle within a circle, a series of concentric circles.[43]

Again, it should be noted that this translation is unlikely to have been Cha's own work. Rather, like several other examples littering *Dictée*, its borrowed presence in this collaged text would be akin to a picture that inspired or indexed something important to its composition, or indeed an ideogram that served alternately to stabilize or disorient. Perhaps this is why, two pages later, the description of the tenth form is *repeated*, this time only in English and without its transliteration: "Tenth, a circle within a circle, a series of concentric circles."[44] These are the only words that appear on the page, its status as translation similarly effaced. Given that *Dictée* is composed of nine sections—which may even plausibly be described as "nine points linked together"—something then quietly inheres in the repeated insistence on a tenth possibility that had not been named from the beginning and that is only made known and available at the "unending" end. May the very form, fabric, and time of the text be quietly mutating through these borrowed and translated forms—from an "unending series" to a "series of concentric circles"? And what may be at stake—glimmeringly, slightly—in this moment?

Some provisional answers may be figured in one of the final scenes of "Polymnia/Sacred Poetry," in which the mysterious woman at the well makes and gives a bundle of medicine to the young girl. In this earlier scene, those concentric circles have already appeared even before the translation itself.

> She took off the kerchief that she wore and placed it on her lap. She took the bowl and said she must serve the medicines inside the bowl. After she had completed her instructions, she was to keep the tenth pocket and the bowl for herself as a gift from her. She placed the white bowl in the center of the white cloth. The light renders each whiteness iridescent, encircling the bowl a purple hue. She laid all the pockets inside the bowl, then, taking the two diagonal corners of the cloth, tied two knots at the center and made a small bundle.[45]

A "tenth pocket" and the round bowl in which everything is to be encircled are meant not for the mother but for the young girl. Even the language of this scene—perhaps a metatextual allegory, perhaps not—offers a reprieve, a gift: its sentences attentively follow their subject's every movement, each clause and action falling with a precise clarity unmatched in the rest of *Dictée* and the other textual examples I examine in this chapter. A new cadence sends the young girl toward home and her mother: "Her steps seem to move lighter than before" even as she registers the weight of the bundle she holds.[46] The color white—previously the color of a pure, abstract melancholia elsewhere in Cha's work and most especially as marked in *White Dust*[47]—is redoubled, and "each whiteness" is still singular, distinct, and glowing with a material integrity difficult to locate in this text. Through these shades of white, our guiding metaphor mutates from dust to iridescent vessel, from that which is scattered to something that gathers and binds. As the light in this scene "encircl[es] the bowl a purple hue," the bowl, and each of its whitenesses, even takes on other unseen colors as it becomes "a series of concentric circles"—bowl, cloth, light, all bundled together with the young girl herself.

And if this bundle is to be a metatextual allegory, then the way in which it is gathered and formed must be as important as the way in which it is given and sent off: from her to her. In a beautifully persistent difficulty—so lasting that it is by now familiar—the young girl and young woman do not go by any proper names and are not referred to in any way other than their simple pronouns.[48] Each of them has the same pronoun, and each use of each pronoun refers differently depending on where we are in the sentence and scene. When we read that "she was to keep the tenth pocket and the bowl for herself as a gift from her," gifter and giftee, woman and girl, stranger and familiar, subject and subject become equivalent, indistinguishable from one another.

And so even as one may suspect that the strange arrangement of Cha's delayed translation has indeed concealed the translation's *status* as translation, it may not exactly have concealed the translation's *work*. Rather, that work has been written—concretized—into the most deceptively simple of stories. After all, what it tells is a story about a transformation taking place in the space between, a translation that is not marked by semantic or graphemic change but only this enigmatic vignette of inheritance within which the colonial ideology and imposed necessity of translation is well concealed by the layers of history accumulated over it. For if the narrative of girl and woman given here may be read as a metatextual allegory for the work of translation, then it demands an even greater seriousness about those transformative yet fragile arrangements of equivalence, offered up first in the spatial shapes of a borrowed cosmology, then an equally borrowed classical tradition of muses and goddesses, then an "unending series" that imperceptibly, unnoticeably involutes—precisely near the very end—to become "a series of concentric circles."

**

The argument has come full circle. Beginning with the correspondences of reading and translation that opened *Dictée*—one language carefully arranged on top of another so that their frictions may be apparent—I have traversed a series of yet other arrangements persistently stretching what is possible in translation's critique, ways in which that critique may live and die beyond the spaces of differentiation between. Within this short story of a mutable concept, the work of translation has become a system of images and voices, layered in order to test or even annul the histories that have produced them— to un-live the pain of those lives that have been lived. By focusing on the visual trope of superimposition in Cha's work as it contests the organizations of geopolitical space and its manifestations as time, I have recalibrated the old stories of equivalence for another time: although translation in Cha is most often understood as an insistence on nonequivalence between a radically absent origin and destination—as well as a static nation-state and resistant subject—it instead emerges as a zone of poetic regulation in the transpacific space, eliminating distinctions not exactly from a drive to wish fulfillment but a drive toward renouncing the violations of the present and reducing an always malleable history within which one must still live. What is more, Cha's work suggests ways in which the ideographic thinking and arrangements of translation that opened this book—already a bundle of contradictions in their abstraction—may confront their formal debts in the space of a transpacific theater saturated with global capitalism, imperialisms both present and past. Whether those debts will ever be repaid—in translation or otherwise—is a question that no book like this one can answer with integrity. In the next chapter, however, a similar question is uttered with only more questions and no firm answers, its ghosts murmuring in dissonant harmony with the ones encountered thus far.

4 Translingual Erasure
Yang Lian

A Grammar of Equivalence

"Write down a poem," commands the poem. One short space and a beat later, "the world can disappear too."[1] The one command has already been done; the other disappearance is impossible to realize, yet it is tenuously correlated to the poem's writing in a common fate that is impossible to fully identify as causation.[2] This is the odd frame within which Yang Lian imagines and visualizes his poetry as conceptual art, a frame of reference he gets from the Western aesthetic tradition. Yet his mode of conceptualism can be difficult to pin down, seeming to be at once conceptually driven, always on the verge of an ontological vanishing act, but also doggedly representational in moments. In one book, its five chapters have no titles and are distinguished only by a wordless series of circles accumulating onto one another: first one, then two and three and four and five concentric circles. The book's title? *Concentric Circles*. I thus highlight his narrative not in order to make a point about his poetry but in order to suggest something stranger about *how* that poetry engages in the gathering, signifying, and even pseudoequalizing abstract functions that are commonly called conceptualism, in the process betraying the foundations of conceptual thinking through a poetry found in translation. The specific concept under consideration here is Poetry as it is visually signified, this time taken apart and gathered back again under the same umbrella.

> You may say that chapter five of *Concentric Circles* is 'conceptual art' [*guannian yishu*; single quotation marks in the original] using the Chinese language: I divided the Chinese character *poetry* 詩 into its three constituent parts (言, 土, 寸—each of which is a character by itself), and used each of them to develop a set of seven poems with a single-character title containing the same radical; the three sets are all ended with a poem entitled 詩. These twenty-one poems together compose a "*shijie, world* inside a character."[3]

The character may be translated in two ways, legible on two levels of abstraction as *Poetry*, the concept under pressure in this account, and its conceptual gathering of smaller *poems*, a common noun. What is more, in this poetics reminiscent of the ideographic method, the concept of Poetry is parsed into a series of three radicals—or ideas—contained within it: *Speech, Earth, Inch*. Semantically unrelated, these three entities live together within the fictional structure of a long poem as if to suggest a meaningful relation between all three. Yet unlike Fenollosa's recourse to nature and cultural otherness—framed as an empirical reading—to trace and elaborate the diachronic relations of ideographic meaning, Yang seems acutely aware that the meaning of his speech, earth, and even poetry is purely and simply the sum of those parts, pointing not so much to the limits of empiricism but to the very complexity of the ideal. The concept of Poetry inheres no more and no less in its composed and *arrangeable* word—and the repeating and recitative world that can be written of it.[4]

This is no simple defense of the poem's aesthetic autonomy or involutionary manner. For in the same breath, Yang is also deeply invested in at least one important *use* of his *Poetry* in the long poem he describes: its potent—and potently abstract—ability to "efface the fantasies of history" through translation.[5] How might Poetry and translation fulfill such a far-reaching task—and what indeed are those fantasies woven by history? His theory of erasure is derived through a strange (and untheorized) method of reading that builds an untranslatable crux of four harmophones in Mandarin: first, the translating term for *epic*—the poetic genre originating in the Western tradition and taken up by Yang—is given as *shishi*, a compound term literally translating as *history-poem*. One *shi*, history, is sounded in the third tone, and the other, *poem* or *poetry*, is sounded in the first tone. Bluntly stated, his argument is that the second negates and erases the "fantasies" of the first. Its weapon of negation is the gesture of translating yet another *shi*, this one sounded in the second tone, from a language with grammatical tense to a language without tense: *time*.

Poetry in Yang's account thus provides a cogent demonstration of Bachner's insight that the sinograph "foregrounds the multiple possibilities inherent in any writing system: connecting the visual and the sonic, the iconic and the symbolic, the combinatorial and the gestaltic."[6] But what exactly may lie at stake in triangulating these similar and repetitive sounds alongside a visual decomposition of poetry—*and* (with Yang) reading seriously the conceptual and semantic pseudo-equivalences that attend such a gesture? That a crux of sound and a play of visual arrangement come together to form the concept of Poetry—working on the edge of meaning and without any guarantee of it—brings me to the final step in my argument across this book. In this last chapter, I bring together the arguments of the two previous chapters in order to consider what John Cayley calls a "*necessary* synesthetic operation of all systems of writing[,] . . . [an operation that is] intrinsic to inscription and subversive of any hierarchy of media and its agencies."[7] However, my interest lies less in the hierarchy of media and its distribution of the senses—even as it indexes the questions of linguistic and cultural hierarchies previously examined through Pound and amply treated by many writers on Chinese script.[8] Rather, I am interested in how that synesthetic operation carves out an aporetic tension *within* the politics of inscription—the act of putting something into writing—and what in Yang's work becomes the felt anxiety and even tragedy of its survival. At the heart of this aporia is the fourth and final harmophone in the sequence: *loss* or *disappearance*—an exact homophone for *poetry*. For Yang, a single phoneme and its rich tonalities gather a tremendous resonance between poetry, history, time, and loss: by surrendering meaning to the movement of sound, *poetry* becomes far more than it means.

Like the final movement of a sonata, this closing chapter recapitulates the foundational and utopian ideas raised in the first chapter on transpacific abstraction—this time in a minor key. In the second and third chapters, I sought to develop and refine the striking theories of translation emerging from those modes of abstraction, contrasting them to two important ways of understanding translation and its raison d'être in the historical and critical contexts of each author. First, the interpretive and exegetical reading of translation fades and burns away for Eileen Chang, leaving only the insignificant echo chambers of sound translation in their wake. Bereft of any imaginary reader as a subject and translator, I looked instead to how translation is spatially formalized in the work of Theresa Cha—a process of concrete translation—to promise infinitely variable arrangements in the realm of language: a formalism that *subsumes* the epistemic divisions and physical distances of the transpacific space in order to negate and transform them. How then might writers and thinkers like Eileen Chang and Theresa Cha—those who have followed the language of abstraction to its limits and compelled us to hear the depths of its silence—respond through their sounds and arrangements to the ideologues who came before them? My goal in this argument is to extend their insights to the transpacific abstractions of the first chapter: where *transpacific abstraction* was the name for a series of complex internalizations of ideographic thinking and its ideological work in translation, I finally reassess its foundational idea of inscription—a transcription without representation—in order to argue for a politics of *translingual erasure.*

The term *translingual erasure* seeks to conjugate Yang's unusual ideas about history and time with Lydia Liu's argument about the translingual *practices* at the heart of modern Chinese literary production. Somewhat counterintuitively, I want to ask, can a carefully articulated epistemic *erasure* be a potent translingual practice too? In Liu's argument, the term *translingual practice* designates a broad range of practices beyond the purview of translation, naming

> the process by which new words, meanings, discourses, and modes of representation arise, circulate, and acquire legitimacy within the host language due to, or in spite of, the latter's contact/collision with the guest language. Meanings, therefore, are not so much "transformed" when concepts pass from the guest language to the host language as invented within the local environment of the latter. In that sense, translation is no longer a neutral event untouched by the contending interests of political and ideological struggles. Instead it becomes the very site of such struggles where the guest language is forced to encounter the host language, where the irreducible differences between them are fought out, authorities invoked or challenged, ambiguities dissolved or created, and so forth, until new words and meanings emerge in the host language itself.[9]

As an inherently negating gesture with no conceptual integrity and only a limited investment in inventing new meaning or neologisms in the translingual encounter, the *erasure* of a metaphysical category like time does not easily fit into this narrative. Yet the radical contingency of its formation—built on that chimerical arrangement of harmophonic *shi* and articulated through Yang's lifelong reading of Ezra Pound—may well suggest that Yang's theory of erasure in translation is a translingual artifact in itself. At the same time, however, the *poetic* formation of Yang's metaphysical thinking suggests that the mode of linguistic struggle in his work is less concerned with the conceptual or discursive formation that Liu traces across her book. Here, Sarah Dowling's concept of translingual *poetics* (also built from Liu among others), a mode of destabilizing settler logics of monolingualism in the North American context, may be helpfully transposed for my argument. While Dowling centers the critical work of translingual poetics on how collisions of language strain the formal bounds of lyric and legal *personhood*,[10] I want to consider how collisions of language strain the formal bounds that encode a politics of *mourning* within a monolingual complex of Chinese haunted by a guest—or ghost—language, English, that is far from a minoritarian one (as is the case in Dowling's study). In my argument, Yang's translingual erasure seeks to confront—without resolving—the dispossessing conditions of writing in the Chinese language *and* in the language of a transpacific translation qua ideographic imagination. Led to that translingual erasure by a poetic equivalence of sound without meaning, Yang ultimately inscribes—in the movement and remains of its negations—a series of ghostly equivalences that animate his work of mourning.

At the heart of this argument is an unusual poetic text that raises the stakes for thinking about translation as it generates a world poetry and world literature often considered stateless. Its author, Yang Lian, was born in 1955 in Switzerland to a diplomat family, and the sum of his work across the years evinces a cosmopolitan sensibility born of an international upbringing throughout Europe and the Western world. As an adult, Yang became a pro-democracy dissident critical of the Mao regime. Earlier in his adult life, in the 1970s, he spent three years in a labor-correction camp, working as a gravedigger and coffin bearer: the experience seemed to have left him with a surreal lightness in handling death and mourning that pervades his work. He left the mainland in 1983 upon receiving news of an arrest warrant issued for him on account of his writing and continued to organize forms of dissent against the martial actions of the Chinese government from his life in exile. After he organized a silent protest in Auckland against the government's martial crackdown on the Tiananmen protests in 1989, his citizenship was revoked. After many years of exile in New Zealand, the United Kingdom, and Germany, Yang was only recently able to travel freely to the mainland, dividing his time across those places so formative for his writing.

Written in the emotional wake of Tiananmen during his stateless existence from around 1994 to 1997, *Tongxinyüan*, literally translated as *circles with the same heart*, is a long poetic sequence written primarily in Mandarin and, as is typical for Yang, draws upon sources as varied as premodern Han Chinese writing, the myths and cosmologies of the Indigenous people of occupied Han China, European modernism, and world literature. In 2005, it was translated into a radically poetic English, titled *Concentric Circles*, by Yang's longtime UK-based translator, Brian Holton, who was then working with his frequent collaborator Agnes Chan.[11] Its thematic focus is a survivor's allegiance to those whom he calls *sizhe* or *the dead*, alternately buried and exhumed in a poetics of disappearance that never directly names the specter of Tiananmen.[12] In this regard, *Concentric Circles* stands somewhat apart from the often masculinist, ethnographic, and aggressively dissident overtones of other works in Yang's oeuvre. Its poetry is typified by an effusive form—a fragile form because it is so effusive—and an almost surgical eye for assembling intractable paradoxes within the smallest of spaces.

Its intricately plotted—and incessantly diffusive—structure belies its simple title and relies equally on repetition and pattern across all aspects of the language (writing, sound) to constitute that structure. Such a structural complexity, however, is most usefully imagined as a simple complement to the private language of the poem. As Jacob Edmond observes of Yang's earlier and related work *Where the Sea Stands Still*, "The poem remains poised between the assertion of an idiolect poetics and a poetics of repeated 'collective images' and cultural stereotypes that moves easily, like the ocean or Owen's modernist waves, from one nation and language to another."[13] Moreover, its patterns stand in a complex relationship to the standard principles of classical poetic form that Yang seeks to revive through his quiet dismantling. The whole is composed of five *zhang*—*sections* or *chapters* and the translating term Yang uses for *canto* in his discussions of Pound's *Cantos*—with no titles, each only marked at the beginning by a printed image of one circle, then two, three, four, and finally five concentric circles. The visual cues suggest a series of poems that accrue or accumulate onto one another in a mode of nonlinear progress, but any impression of a cumulative process gets roundly contradicted as the poem's narrative develops instead toward a slower work of disappearance and transformation. And as Yang tells us in the commentary that opened this chapter, when this poetic world accelerates to a close in the fifth and final section, every one of its poems has the same minimalist title, *shi* for *poem*.

What does this strange text have to do with translation? I am not the first to read Yang's work with translation in mind: in fact, the first to do so was Yang himself, who across a long and varied career has repeatedly and fulsomely articulated his transformative debt to classical Chinese poetry and its peculiar manifestation in Ezra Pound's Chinese starts. This was to such a point that he has received criticism for being *too* indebted to Western poetics—even deliberately skewing his work and ethos for the sake of being legible to a Western audience, writing a version of China and Chineseness that is unrecognizable to Chinese readers.[14] More sympathetic critics see Yang's modernism as a wholesale transformation of its Western counterparts, pointing especially to his use of poetic repetition as a dynamic state of rest rejecting oppositions of sameness and difference—what Edmond describes (via Yang) as the iterative sweep of a wave on a shore.[15] And so although (or because) Yang is one of the most widely translated contemporary Chinese poets into English, it is not a stretch to suggest that his work has already been "born translated" in much the way commentators like Cosima Bruno have read the linguistic and translingual experiments associated with Pound.[16] The critical controversy surrounding his work has not prevented Yang from being frequently considered a leading voice in world literature, receiving nominations for the Nobel Prize for Literature several times. Even the details of Yang's poetic life, one can surmise, point definitively to a career lived in and through translation in both the broad and narrow senses of the term.

What is more, Yang's intimate association with the work of translation and the ethos of world literature has tended to be read as an aesthetic event melding a nativism of the spirit with a cosmopolitanism of the flesh, an unresolved quarrel of East and West that is not typically reconciled with the ambitious political and philosophical critiques embedded in his work. With a temper that is often described as modernist, experimental, and conceptual, and working from a Western point of view, Yang tends to be grouped with a school of poets known as the *menglong pai* or *Misty school* for their difficult and astringent work. The term, apocryphally a translation from Baudelaire, was originally a disparagement by political enemies seeking to denounce their supposed obscurantism. Despite or because of their trademark opacity and often macabre fascination with violence, the Misty poets are most often read through the lens of political allegory both at home and by Western observers, typified by the Misty anthologist and translator Tony Barnstone's well-known observation that

> due to China's troubled literary history, the use of a common metaphor in unsanctioned ways, a poet's experimentation with Modernist

techniques eschewed by the official literary establishment, even the writing of a simple love poem can be a dangerous political act. . . . Many of these poems are ephemeral, glancing encounters with brutality, an execution in half-light, a nightmare glimpsed through the mists; thus their authors have been nicknamed the "Misty" poets.[17]

Barnstone's account defines Misty poetry as political acts seeking to evade or contest state censorship, suggesting too that his own translations have often sought to translate the difficult context from which the poems emerge. Some years later, however, Edmond's study of Yang's publication history on the mainland problematized Barnstone's account of the Misty mythos by noting the small but significant forms of accommodation Yang made to censors on the mainland in the years following Tiananmen—as well as the ways in which his dissidence was domesticated and commodified for the literary marketplace.[18] And in a similarly complex take on the politics of Yang's work, Lucas Klein is dissatisfied with a Derridean mode of reading—exemplified by the collaboration between Cayley and Yang himself—that "not only returns to a vision of translingual poetic writing, to a poetics of translation, but does so with an emphasis on the parataxis of 'systems of inscriptions' that, like the ideogrammic method, would be non-'hierarchically ordered.'"[19] As Klein points out, asserting an absence of hierarchy is indeed easier said than done, requiring, in his argument, a careful consideration of what he calls Yang's ethnopoetics—a writing of Chineseness in its linguistic and political dimensions.

And indeed the Chinese poems themselves are—as Yang's commentary and mixed critical reception would indicate—*already* translated artifacts and mediated objects in their own right. Building on the critical consensus that Yang's poetics and commentary on his own work are indissociable from his thinking of translation from the Western tradition—such that, to take this argument to its furthest possible conclusion, his every work may even be seen as a secret translation of Pound—I want to propose another way of brushing Yang's poetics and politics of translation against its grain. Might its antitotalitarian gestures lie beyond the semantic and allegorical productions of his writing? After all, as Cayley notes, one does not have to accept Yang's inaccurate and essentializing ethnographic claims about the Chinese language in order to entertain the possibility that there can be unexpected points of convergence between the English and Chinese traditions especially if abstracted to the level of poetic language;[20] and my argument precisely seeks to raise the political stakes for that untranslatable and aporetic convergence between those languages and traditions. More than a nativist experiment in cosmopolitanism or a desire to be admitted into the canon of world literature or even a style developed to evade censorship, Yang's unusual and often transformative reading of the ideographic tradition inherited from Pound and Fenollosa has the startling effect of abolishing its conceptual foundations in the fantasies surrounding Chinese script, exceptionalism, and futurity broached in the first chapter. Reading Yang through a transpacific imaginary—and indeed through the theories of Eileen Chang and Theresa Cha—reveals a hidden grammar that distributes the perpetual work and time of mourning beyond the language of the nation-state's violence, disappearing it into that stateless and nameless language whose best name is simply translation.

In what follows, I derive the argument in three moves. The first is a detailed examination of how Yang arrives at his theory of erasure through a sleight of hand in translation, which offers a provocative contextual frame for approaching his *Concentric Circles*. Then, I extend his theory of erasure to the concerted mourning at the heart of its writing, arguing that the grammar of mourning lies beyond the discrete boundaries of either the Chinese or English language, its translingual constitution opening a space of nonexceptionalism and suspended futurity. Finally, I animate these ideas through a close reading of the final section of *Concentric Circles*. In the hushed and haunting rhymes of *poetry* with *disappearance*, Yang's poetics of equivalence creates the world of the poem as a space of perpetual mourning, taking on blind faith the possibility that two words that sound the same do, after all, fully negate one another—erase the conditions of value, to use the vocabulary of my argument—in defiance of their inscription. In the rituals of the poem, neither disappearance nor death nor survival are to be affirmed. Rather, one mourns survival itself—indeed the self who has been *exempt* from death—and the irredeemable experience of remaining alive in this world. To write a poem is to be born in translation and to live in an untranslatable yet unexceptional Chinese of state violence—from which the only deliverance is erasure, a disappearing act.

Erasure, a Translingual Gift

The first step of that erasure lies in a play of translation into and out of a compound word, *shishi* or *epic*. Upon the publication of the English *Concentric*

Circles in 2005, Yang's author's introduction drew a connection between the English translation of his book and a Chinese translation of Pound's *Pisan Cantos*.

> When the Chinese translation of Ezra Pound's *Pisan Cantos* was published, I wrote a short essay for it, entitled "In the Timeless Air" [a quote from Pound's *Canto LXXVI*] in which I come to a sensational conclusion: only with its Chinese translation was the *Cantos* finally completed. The argument is not actually complicated. To me, the most impressive poetic quality of the *Cantos* lies in the contradiction between the synchronic nature of its poetic ideas and the diachronic nature of its language. The startlingly, inexplicably large-scale collage of episodes that seems out of control cannot be obviously explained by Pound's simple intention to write the longest poem in English. I think Pound's real focus was to break through the limitations of *time, shijian*, especially those temporal limits which exist in the grammar of English. His *Cantos* ramify through all time—it is by embracing all cultures, past to present, east and west, that he is enabled to peel away the illusion of the differentiation between the different presentations of life, and touch directly on the changeless core of existence. In other words, the *Cantos* is not an epic or *shishi*, i.e., a poem about history, but on the contrary, it aptly uses poetry, *shi*, to efface the fantasies of history, *shi*.[21] That self-sufficient universe of poetry, without beginning or end, completely undermines the European epic tradition. I do not know whether or not Pound got this creative idea from his "reinvention" of ancient Chinese poetry. But the Chinese language does give him the best return of all: by way of the constant form of Chinese verbs—which are unchanged, even if person and tense change—the Chinese translation of the *Cantos* eradicates all traces of the struggle between the poet and his language, and finally, completes Pound's wish to break away from the diachronic grip of the English language. What the Chinese reader sees is the *Cantos* re-invented by means of the unique qualities of the Chinese language, an entirety which is transparent, stable, omnipresent and flawless.[22]

The posited relationship between the *Cantos* and its translation is a *completion*, a desirous lack surprised by a gift perfectly shaped to itself—one might even say a restoration of equilibrium.[23] In this regard, Yang seems to hew close to the argument central for translation studies in recent years: translations are not derivative but rather are creative works of reading, growing new and transformative meanings that were always immanent in the source text and consequently enriching our understanding of the source. Yet a closer inspection of *how* he *derives* this claim may induce some skepticism. What chimerical gift economy does this institute, and may its gifts harbor any unforeseen dangers? The Chinese translation is said to complete the *Cantos* not by *explicating* or *interpreting*—that is, rendering meaningful and legible through analysis—the many ideographic moments littered throughout its pages. Rather, its work lies in two aspects intrinsic to the very *grammar* of the translating language. The first aspect is the way verbs or actions are handled: whereas Pound's English language works through tense, the translating Chinese language requires more inventive, sometimes contextual, and nonschematic strategies for indicating the passage of time and the status of an action. But Yang instead—and apparently intentionally—frames this as a lack or erasure in tacit relation to the Western tradition. For him, translating the *Cantos* into Chinese de-temporalizes it, imbuing it with metaphysical claims to transcendent timelessness and a totalizing suture of signifier and signified. Chinese writing transcends time because it does not *have* to *register* and to make decisions about what kind of time it finds itself in. This linguistic property—which Yang somewhat recklessly calls *timelessness*[24]—then explains his enigmatic claim that "the Chinese translation of the *Cantos* eradicates all traces of the struggle between the poet and his language, and finally, completes Pound's wish to break away from the diachronic grip of the English language."[25] In Yang's argument, it is *because* of the Eurocentric commonplace that the Chinese language has no linguistic tense that it would whittle away the temporal grounds of history, allowing Pound's desire for a "timeless" *Cantos* to be "completed" by the Chinese *Cantos*. By the same token too, translating Chinese verbs and actions into English—that is, translating Yang's *Concentric Circles* into English—cannot but bring it into a form of time that is irreducibly contextual and relational. Built between the two translating languages is a semantic economy in which time is lost and gained in equal measure, embedded in the Eurocentric mode of unequal equivalence that this book has set out to unlearn—and now happily corrected, all too easily, its asymmetries erased in translation.

At this point, it may be fruitful to step away from the particulars of Yang's narrative and look to the larger contextual picture for more pieces of this puzzle.

First, the direct referent for this discussion is not *exactly* Yang's own poetry or its translation. Instead, the direct referent is the difficult task of translating the Pisan *Cantos* into the Chinese as was done by Yunte Huang in 1998. On the other hand, however, extending this commentary to Yang's own work is certainly justifiable: after all, his thoughts are being offered on the occasion of his *Concentric Circles* being translated into a complex and multifarious *English*—that is to say, in the *opposite* direction of the translation discussed in his commentary. What is more, that "startlingly, inexplicably large-scale collage of episodes that seems out of control"—a formulation adopted by Yang to describe the *Cantos*—is also an uncannily accurate description of his *Concentric Circles*. All things considered, Yang's comments on the Chinese translation of Pound do seem firmly identified with his thoughts on the English translation of his *Concentric Circles*. If so, one may further wonder, *to whom or what* is that gift of the Chinese language being offered? By means of a muted identification, may that gift of timelessness be extended not just to Pound, but perhaps *also* to Yang's work?

But timelessness and its erasure may be both gift and curse. After all, time in Yang's account has emerged as an intractable and affectively rewarding problem of translation from the diachronic to the synchronic. If the *Cantos* have had their central contradiction resolved through translation, then they are also bereft of the opacities animating Pound's ideographic writing in the first place: one erasure that simply displaces yet another. Where previously the disjointedness and disorientations of Pound's *Cantos* were its primary drama, now the Chinese *Cantos*—and by extension Yang's *Concentric Circles*—have achieved a totality that is "transparent, stable, omnipresent and flawless" through the erasure of time. Yang's pathos-ridden account locates the flawlessness and universality of the translated *Cantos* in their belated fulfillment of what he takes as Pound's central poetic mission: the attempt to linguistically transcend the linguistically imposed limits of time in his poetry. Yet this transcendence of contradiction is a highly qualified one, possible only when translated into a different language—the different language that prompted the initial contradiction—that cannot register and mark the passing of time within a single verb, and for which the passage of time can only be read in relation and in context.

This problem of a desired *and* undesirable time then returns us to the problem of ideographic inscription with which we began. For, put simply,

Yang needs the idea of history if not time. Time and the writing of poetry are intricately connected in his work: unlike Derrida (a fellow reader of Pound and Fenollosa) for whom inscribing something in writing is to give it a chance of survival—even a life in and through time—Yang instead invests *his* gestures of historical inscription with a persistent and indeed inescapable fantasy of disappearance. Just as Pound's work is not an epic, so too is Yang's work not an epic but rather a work that calls the fundamental assumptions and conceptual organizations of the epic poem into question. Its reason for this erasure is perhaps the clearest thing about this poem: in a final and striking departure from the *Cantos*, *Concentric Circles* is not a multilingual or translated epic. Better read as a translingual elegy, its uncanny echoes erase the lines that separate the living from the dead.

A Word of Mourning in the Language of Translation

In a chapter on Yang, Lucas Klein skeptically points not only to Yang's essentializing takes on the Chinese language but also to his tendentious desire to separate the language of his writing from its inevitably nationalist dimension.[26] While Klein argues that Yang's distinction can only be a naive one (an assessment with which I fully concur), I nevertheless wish to dwell a little longer on Yang's clear ambivalence about writing with the language of the nation-state, its stakes quite a bit heightened by the project of writing the *sizhe* or *dead* in the unnamed shadow of Tiananmen. The epic—qua inscription of history, qua European aesthetic category—and the ideograph are then not the only things at stake in Yang's gesture of mapping the translingual onto an intricate concept of transhistorical erasure. More simply, at stake is an oblique and unresolvable struggle for a language in which to grieve—especially given the tacit suggestion that the Chinese language may be the most impoverished and challenging choice in this regard.

What does it mean to write *and mourn* in "the" Chinese language—and how? How does this question compel a reconsideration of what constitutes the language at all? After all, Yang's insistence on the high-modernist aspiration to "break through the limitations of time" in connection with his own work was always going to sit uneasily with his stubborn motif of mourning the dead. On the one hand, we might understand mourning as unproblematically incorporated into the drive toward timelessness, effacing the fantasies of a linear history that would leave its dead behind. On this initial reading, the dead would be changelessly preserved within an unchanging poetic present: translation thus commits an ultimate act of mournful fidelity and even defiant ventriloquism that exceeds the grave. Yet pursuing the implications of Yang's account turns up further questions without ready answers, particularly when one considers that Yang's work is always written first in Chinese (even if destined for translation). Provisionally accepting Yang's essentializing and Eurocentric view of the Chinese language, one is left with Yang in a milieu in which marking time is impossible in a single instance and only possible through contextual imbrication and/or translation outside its own linguistic system. If nothing else, this is an essentialist formulation of language that propagates a radically *non*essentialist conception of time and the possibility of mourning. Amid this contingency, how exactly would the dead and their deaths then be marked? Is it possible to mourn in a linguistic space in which the temporal conditions that enable mourning—those "fantasies of history"— cannot quite be taken for granted as such?

A moment in *Concentric Circles* seeks to theorize at least one side of this equation: the notion of life and survival, built into the metalanguage of the poem itself. "To Live   This Word" functions as a relatively self-contained formal catastrophe for the second section of *Concentric Circles*.[27] The sixth poem in a sequence of eleven poems, it is also the longest and most formally innovative in that section. The poem is further divided into five subsections that each have a relatively stable—if unusual—form. With sections consisting mostly of disjointed lines and indefinite stanzas punctuated with spaces and meeting one another at unexpected junctures, the poem's third and fourth subsections stand in contrast to the others in being structured not as stanzas but as rectangular blocks of text in precise alignments, with the occasional word or phrase breaking out from the rectangles in seemingly meaningful fashion.

A similar strategy extended to the title, which performs the trials of language posed by living and survival. Maintaining a larger than usual space between its main parts—on the one hand, *huo* or *to live* or *life* and, on the other, *zhegezi* or *this word*—seems to call into question the relationship between the two. On one reading, it may simply be announcing its focus on defamiliarizing this word *life*, what it means *to live* or even *to survive*: the poem that follows, it seems to be saying, will be tarrying with this difficult word and everything that attends it. Yet on another reading, one might also wonder: if the act of living is coming under scrutiny, then is the poem also interested in thematizing *living* as a transitive verb—and so in thematizing and performing the impossible and transgressive task of living a word, "living this word" whatever it may be? The ambiguity legible in my English translation is also possible in the Chinese with the addition of a particle, such that what is most challenging is the elongated space between the two, marking the illegible and withheld transitivity of the verb (if it is one). Somewhere in the space between living and "this word" is a simultaneous promise *and* denial that one might actually be able to live, even to survive, in a word, "this" word.

All these questions hover over the poem, which is somewhat more autobiographical than many of the other poems in *Concentric Circles*. Earlier sections contain occasional cues like specific place-names and date markers that act unambiguously as callbacks to places where Yang had spent some time, but "To Live" in particular contains several references to someone and some things that are forty years old (Yang was born in 1955 and would have turned forty around the time of writing *Concentric Circles*, from 1994 to 1997).[28] In the closing moment of this difficult and dispersive poem, the vertiginous problems of a life in duration—and the possibilities of living a word—are gathered together in a dense passage that begins to break up the rigid rectangles of his form.

四季　　孤獨更明亮的形式
　　　四十歲的一千年
你脫下這口釘牢的棺材而我在其中醒來
聆聽　　你緊貼白骨時靜靜聆聽的
厭恨　　被水泥花朵唯一等到了
我　　還是一個字里無力發生的事故
　　　　還活著　　還
　　　沒被說出[29]

        Four seasons　　a form more luminous when lonely
        Forty-year-old millennium
You strip off this nailed coffin yet I wake amidst it
Listen　　　　you cleave to white bone while quietly listening to
Hate　　only awaited by concrete flowers
I　　still am an accident powerless to happen in a word
        Still living　　Still
        Unspoken

Precisely aligned, Yang's words also work to showcase moments of unevenness and transgression, as if to echo the somewhat metatextual commentary provided in the luminous and lonely form. In this long sequence, death is incessantly challenged as a matter of the flesh, so that by its end the work of the poetic speaker at once equates the potential of survival with the extensive trials of writing evident in the poem. Indeed, the *shigu* or *accident* waiting to happen here draws its powerlessness from the fact of containment, being *in* a word—perhaps providing one answer to what it is like to *live* a word. Being a living accident waiting to happen may look like waking up in a coffin that another version of oneself seems to have thrown off, and also like listening to white bone amid the quiet. And its life of waiting also sounds like an untranslatable invocation in the 還 of the final lines: the accident that is powerless to happen is *still, still, still* caught somewhere within life itself—and yet the very same word, if used in other contexts with other words and spoken in another way, may also mean *return, huan*, a return still possible in a word. To survive is to wait in the aporia of a word and language—unable to signify the passing of time, unable to indicate the status of an act. This may seem to make death impossible, render survival preposterous, and ensure that the future is unimaginable—yet the series of deeply felt affective logics also becomes transformed within the space of a single word, inscribing a mode of living that is suspended between stillness, survival, return.

In the unresolved search for a language of grief, the poem's relationship to its own language is profoundly transmuted. Does a name exist for this new kind of language? It may be instructive to consider an argument from a somewhat unexpected source: the very translator whom Yang so ardently cites. Responding with some bemusement to Yang's "absurd and inspiring praise" of the Chinese *Cantos*,[30] Yunte Huang first disputes what seems like an ethnoexceptionalist reading of Chineseness implied in Yang's claim.[31] But his real target is the very premise of "the Chinese language" *as* translating language and untouched whole to begin with. Instead, Huang argues that "Pound's poetic project is realized not in the language of *the* translation, but in the language of *translation*."[32] Because everything Pound writes is already a translation, there can be no distinction between source and translating language—or, the two should be understood as mutually constitutive, even fungible. For Huang, Pound's Chinese-English is a "Joycean portmanteau whose meaning hovers between languages, beyond any one language,"[33] undermining Yang's thought of a translational economy and equivalence of take and give between two distinct texts and languages.

Huang's insight about the nonexceptional and always impure status of the Chinese language qua translating language—coupled with the strange mechanics of survival within the poem—thus offers another way to read *Concentric Circles* and its political project of mourning without naming its objects and the trappings of state power. For this too is an equivalence—built from equivalences of sound and in space into an equivalence of languages—by another name. More, this translingual equivalence crafts its equivalencies not by means of the nation-state's power but in *spite* of it, indeed in the quixotic and ultimately naive struggle to evade it. What is more, I would argue that a similar point can be made about the portmanteau grammars of grief in *Concentric Circles*: it takes on new dimension when it hovers between languages and traditions. Because everything *Yang* writes is already a translation (propelled less by meaning than by the prospect of its vanishing), the borders that define his Chinese language are rendered porous by a more malleable grammar and a more resourceful, duplicitous lexicon, their arrangements and repetitions even stretching stasis and stillness into an indefinite waiting and suspending accidents before they happen, crafting a state of perpetual vigilance. Imagining the translingual relationship of Chinese to its many other linguistic counterparts—radically unexceptional in its constitution, stubbornly demanding a translation of the untranslatable—then gives a startling new form to Yang's poetics of disappearance.

Forms of Disappearance

In the final poem of *Concentric Circles*—which is also the last of three poems simply titled *Shi* or *Poem, Poetry*—the notion of the poem and its poetic constitution comes under immense pressure, opening into a final incomplete fragment like a question with no answer. The poem is reproduced in full; it does not break where the page breaks. Moments salient to my argument are translated in commentary.

零

消失成三

字

三个秋天越過國界

遠
離
自
己
的
過
去
肯
定
此
刻
詩
是 [34]

三次　鳥向光輻射藥味的影子

但丁就是被鑰匙拒絕的

消失就是思想

挽回不了的　偷渡成下一行

合唱的土黃色　虛無

停著　故鄉死了的路被鐵軌指著

三章　三塊最遠的雲

分泌

落葉　成百萬塗得猩紅的指甲

擾破樂譜　存在沒有下限

消失進親愛的

死後　美麗的情節

Meticulously arranged to interfere with existing protocols of reading, the two-directional reading that the poem invites also sets up an intersecting dialogic system wherein the questions on one hand find quarrelsome and antagonistic answers on the other. In fact, it would be helpful to imagine

Yang's poetry as plotted out on a grid that would be difficult to accurately reproduce in the present format: Chinese writing paper is often lined in a grid, in keeping with the spatial forms of the script. The ending may be read in two ways, depending on whether one reads the poem vertically along its first column—as is traditional for premodern Chinese script, an important touchstone for Yang—or horizontally from left to right and top to bottom, as is conventional for Western languages and modern Chinese. (Though the latter mode is typical for Yang, he also makes the occasional exception as we see here.) Suspended between two spatial organizations of language, the poem and its sound patterns of *disappearance*—after all, a homonym for *poetry*—continually exploits the possibilities of both.

On a literal translation, the one vertical line reads, "The word zero leaves its past confirms this moment poetry-or-poem is." Yang's characteristic absence of punctuation—likely an influence from classical Chinese prosody, which uses its internal tonal patterns, meter, and line breaks to lend structure—compounds the ambiguities suggested in the English translation, although the line could well be rendered more meaningful by a reader interpolating some interpretive pauses. Certainly, when read in both vertical and horizontal directions, the final word of the line is *shi* in the fourth tone or *being*, *is*: a lingering question asking what exactly *shi* or *poetry is*.

Yet in the same poem, some tacit answers are quietly sounded: when read horizontally, the first word is *ling* or *zero*, which status as *zi* or *word* (also a homophone for *self*, an idea that surfaces later in the poem) is revealed by way of an intervening *xiaoshi chengsan*, a *disappearance becoming three*.[35] In this reading, the first three lines might alternatively be understood as "Zero / disappears becoming three / words." This disappearance—a homophone for *poem*—is picked up again in the tenth and twenty-sixth lines. First, it is revealed that *xiaoshi jiushi sixiang* or *disappearance just is thought*, suggesting that the operations of thought compel the transformative disappearance of zero into words. And as the poem draws to a close, the operations of thought may continue to be at work as an unknown object "disappears in *beloved / poem*" or, on a different reading of the ambiguous genitive *de* at the line break, "disappears in *beloved's / poem*" (emphasis mine).[36]

Do these disappearances bring the full weight of their enigmas on the ending of the poem—which is also the ending of *Concentric Circles* and an unresolved question over the ontology of poetry? Perhaps yes, perhaps no: it is not clear if the twenty-sixth and twenty-seventh lines *should* be enjambed. To be sure, Yang's work elsewhere does contain instances of enjambment, which is a modern innovation in Chinese verse popularized through the reading of Western verse. However, this line break and the poem in general require more circumspect treatment considering their insistence on fragmentation and the unfinished. Indeed, the fact that this disappearance does not seem to take an obvious object might be a signal to read the disappearance as already having happened, already performed by the poem's surreptitious operations: a zero disappears into words, first enumerated and then beloved.

 The enigma of the poem's end is compounded by another intervention that comes between the question asking what *poem* or *poetry* even *is*. The penultimate line reads literally "after death beautiful plot" (where *plot* refers to the narratological term),[37] with the result that the last three lines may also read, on another semantic level and preserving the syntax that is crucial to its ambiguity, "poem / after death, beautiful plot / is." That such a reading is even possible is already against the grain of Yang's analysis, which insists on the ontology of poetry as a rhetorical and open question. Indeed, if one reads the poem on the level of meaning as well as sound, the "beautiful plot" "after death" (a kind of survival, perhaps) *spatially* intervenes *between* the poem and the harmophonic possibility of its being.

 Why and how does the poem present death as the condition for beauty in this poetic cosmology? Indeed, why is there a plot, and more to the point, why would such a plot be *beautiful*? Elsewhere in the fifth section, in a poem titled *Xu* or *Ruins*, there seems to be a relatively straightforward answer: "唯一没背叛這首詩的是死者," "the only ones who do not betray this poem are the dead."[38] The postmortem beautiful plot might then be the fidelity that comes with being dead. Such a pronouncement begins to implicate everything and everyone in the implicit betrayal of the poem as ruin: the poet, readers, and, more broadly yet, those survivors who are often distinguished from the dead in Yang's work.

 Indeed, I would suggest that these emphases on survival and death may be productively read alongside the other modalities of loss proliferating throughout this fifth and final section. What Yang calls in another poem *xiaoshi de xingshi* or the *form/s of disappearance*[39] is further suggestive of how the sounds of the language arrange a textual intimacy between poetry, disappearance, form, and mourning or death as almost coterminous or even fungible textual operations. Such an argument may be augmented and developed through a poem accompanying the one above, this one also titled *Shi* or *Poem* or *Poetry*. The poem comes at the end of the first subsection of the fifth section, and is one of seven in the subsection titled "Speech" or *yan*. It is reproduced here in full; the lines do not break where the page breaks. Translations of relevant moments are provided in commentary.

零
　　日期停在危險的一刻
譯成
　　小小心臟失血的藝術
水滴與水滴的界線
　　比喻歷史
鳥鳴邊緣
　　但丁躺在拉文納
雲起源之處
　　地下挖出的手錶戴到薩拉熱窩街頭
復數的黑暗
　　孩子們作曲
風和風的間隙
　　紅色大理石切成薄片
疼握住手
　　黃昏　　撤離窗戶
葉子　　蠶食自己的綠
　　從背後射擊秋天的建築
語言學
　　容納現實
火舌
　　舔中愛情的要害
一次內分泌　　我們搖搖欲墜
　　但丁　　背上遍佈童聲的彈孔

躺在海底
　　作為行刑樂隊的讀者
被零變成
　　像零的　　一根晦澀的食指指著中文
此刻　　什麼不是詩 ⁴⁰

As in the previous poem, the first word of this poem is again *ling* or *zero*. However, much of this poem's labor does not consist in making the zero disappear but in transforming its status. At first standing alone and seemingly unrelated to any of the words or lines that follow it (either vertically or horizontally), this *zero* is crucially placed a word's distance away from the poem's next line: "date stops at a dangerous moment."⁴¹ Begging the question of what this dangerous moment might be, this conjunction of ideas gets picked up again at the poem's end, where in the final three lines we learn that an implied *something* has been

by zero changed into
image of zero　　an obscure index finger points at Chinese-writing
at this moment　　what isn't poetry [*shī*]

In these lines, *zero* has become an agent that changes something into an image of itself. That object is open to question: if the two lines before are enjambed, then it is possible that the object of change is "lying at the ocean's bottom / as reader of an execution band."⁴² The possible ambiguity in my translation's "of" is at work in the source as well: it is unclear if the reader *reads* the "execution band"—the composite image is of an organized musical assemblage that performs capital punishment—or if the reader is *a part of* the "execution band." If this ambiguously implicated reader is being transformed into an "image of zero" or something that *resembles* that zero, then it might also be implicated in the poem's final and somewhat counterintuitive question that reprises the same word *ke* meaning *moment*: "[in] this moment what isn't poetry."⁴³ Given the characteristic disjointedness of Yang's poetry, one might be forgiven for wondering if the deictic for "this" moment is being preemptively explained or prematurely strained by the line that came before it. With the well-worn image of a finger pointing at its own language and performance, it seems then that "this" moment might, banally enough, be *this moment*: a moment of plenitude wherein self-referentiality can turn its very instant of reference into the poetry and the poem it names. Yet this moment is also a moment that has previously been labeled "dangerous": a moment of danger in which a date stops—perhaps at its moment of inscription. The strangeness of the formulation—dates do not often stop in any literal sense—betrays already the temporal difficulty and thickness accrued to "this moment" over the course of the poem. If at this moment nothing is not poetry—nothing is to be excepted from the claims and reaches made by "this moment"—then we might wonder if, under the terms of the poem's rhetoric, writing about *another* moment is even possible at all.

These two "moments" of poetic temporality frame the meandering and diffuse work of a long poem that at times overtly privileges the possibility of reality and at others extensively distorts images of nature and matter precisely through the nonrepresentational aspects of language, perhaps in order to collapse both forms of the material on themselves. Indeed, nowhere else in the poem is the question of time raised at all: moving from one time to another in the poem necessitates traversing an unstable territory of fissures only implicitly beholden to the structures put in place by time. Two examples of such fissures require a conjoined reading, providing a demonstration of the inseparability of history and nonrepresentational language as worked over in these poetic sounds. The first fissure comes in lines 5 and 6—a "boundary between water-drop and water-drop / history [*lishi*] of parable" or alternately, "comparable to history."[44] The second fissure, in lines 13 and 14, only half reprises the early syntax, but its second line recalls the sound of *lishi* or *history* returning through harmophony—an "interfissure between wind and wind / red marble [*dalishi*] cut to slivers."[45]

Imagining impossible interstices within the fluids of nature, the first lines in each example eventually give way to two different activities and forces of history. It is unclear what kind of relation is being drawn between "history" and "parable" and/or "comparable" and whether the possible parable for history might indeed be the hallucinated boundary that slices water into drops. The later example deepens and complicates matters further, for it remains unclear if it is the wind's "interfissure" that is cutting the marble into its slivers or if it is the marble that is slicing the wind into slivers (assuming that the two lines are to be read enjambed). Yet the tension that exists between these two pairs seems to animate a diffusive parsing of history into components that cannot quite be named as natural *or* material *or* poetic *or* auditory.

For if one further pursues the harmophonic traces given in the poem, then one is also led to lines 19 and 20, where Yang writes "linguistics / accommodates reality [*xian shi*]" or perhaps, reading the verb as an imperative, even "accommodate reality."[46] The notion that linguistics (the academic discipline) and reality might exist in some relationship of uneasy or demanded accommodation is not a new one, but given the implicit harmophonic *and* semantic relationship suggested between *xianshi* or *reality* and *lishi* or *history*, it then seems clear that both concepts are certainly being rendered abstract through linguistic means, and within the same mesh of signifiers. However, this is not to suggest that they emerge on the other end affected in the same way: although Yang is by no means the first person to suggest a correspondence between reality and history, he recalibrates their correspondence by drawing them into relation with yet other concepts further afield.

Most notable is the final harmophone to be read in lines 3 and 4, which brings reality and history into the same realm as a far more vivid loss.

translated into
little heart-organ's art of losing blood [*shixue*][47]

Perhaps it is the stopped date in the previous line that is being translated—or will be translated—as a waning aesthetic wound whose *loss* sounds just like *poetry* in its saying. For this is also a moment to be recalled later on in the sequence, in which *disappearance* and *poetry* become fungible as textual processes: the character that invokes *shi* or *loss* here and the *xiaoshi* or *disappearance* of thought and poetry elsewhere then gathers those disappearances together with this corporeal work of translation in loss.

Yet elsewhere in *Concentric Circles* Yang writes also of a different and more idiomatic kind of loss: "which hand writes—or wrote—the nursery set on fire in the air."[48] The idiomatic phrase for an accidental fire, *shihuo*, translates literally as *loss fire*, a compound term that presumably seeks to capture the loss of control or consciousness that leads to the fire itself. And it also encodes within its idiom a mode of loss that precipitates a conflagration, murmurously aligning poetry, history, reality, and matter too with an uncontrolled loss that is both active and vulnerable at the same time. At this point, it almost comes as no surprise that *huo* or *fire*, spoken in the third tone, is also a harmophone for *huo* in the second tone, the same word meaning *to live*. A conflagration nestled with survival and life, a lively survival that may also be a devastating conflagration: the sounds of disappearance were the mournful wick for survival across this poem.

***

How does one write so faithlessly at the limits of the Chinese language—and how does one write a Chinese that was already a translation, awaiting translation into another language? How does one survive while waiting for translation? By mounting a series of disappearing acts, the poem seems to say; by executing the protocols of reading demanded by that translingual erasure, its compounding whispers of *shi* sounding just like the depths of silence. Which is why Yang's politics of grief has required a contrapuntal reading. In this chapter, I have sought to take seriously his insight about the Chinese language in all of its resources and all of its gravest disappointments. Second and equally, I have also sought to think generatively at the limits of those claims in order to chart the shape and stakes of a translingual erasure in Yang's work. By focusing on the trope of *disappearance* as it was consistently coupled with and theorized as *poetry*, I have traced the intertwining work of sound and concrete translations as they produce a dispossessing work of mourning, forged finally in the poetic equivalences of a history never equal to time.

Conclusion
If Babel Had a Form

Vanishing Babel

In a curious moment of the Babel myth, Jacques Derrida imagines the tower hollowing itself out from within, vanishing within the mind's eye. One may imagine that the tower is dissolving because of the divine anger visited on everything it represents: one language for one people, a pure and fluent universal communication of meaning across all humankind. "Let us confound their language, that they may not understand one another's speech," intones the law that results in our multiple tongues and scattered homes, calling for an eternity of translating across zones of mutual misunderstanding.[1] Yet in Derrida's telling, that divine retribution seemingly visited from above does not fully explain how a once-sturdy myth must yield its architectonic form. Instead, the hollowing tower suggests "the need for figuration . . . an internal limit to formalization."[2] In other words, the tower is vanishing because the language for its building was *never* pure, with or without divine intervention. Even his title—*Des tours des Babel* or *Towers of Babel*—desacralizes the myth by multiplying it.[3] In that impurity—a flimsy structure of what I have been calling meaning and value—lies a tower that could never have been built, a figure standing in for the impossibility of its law. Indeed, the Babel myth was never about communication, or understanding—or even about how we came to need translation. Instead, its interest for Derrida lies in how and why its empty catastrophe becomes the primal law for translation.

Like that hollowing tower that could never be, this book has also been built in the subjunctive. Yet unlike Derrida, I have not been writing against purity or the sanctified borders of language, an argument whose insights I have been lucky to assimilate and even take for granted from the start. Instead, my argument lives and thinks with the formal principles at the heart of translation—up to and including those internal limits of alterity and opacity that Derrida illuminates. These limits are the fulcrum of a poetic *equivalence*. Thus far, I have argued for a new and situated equivalence that opens the epistemology of translation beyond protocols that assign meaning-value in often violent ways. In relinquishing the powers of differentiation, recognition, and even the interpretive task of reading, these translators and writers instead have recourse only to the abstract poetics that lie on the wayside of those processes. With the untranslatable fragments and arrangements of literary language—and their contradictions embedded in the transpacific scope and ideographic shadows of this book—they have staged yet more scenes that theorize oblique and often rigorous translations at the hands of a reductive sameness. If Babel had a form in these hands, it would look something like a series of mistaken transcriptions, the sound of a voice bleeding into the waves of a radio, translations formless but as souvenir and sediment, figure and machine. Working from abstractions that embed capital in poetry, the writers studied across this book suspend the value-making logics of translation and rest in hiding places within those tangled forces, those "internal limits" marked by flashes of sameness that vanish before too long. In that finitude, they understand and even embrace translation as an imprecise scalpel through which it becomes impossible to carve out zones of exception—a poetically transitive sameness that flattens worldly hierarchies without flattening the world.

In these final pages, I work through the two-step argument of the book and situate it alongside a sustained account of critical conversations on equivalence, foreignization, and untranslatability across translation studies and comparative literature. After all, what I have rashly called a *new* equivalence is—properly speaking—not new at all. Rather, it is a work of critique and reconstruction taking shape obliquely around the precepts of my fields, bending theoretical frames to better accommodate the cast of characters that I have placed in their view—and in the process discovering new rigors to my conception. If there is anything new about these thoughts and things, it is only the effort of unlearning old frames in order to name and shape a certain shift of the light: an equivalence formed and contained in the glimmers of signifiers we do not look for—before they slip back into those systems of meaning whence they came. Distilled to the most schematic, this poetics of equivalence rests only on a double gesture: a contestation and a displacement. It is neither protocol nor prescription, only a gambit with no endgame in sight.

Contest the Foundations of Equivalence in Exchange-Value

Equivalence has principally been a problem mortgaged to the value and valorization of difference; to critique equivalence then entails calling on its antecedents in the logics of capitalism.[4] Central to those critiques is the question of exchange-value—or exchangeability—within an implied political economy of translation. Equivalence in meaning, Naoki Sakai notes, has been the ideological and policing drive of a "regime of translation . . . that makes translators imagine their relationship to what they do in translation as the symmetrical exchange between two languages. . . . A translation is believed to become more accurate as it approximates the rule of equal value exchange."[5] In a similar vein, Lydia Liu observes that positing a "hypothetical equivalence" has been the a priori condition or principle for any translation at all, insofar as one has to first delineate and then juxtapose at least two texts, languages, or cultures into relation with one another in order to translate them in the conventional sense of the term.[6] For Liu as for Talal Asad, this foundational hypothesis is a speculative gesture that disingenuously represses—or even seeks to overcome—the material conditions of inequality from which it is founded, and is understood as a forceful act of epistemic violence. Hypothesizing equivalence qua exchange-value then becomes the discursive and quantifying terrain on which lesser or greater values are distributed, itself mimicking and even reproducing the unequal conditions from which it arises.

Critical efforts to evade this regulative law of value have prompted a shift away from the concept of equivalence in toto, aided by a major precept of literary and critical theory. Working without the illusions of equivalence gives way to meaningful and clear-eyed acts of *differentiation* and a deeply transformational reckoning with forms of otherness that already exist in our midst, providing "a vital clue to where the self loses its boundaries," in the memorable phrasing offered by Gayatri Spivak.[7] For his part, Sakai identifies such a difference as the a priori condition for a heterolingual structure of address in translation, prior to any communication or meaning and unrepresentable insofar as it escapes from the regime of equivalence.[8] In this proposition, he echoes Homi Bhabha's pioneering articulation of cultural translation, in which "the power of the postcolonial translation of modernity rests in its *performative, deformative* structure that does not simply revalue the contents of a cultural tradition, or transpose values 'cross-culturally.'"[9] Rooted in the specifics of the postcolonial Asian context, Sakai's and Bhabha's arguments nevertheless exemplify a more general shift in how literary and cultural theorists have come to approach translation. "Translation is not a mere mediation," wrote Antoine Berman. "It is a process in which our entire relation to the Other is played out."[10] Unlike for Sakai and Bhabha, the claim is made with some confidence as to who "we" are and who or even what the (tacitly nonequivalent) "Other" may be, even if its surprise will be to lodge the Other—that is, the difference of the foreign and feminine as unevenly mobilized across the Western literary-theoretical tradition—within oneself and one's own translating language and writing, a propriety or ownership that has thereby been unsettled and is inherently alienated.

Thus conceptually entwined across major strands of literary and critical theory, the relation of self with other has become the ethical ground for the tactic known as foreignization in translation studies. To foreignize is often taken as a gesture of hospitality and accommodation: it calls on one to translate by changing the fundaments of the receiving language, inflecting it with the peculiarities of the translated language. While its roots are in the German Romantic and Idealist tradition of Friedrich Schleiermacher, the notion has recently been given a stronger critical presence by Lawrence Venuti, whose concern is to heighten the visibility of translational work by "disrupting the cultural codes that prevail in the translating language. . . . In its effort to do right abroad, this translation practice [of foreignization] must do wrong at home, deviating enough from native norms to stage an alien reading experience."[11] For Venuti, the "foreign" is not a given but "a strategic construction whose value is contingent on the current situation in the receiving culture."[12] This latter formulation prepares us to think through the unequal conditions that also subtend any foreignizing disruption—and indeed the fact that alien reading experiences may often take place outside poetic intention and as a matter of political determination rather than being conscientiously staged by a responsible translator. As Asad argues in his critique of equivalence, languages and cultures are assigned or inherit values in unequal and unpredictable ways, so that some translating languages "are more likely to submit to forcible transformation in the translation process than the other way around."[13] If given a conceptual movement from its ethnonationalist roots to an "ethnodeviant pressure" per Venuti,[14] the tactic of foreignization presents a powerful corrective to the stubborn problem of an equivalence sprung from unequal material conditions: an agile tactic to respond to myriad existing wrongs.

Yet by disrupting or reassigning the codes of signification along a one-way vector, the model of foreignization is difficult to square with the problem of exchange-value, and moreover continues to presuppose a conceptual integrity in the colonial structures of value that I seek to rethink. After all, in moving away from equivalence as an interpretive orientation, one still does not address the matter that had caused us to abandon it in the first place: the *speculative* violation of concrete fact—and the animating question for my argument. As Liu expresses the problem, "Exchange-value is to political economy what simile, metaphor, or synecdoche is to the linguistic realm of signification, as both involve the making of equivalents out of nonequivalents through a process of abstraction or translation."[15] Abstraction in the Marxian account, and as taken up by Liu, is dangerous because of its ability to create—and conceal—false equivalences in the process of creating surplus value (isomorphic with meaning-value in this account). I thus suggest that continuing to think with equivalence—refusing to throw the baby out with the bathwater—indeed allows for a more direct confrontation with those very problems.

What is more, Liu parses a *twofold* foundation of equivalence: one must approach it through both a transformational critique of the global political economy and the need to think carefully about if and how language—and especially as it is expressed through those figures of speech often attributed to literature qua mode of thinking—engages or contests the problem of exchange-value. To build on Liu's earlier work, the former task has more recently been taken up in decolonizing and anticapitalist projects in and beyond the Global South: as Mona Baker notes in the introduction to a special issue, "Translation is a core mechanism for the production and circulation of all forms of knowledge. . . . [L]eading scholars and activists such as [Boaventura] de Sousa Santos [theorist of the Global South] have long acknowledged the potentially transformative role that translation can play in reconfiguring social and political relations by articulating new forms of knowledge based on the responsible confrontation of diverse cultural experiences."[16] With a similar ethos in mind, I have sought to engage the second task: rewriting our figurative economies of translation. In doing so, I have been led toward an argument beyond exchange-value—and toward other imaginations of equivalence marked by their often cursory relationship to semantic reading. For this task, Liu's work continues to afford conceptual resources, in part because she does not confine herself to articulating the paradox by which equivalence enforces a rule of cultural difference through the logic of value. Rather, her argument

> demand[s] that we reconceptualize the ways in which meanings circulate *meaningfully* from language to language and culture to culture. As a migrant deixis of potential value, meaning acquires value in the process of exchange

between actual signs. The circumstantial encounter of one sign with another (in a sentence) or another language (in translation) decides the manner in which the actualization or sabotage of meaning takes place.[17]

In other words, what happens when one structure of language intersects with, or is interrupted by, another when they live in one economy of translation and circulation? Liu retains the structuralist understanding of how meaning is made—through a system of differences without positive terms—but erodes its regulative and deterministic character in favor of a "circumstantial encounter," that is to say, a chance or contingent event that yields not meaning itself but rather its openness to determination such that it may be alternately actualized or sabotaged (or something else altogether). In this regard, Liu's analysis of the *happenstance* of "meaning-value" departs from the Marxian analysis of the law of surplus value and the Saussurean analysis of structural linguistics: unlike those deterministic accounts, the meaning-value of translation is conditionally bound to what she elsewhere calls the "bonding of heterolinguistic elements through a mobile process of translation."[18]

I want then to take Liu's argument on the contingency of linguistic-structural encounter seriously and one step further: Can there be translation with, so to speak, the signifier uncoupled from the signified? What is more, can there be *equivalence* with the signifier uncoupled from the signified and as they have already been uncoupled from the referent? To ground this move, I also mobilize Sakai's argument that the multidirectional force or regime of translation simultaneously calls attention to the concept of *literature* as a historical and political formation offering the possibility of intervention.[19] If, as he argues, it is possible to intervene in that translated regime called "literature" by rethinking the labor and protocols of translation,[20] then might it also be possible to extend a similar intervention toward the disavowed law of value in equivalence to confuse its protocols? For even as I lean on the explanatory power in Liu's dialectical synthesis of literary language and political economy, I would also argue that such a dialectic needs to hear the finer mechanisms and operations that work between the two. After all, this is what gets the dialectic going to begin with. Between the Marxian and Saussurean accounts of economic value and linguistic value, there were always two different ways of being diachronic, two ways of entering an object or word or sound into circulation. Must meaning *circulate*? Can there be translation by other means? Even as literary language and political economy are isomorphic with one another, I also invest my argument in the nuances between them. Within those spaces are the interlocked forms of abstraction that function where the signifying processes of translation appear to be impossible.

Ground Equivalence in the Aporia of the Untranslatable

The argument's second move displaces equivalence from its systems of exchange and grounds it in a surprisingly transitive aporia known as the untranslatable—revising one situated abstraction to another, and a move from the poststructuralist convention of a radical alterity toward a new task of equivalence. After all, for those who work in translation studies, there is a *pragmatic* definition for the untranslatable: a word or term that is reproduced and included in its untranslated state within the body of the translated text, often without further commentary. At first legible as the record of a failure—as if a translator has arrived at an impasse—the gesture nevertheless seems to defer the task to a future reader, opening a stranger afterlife not in translation but indeed in the untranslated that can no longer quite be called the original. My argument thus conjugates both the simple and complex senses of the term: much like the untranslatable jokes that opened this book, I have found a drifting equivalence in those pieces of language—harmophones, homographs, words that become shapes and others in between—that catalyze aporias of meaning into a political aesthetic of translation that is not so different at all. Throughout this book, I have sought to trace a *poetics* of equivalence as an unlikely pendant to the politics of untranslatability: where Emily Apter's influential argument orients her localized sense of "world literatures"—against the freighted "World Literature"—around untranslatable *philosophical* concepts and geopolitical nodes in our world systems, I also orient the question of equivalence around the untranslatable *literary* elements of translation with which every translator grapples. The abstractions of literature afford what Vicente Rafael calls "a kind of semantic *bouleversement*" underwritten by the aporia of untranslatability, which "persist as sources of continuous bewilderment in need of further explication, calling forth imaginative revisions."[21]

Such an argument sits within a long history in which translation has a developmental and dialectical character, most saliently tied to the central status of Walter Benjamin and his readers in the field of translation studies; indeed, Benjamin's foundational questions of how translation unsettles questions of origin, historicity, and futurity have most recently been politically radicalized by thinkers interested in its decolonizing and universalizing possibilities.[22] Yet the volatile history of developmental logic—especially as embedded in its Asian and Pacific avatars, abstract and flexible into perpetuity as we have seen—calls for a careful reinvention of what exactly it means to think translation with *and* against the circulatory processes of capital. In translation studies and comparative literature, that relationship has typically been routed through materialist and sociological considerations of world literature as a global market economy (which critique does not in itself preclude alternative senses of literary production qua world literature). Where recent interventions have extended that conversation by prioritizing the literary and material praxes endemic to the simultaneous goods and ills of world literature,[23] I instead take a closer look at the ways in which untranslatability and its conceptual genesis in an anticapitalist impulse may craft a robust poetics of equivalence beyond value.

As Marx notes in the *Grundrisse*, the processes of capital perform (a kind of) translation; that the same may be true the other way around has by now also become virtually axiomatic.[24] Those very axioms of capitalist abstraction are the target of Apter's insistence on a politics of untranslatability: a "resistant yet mobile" political symptom, the untranslatable deflates the transactional and imperialist fetish for a homogenized World Literature. To oppose that uppercase version of the term, the political force of Apter's argument sits squarely on the lowercase counterparts: untranslated world literatures made in local and polycentric modes of literary production that do not always enter global circulation for reasons ranging from defiant resistance to simple incapacity. Thinking with the untranslatable thus demands a sustained reflection on the infrastructures that stratify those two worlds of literature, inhabiting a contradictory tendency to "impede translational fluency yet enable critical faculties nonetheless" (a critical refusal of fluency that suggests a close resonance with Venuti's classic argument).[25] In this gesture, Apter does not thereby suggest that some writing *ought* not be translated or that what translation does take place should not have taken place; that is to say, her proposition is neither prescriptive nor prohibitive. Rather, Apter describes a new epistemology of translation beyond equivalence and foreignization: untranslatability is born of the relationships that translation makes, so that translatable and untranslatable are not simple opposites but orbit the same theoretical and political problem. Reading for untranslatability bears down on points of disconnection or withdrawal that themselves generate heuristics of knowing *through* and *about* the violent conditions of colonial capital: an intervening caesura within which the possibility of difference is inscribed.[26] Apter's polemic thus suggests a critical praxis of untranslatability in which translation and translators have always been the agential knower—or subtle un-knower—of violence rather than the known or the objectified. With these modes of praxis in hand, speculation is not a realm separate from the material base but an entangled way of knowing and making something different and new—such that speculation may then in turn be vigilantly wielded against itself.

And as we have seen via the transpacific core of this argument, translation is abstract *not only* in relation to the thought of capital and indeed may demand ways of thinking about literary form in and beyond an economic frame. If the first task of imagining an equivalence after capital has been to—conceptually and not materially—disentangle translation from its law of meaning and exchange-value, then I would suggest that the heuristic of untranslatability is a helpful conceptual friend in both diagnosing and taking a step beyond such a critique. Indeed, Apter's argument may well be usefully recast as an invitation to address its precept in those very questions: *Is* translation instrumentalist and complicit with the global conditions of which it is a part, a matter of exchange-value? If one answers yes, then the method of resistance lies with a strategic and considered untranslatability; if one answers no, then translation *is* the method of resistance in itself. Yet of course the answer will always be *both* and *more*: my reductive question has presumed that we already know how the work of translation is done—and, for that matter, flattened the sophisticated maneuvers of capitalism *and* anticapitalist critique. If abstraction is a capitalist form paradoxically defined by a fundamental in-definition, then the related question of translatability also demands a similarly volatile sense of literary language.

Yet mobilizing an aporia requires careful treatment—and looking to literature brings as many limitations as possibilities. To explore this question, I follow Apter in looking at a moment from Derrida's *Le monolinguisme de l'autre* (1996) (translated two years later by Patrick Mensah as *Monolingualism of the Other*), which is written in a quasi-autobiographical mode reflecting on his relationship to the colonial insistence of the French language, especially in light of his Jewish and Algerian heritage. Here, Derrida unfurls an economic system of writing that seeks to think outside the economic and exchangeable senses of equivalence.

> Not that I am cultivating the untranslatable. Nothing is untranslatable, if only one give oneself the time for the expenditure or expansion of a competent discourse that measures itself against the power of the original. But what remains untranslatable—should remain, as my law tells me—is the poetic economy of the idiom, the one that is important to me, for I would die even more quickly without it, and which is important to me, myself to myself, where a given formal "quantity" always fails to restore the singular event of the original, that is, to let it be forgotten once recorded, to carry away its numbers, the prosodic shadow of its quantum. Word for word, if you like, syllable by syllable. From the moment this economic equivalence—strictly impossible, by the way—is renounced, everything can be translated, but in a loose translation, in the loose sense of the word "translation." I am not even talking about poetry, only about prosody, about metrics (accent and quantity in the time of pronunciation). In a sense, nothing is untranslatable; but *in another sense*, everything is untranslatable; translation is another name for the impossible. In another sense of the word "translation," of course, and from one sense to the other—it is easy for me always to hold firm between these two hyperboles which are fundamentally the same, and always translate each other.[27]

Even as he breaks the one-to-one calculus of equivalence, Derrida also insists on another kind of economy: the "poetic economy of the idiom" that will always exceed any attempts at formalization or quantification. By conceptualizing a poetic rather than formal economy, the passage recapitulates the theme of incalculable loss and untranslatability in translation—familiar to us by this point in the argument—yet crucially reads that aporia *beyond* any equivalence and does so through a distinction between *la poésie* or *poetry* and *la prosodie* or *prosody*. The two senses of un/translatability are disambiguated and still braided: an expansive, loosening sense and a restorative sense. Cast in nonoppositional terms, translation might be an expansive attempt to account for and bear witness to the singular event of *parole* (this is the sense in which everything is translatable), which in its growing scale still cannot restore the poetic economy or prosody of the event (the sense in which everything is untranslatable).[28]

This is because, as Derrida argues, the word-for-word (or even syllable-by-syllable) economy of equivalence between two languages is strictly impossible. Everything is "loosely" translatable given time, competence, and a willingness to break or at least loosen the promise of equivalence by renouncing it in its quantifiable dimensions while still rigorously holding oneself accountable to the original. This is one sense of translatability: a translation that must dissolve an economic and quantifiable equivalence. It is in the aftermath of that dissolution that Derrida works in the second sense: the poetic economy of the idiom that must fall away. Where a translator cannot give one word for one word, they may still be able to give a sentence, or a paragraph, or even a book: yet more words as prosaic yet meaningful substitutes for something that began only as a single word. What this exuberance of meaning does not restore is the event of the poetic idiom, its prosody. This is why the two hyperboles are contiguous to one another, at once a generative gift of time and an irrecuperable loss of the event, two operations operating on one another in a manner that Derrida still calls "translation."

In renouncing the economic and quantifiable sense of equivalence while continuing to affirm the (by now familiar) loss of idiomatic language in the service to meaning, Derrida's argument is necessary but not sufficient for fleshing out a poetics of equivalence *without* meaning. After all, at stake in the rapid move from "*nothing* is untranslatable" to "*everything* is untranslatable" is more than his point about the overdetermined and multiple definitions of untranslatability: even more challenging, it would seem to totalize the expansive and uncontainable sense of equivalence he offers via the first (which still operates via an equivalence of meaning) into the absolute finitude of the second. How does that chime with the account of meaning and value organizing this discussion thus far? For a surprising way to grapple with this question, I have looked to Marx's discussion of surplus value, which account of how difference vanishes in value formation may almost be legible as a sinister underbelly for a poetics of equivalence.

> In the circulation M-C-M [the circulation from money to commodity and then money again, i.e., buying in order to sell—Marx's primary concern in the diagnosis of capitalism and the chief formula and process by which surplus value is generated], value suddenly presents itself as a self-moving substance which passes through a process of its own, and for which commodities and money are both mere forms. But there is more

to come: instead of simply representing the relations of commodities, it [value] now enters into a private relationship with itself, as it were. It differentiates itself as original value from itself as surplus value, just as God the Father differentiates himself from himself as God the Son, although both are of the same age and form, in fact one single person; for only by the surplus value of £10 does the £100 originally advanced become capital, and as soon as this has happened, as soon as the son has been created and, through the son, the father, their difference vanishes again, and both become one, £110.

Value therefore now becomes value in process, money in process, and, as such, capital. It comes out of circulation, enters it again, preserves and multiplies itself within circulation, emerges from it with an increased size, and starts the same cycle again and again. M-M, 'money which begets money,' such is the description of capital given by its first interpreters, the Mercantilists.[29]

An autopoetics of value: only by the surplus does the sum become capital; only by translation does the source text become the original; and on it goes without end. Both Derrida and Marx, one may now see, mobilize the dialectical structure in ways that have strikingly different consequences for tracing the operations of value within a theory of translation. Writing about a contradiction endemic to capitalism and that will precipitate its crisis, the passage demonstrates how Marx has classically derived that ideological cliché: only money can make money. What Marx suggests is that this is not quite the full picture. Lost in citations of the phrase today is how exactly that may be so: here, it is through the abstract driver that Marx also calls "value"—encrypted from the labor of workers and instantiated in money and other commodity forms—so that in its reproductions we cannot differentiate origin from surplus, source from target, the origin from the end, the owner from the dispossessed, the knower from the known, father from son: all are the same and conjoined just like the Holy Spirit is analogized to the dispossessing and self-sufficient process of capital. Presented here as a self-making of value and growth, the mode of violence that Marx is diagnosing here is not the breaking or fracturing of divine law or even the Tower of Babel before God's Word but by analogy a radically protean quality of value, able to seamlessly assimilate and convert past to present to future through the process known as capitalism.

Marx's account thus permits a surprising deconstruction of singularity with excess, unmooring the grounds of equivalence.

Moreover, through this indeterminacy of origin and end, Marx radicalizes value beyond its status as a representation of the commodity form, "a fantastic form of relation between things."[30] Instead, the form of value, with which I have been working thus far, is transformed into an involuntary and fully tautological "private relationship with itself."[31] Value here is not so much representational as it is a self-contained form-in-itself that functions on its own terms. For value to grow, it must still live with these two contradictions that serve as its conditions: (i) it must be unable to be differentiated; and (ii) it must be privatized but only unto itself. Such a radical *indeterminacy* of value should not then be understood as the *absence* of regulation as it is still, at least for Marx, its own mode of *self-contained reproduction*—both law and contradiction by which capitalism not only grows, but indeed sustains itself in the time of development, an aporia of translation that is always on the move.

Yet as commentators of transpacific abstraction have suggested, this portrait of a self-sustaining value formation—which in the Marxian narrative promises an ignominious end to capital—may contain not an inevitable crisis but only the germinating seeds of neoliberal mutability.[32] As Iyko Day points out, the neoliberal landscape of today also entails a certain formalization without codification, one whose ideological force de facto lies in its inability to harden into any law or forceful determination— and in that specific regard, brings us to the work of translation. Marx is writing in a nonaffirmative register, yet in this critical fidelity to describing the topsy-turvy laws of capital, he also excavates its poetics of translation: one in which numbers craft their own vanishing acts so that an expansive, loosening, and nonquantified sense of equivalence may encounter only a "private relationship with itself" that ultimately sublates any possibility of loss—and one in which, pace Derrida, an equivalence that vanishes a word for a word even begins to look less impossible. Under the laws that Marx seeks to diagnose, money *can* only *make* money; and if perchance money *loses* money, it is only due to contingent errors by the players involved rather than a symptom of a failing system writ large: careless calculations, imprecise speculations, sheer unluckiness. Yet words do not obey exactly the same laws in translation: across the readings in this book, they lose themselves in other words and gain new proxies and collapse their distinctions in ways that are more complex than the Marxian model of contradiction and development. Odd as it may sound, the conjunction of Marx with Derrida brings to the fore a renewed thinking of loss, such that each radicalizes the other *not* on the question of how value—and meaning—may be *reproduced* in translation but rather how it may be *contained* within that aporia that I—with Apter and Derrida—have been calling the untranslatable.

The conjunction of both thinkers suggests that the differentiation between origin and surplus is in the end untenable because of the formal structures within which they live. But if the laws of capital present a monstrous tautology that is nonrestorative and that we now know cannot be counted on to end itself, I instead suggest that Derrida's insistence on the *finitude* of translation—identified throughout with the untranslatable poetic idiom—presents a way of limiting the forces of value formation in a provisional sense. Given everything I have argued thus far, such a finitude can no longer quite be called a singular event or indeed a poetic idiom: both befall from the incalculable unknown of the future or haunt in their absence, notions of finitude that still operate on a relatively static and ahistorical concept of difference, alterity, and origin from which we have already departed. A better name for this finitude, now riven by sameness, might then be *equivalence* after all.

A final functional equivalence, this one between that migrating animal named *theory* and its many contextual habitats that have ranged from Europe to America and then everything here: just as translation theory has enabled me to reconceptualize the Sino-US transpacific, so too has the particularity of that context helped me to deepen what translation can do and mean beyond this work, to trace and illuminate dimensions that would not have been visible otherwise. Far from a subtractive or parochial gesture, theorizing translational equivalence as embedded in the specific context of the transpacific *and* at multiple levels of abstraction amplifies the political potency of translation studies and its insights.[33] If we have emancipated the proper authority of the translation's original, then what we make from it—theory, universalism, target, translation—properly belongs to no one and everyone. That it has been so improperly distributed finally betrays its partiality and reveals the contradictions that still drive translators to an unending task.

Acknowledgments

I gratefully acknowledge financial support from the University of Oregon, Oregon Humanities Center, and Emory University's George W. Woodruff Graduate and Dean's Teaching Fellowships in the writing and production of this work. At the University of Oregon, the work of United Academics and the Women of Color faculty group laid foundations for my institutional well-being too. And in the end stages, completing a book under the weight of a pandemic always meant drawing on the goodwill of my colleagues and students, itself a kind of material support; for this and more, they have my enduring thanks.

Years ago at the National University of Singapore, John W. Phillips, Tania Roy, and Barnard Turner wrote letters to recommend a determined naïf for graduate school—not knowing that, without their teaching, that determined naïf would have been directionless instead. At Emory's Department of Comparative Literature, a deeply introverted thinker somehow found a place to grow on her own terms. When I first met Geoffrey Bennington, I knew of his intellectual commitments—impatience with dogma, love of precision, respect for how the rigor of thinking may bend and break—but not that those very things would eventually add up to a gentle understanding that I have never found anywhere else. Most of all, I thank Geoff for the simple surprise of a friendship between like minds, which has stayed with me throughout the years. Haun Saussy agreed to serve on my committee as an external reader, and his guidance was indispensable at the dissertation, job market, and book prospectus stages, always meted with an exacting generosity that I have come to associate with the best of intellectual rigor. It is a measure of how perceptively Deborah Elise White and Elissa Marder shaped my thinking in the formative years that they will almost certainly recognize their questions in these pages even now. And to Catherene, Lulu, Megan, Mark, Claire, Taylor, and Ania—I often visit the alternate world in which we are still thinking together under a rickety yurt and cloudless sky.

At the University of Oregon, my colleagues in the Department of Comparative Literature gave this work a chance to breathe, take root, and mature. My deepest appreciation goes to department heads Kenneth Calhoon, for seeing something in me back then and for sharing my quiet love of the depths of thinking, and Leah Middlebrook, for her boundless reserves of intellect, foresight, and cheer. Going on walks with Michael Allan always makes me glad to have his speedy mind by my side. Roy Chan's excellent home cooking is surpassed only by his unyielding commitment to what we may still glean from this topsy-turvy world: his friendship has kept me honest and sane. Many more colleagues unfailingly showed up to give whatever was needed at the time, be it reading a proposal or savoring the sweets and bitters of institutional life: Jenifer Presto, Katya Hokanson, Lanie Millar, Steven Brown, Amalia Gladhart, Joyce Cheng, Mayra Bottaro, Sangita Gopal, Tara Fickle, and Brendan O'Kelly. And at the helm, Cynthia Stockwell's hard work, light touch, and staunch mind made me feel lucky to work with her everyday.

The spirit of Fordham University Press is everywhere in this book, so much so that I cannot imagine publishing this work anywhere else. Tom Lay's very early support gave me the courage to take the intellectual risks now sustaining this book's argument; much later, his steadfast patience enabled me to complete it. And if you admired the cover of this book before now reading it, please know that it was Tom who picked out the image and who detected the book's undertow of quiet surprise. Special thanks to Myeongbeom Kim for giving permission to use his luminous art on the cover. Perceptive reader reports, from Yunte Huang and an anonymous reader, greatly improved the argument's presentation and gave me much to think about even now. Sheila Berg's deft and thorough copyediting (which patiently found room for my abuse of italics and the em-dash), Tim Roberts's steady oversight, Eric Newman's timely responses, and John Garza's efficient emails made for a blissfully uneventful production process despite the stresses of pandemic life. Last but not least, I have a feeling—even in these early days—that the marketing team will help this book find its readers with acumen and care, for which they will have my hearty cooperation and heartfelt thanks.

Even as writing this book has led me far away, it has also helped me see the things that stay and remain the same. Thank you to my parents and siblings for bearing with the distance between us and for giving me a home to miss and hold close. My in-laws treated me as family right from the beginning. And as for B., A., M., and S., who waited patiently—there remain only our golden walks, salty gleaming eyes, your sticky little leaves that come out in the spring, knowing that this is enough—

June 2021
Eugene, Oregon

Notes

Introduction

1. Walter Benjamin, "The Translator's Task—Walter Benjamin," trans. Steven Rendall, *TTR: traduction, terminologie, rédaction* 10, no. 2 (1997): 164. What Rendall translates as *meaning* or *Sinn* may also be translated as *sense* (as is the case in the alternate Zohn translation), the meaning that is signified through language, whereas its frequent kin *Bedeutung* roughly corresponds to the referent, i.e., another axis of meaning. The drift of Benjamin's essay is toward *Sinn*. *Flüchtigkeit*—translated as *fleetingly* by Rendall—has the temporal meaning and is also a scientific term for chemical volatility, the transmuting of substances.

2. This very short story remains a popular translation exercise for beginning learners of the Chinese language. Despite its untranslatable plays of language rooted in script and sound, the story and its jokes are linguistically simple on their own terms and (handily for the pedagogical projects of the vernacular movement) call attention to those new features of modernizing the Chinese language. The title and character *Chabuduo xiansheng* is most commonly translated as *Mr. Close Enough*. This gives the idiomatic sense of being "good enough," but a literal translation would reconstruct the negative dimension explicitly at work in the phrase *chabuduo*—lit., *difference not more*. *Cha* may also be translated as *worse*, so that the notion of inferiority is audible in the idiom as well. As negativity is important to my argument, I have opted for a literal—perhaps worse—approach. Hu Shi, "Chabuduo xiansheng zhuan" [The Story of Mr. Close Enough], in *Hushi sanwen xuanji* [Selected Writings by Hu Shi] (Tianjin: Baihua wenyi chubanshe, 1995), 123–25.

3. Hu, "Chabuduo," 123.

4. *Harmophone* is my translating neologism for words close in sound but usually differentiated tonally. Chinese writing frequently adopts a play on words known as *xieyin*: it mobilizes homophones or harmophones. Mandarin Chinese is a tonal language with four tones that inflect a comparatively small number of phonemes (relative to Western languages). This phonetic structure functions in tandem with a disproportionately large number of written characters in the script; as a result, homophones and harmophones are rife and commonly punned on in colloquial speech and literary writing, their allusive and allegorical dimensions often helping evade state censorship and machine reading surveillance where circumstances demand. The effect of this play is more than a pun in that there is often a strong metaphorical or allegorical connection implied; in the sad fate of Mr. Not So Different, that way of thinking is subject to a didactic reductio ad absurdum.

5. Hu, "Chabuduo," 125.

6. As most influentially expressed in Gayatri Spivak, "The Politics of Translation," in *Outside in the Teaching Machine* (New York: Routledge, 1993); Lawrence Venuti, *The Translator's Invisibility: A History of Translation* (New York: Routledge, 2008).

7. Jean Luc Nancy, *After Fukushima: The Equivalence of Catastrophes*, trans. Charlotte Mandell (New York: Fordham University Press, 2014), 8.

8. Lydia Liu, "The Question of Meaning-Value in the Political Economy of the Sign," in *Tokens of Exchange: The Problem of Translation in Global Circulations*, ed. Lydia Liu (Durham, NC: Duke University Press, 2000).

9. Andrea Bachner, *Beyond Sinology: Chinese Writing and the Scripts of Culture* (New York: Columbia University Press, 2014), 199.

10. *Signifier*: Saussure's term for the part of the sign apprehended by the senses. In Saussure's account, it is "arbitrarily" connected to its other part, the signified, i.e., the imaginary object, idea, or concept that is called to mind via perceiving the signifier. For Saussure, meaning is made through a process of signification within a system of signs differentiated from one another. In this system, neither signifier nor signified is self-subsistent but gains its identity or "value" purely from its relation to other signifiers and signifieds. The Saussurean model of language has a long afterlife of reading and adaptation in the poststructuralist literary theory of Jacques Lacan and Jacques Derrida, among others. For Saussure's explication of "value," see Ferdinand de Saussure, *Course in General Linguistics*, trans. Wade Baskin, ed. Perry Meisel and Haun Saussy (New York: Columbia University Press, 2011), 111–22.

11. Rey Chow identifies the "bracketing of referentiality" in processes of meaning-making as the central legacy of poststructuralism, before going on to explore the tensions endemic to its defamiliarizing interiorization of difference—what she calls "differencing." In short, the valorization of difference turns out to introject and mask an unthought logic of exclusion. To think more responsibly with the powerful insights of poststructuralism, Chow argues that its blunt instrument—differencing after the refusal of reference—should not be adopted in uncritical ways. Instead, one should "let the problematic of referentiality interrupt—to reopen the poststructuralist foreclosure of this issue, to acknowledge the inevitability of reference even in the most avant-garde of theoretical undertakings." *The Age of the World Target: Self-Referentiality in War, Theory, and Comparative Work* (Durham, NC: Duke University Press, 2006), 69. In the indirect brilliance of his naïveté, Mr. Not So Different may have started to fulfill Chow's call before the advent of poststructuralism, before his untimely end.

12. George Steiner connects the hermeneutic translator's faithful restoration of an equitable meaning to the economic realm, going so far as to analogize it to the dynamic equilibriums theorized in Lévi-Strauss's anthropology of social structures. To that, he adds, "Fidelity is ethical but also, in the full sense, economic. . . . The arrows of meaning, of cultural, psychological benefaction, move both ways. There is, ideally, exchange without loss. In this respect, translation can be pictured as a negation of entropy; order is preserved at both ends of the cycle, source and receptor. . . . Within the class of semantic exchanges, translation is again the most graphic, the most radically equitable. A translator is accountable to the diachronic and synchronic mobility and conservation of the energies of meaning. A translation is, more than figuratively, an act of double-entry; both formally and morally the books must balance." Steiner's argument that source and receptor should be understood as co-restorers of the meaning that is lost, circulates, and lies between them has been an instructive one for my own; I would add, however, that the mode of equivalence I seek does not map onto this (somewhat utopian) hermeneutic paradigm. *After Babel: Aspects of Language and Translation* (Oxford: Oxford University Press, 1998), 318–19.

13. David Damrosch, *What Is World Literature?* (Princeton, NJ: Princeton University Press, 2003); Emily Apter, *Against World Literature: On the Politics of Untranslatability*

(New York: Verso, 2013); Ignacio Infante, *After Translation: The Transfer and Circulation of Modern Poetics across the Atlantic* (New York: Fordham University Press, 2013); Rebecca Walkowitz, *Born Translated: The Contemporary Novel in an Age of World Literature* (New York: Columbia University Press, 2017).

14. Per the structural linguistics of Roman Jakobson and refined in a cultural analysis by Eugene Nida. Roman Jakobson, "On Linguistic Aspects of Translation," in *On Translation*, ed. Reuben A. Brower (Cambridge, MA: Harvard University Press, 1959), 233. Nida's thoughts on equivalence are recorded across two works: the first proposes the distinction between "dynamic" and "formal" equivalence, and the second reconsiders "dynamic" equivalence as instead a "functional" one. Formal equivalence may be understood as the word-for-word literal translations that appear throughout this book, often used to retain the grammar and idiom of the source; dynamic or functional equivalence sought to take into account how the receiving or translating culture would receive the translation in order to reconstruct its equivalent accordingly. Both are tied to the mirrored reconstruction of meaning, be it on the lexical, grammatical, or cultural level. Eugene A. Nida, *Toward a Science of Translating* (Leiden: Brill, 1964); Eugene A. Nida and Charles R. Taber, *The Theory and Practice of Translation* (Leiden: Brill, 1969). Another important touchstone is Mona Baker's typology of translational equivalence—understood via meaning—on the levels of word, grammar, text, pragmatics, and semiotics. *In Other Words: A Coursebook on Translation* (New York: Routledge, 2018).

15. I have in mind the work of several thinkers working with postcolonial theory more closely considered later in this book, for example, Lydia Liu, Naoki Sakai, Talal Asad, Homi Bhabha, and Shaden Tageldin. Two exceptions share—and nevertheless seek to rethink—the collective skepticism about equivalence: Rey Chow argues that "the equivalence and coevalness between cultures, however dissimilar those cultures might seem, ought to be a type of potentiality we seek and explore—that is, *regardless of the number of languages involved and even if only one language appears in use*." *Not Like a Native Speaker: On Languaging as a Postcolonial Experience* (New York: Columbia University Press, 2014), 75, emphasis in the original; see Chow's derivation of the claim via Paul Ricoeur on 73–75. The second exception is Gayatri Spivak, who proposes an affirmative location of equivalence in *languages* as a condition of comparison—even while cautioning that its promises, only possible in the realm of simulacra, will remain "upstream from all the historical language battles of postcoloniality and neocolonial power that are still being fought and must continue to be fought." "Rethinking Comparativism," *New Literary History* 40, no. 3 (Summer 2009): 613. I seek to think through the sum of their insights in my particular focus on the transpacific Sino-US world—and with the help of abstraction as a theoretical frame.

16. I have also benefited from Jacques Lezra's reading of the lapsed elision from relative to general value in Marx, as well as his argument on general equivalence as a deconstructive "necrophilology." Lezra's work has enabled me to conceptualize the partial nature of abstraction and untranslatability—with potent stakes for the transpacific context and the divided modes of literariness with which I work. Jacques Lezra, *On the Nature of Marx's Things: Translation as Necrophilology* (New York: Fordham University Press, 2018), 105.

17. This may seem a counterintuitive point. Some of its difficulty is suggested by Lawrence Venuti's polemic against what he takes to be a callow emphasis on translation in comparative literature, which for him is exemplified in Apter's (via Cassin) formulation

of the politics of untranslatability. To my ear, Venuti's argument suggests a serious need to clarify how the loose heuristic and dense conceptuality of "untranslatability" opens up, in no uncertain terms, to possible praxes of translation—as well as (and this is my interpolation) a more radical, inclusionary, and empowered understanding of what translation even *is*, as Mona Baker and Maria Tymoczko have argued. Thus I do not share Venuti's diagnostic understanding of untranslatability as a restrictive essentialism founded on negating translation—and as a comparatist who takes seriously the disciplinary insights of both translation studies and comparative literature, I can only strive to prove his subtitle wrong. Thus, in seeking to think about equivalence *with*—and not against—the analytic of untranslatability, I share the spirit if not the letter of Venuti's observation that "untranslatability is not an aesthetic or philosophical category but a set of lived relations to opposed constituencies, provoking suspicion, insult, and violence," as well as his insistence that work on the politics of translation should leave one with "a renewed sense of the importance of translation in realizing utopian aspirations for social life." As many postcolonial critics have argued before me, translation is precisely a site in which aesthetic and philosophical categories come to reckon with their making and articulation in those very modes of lived power relations that have produced them *and* have been excluded by them, often indeed stemming from the conditions and organizations of social life. To trace those problems of subsumption and exclusion does not entail a rejection of either translation or untranslatability, only a renewed articulation of the work of the negative and its nonoppositional relation. "Hijacking Translation: How Comp Lit Continues to Suppress Translated Texts," *boundary 2* 43, no. 2 (2016): 202.

18. Barbara Cassin, Introduction to *Dictionary of Untranslatables: A Philosophical Lexicon*, trans. Michael Wood, ed. Barbara Cassin (Princeton, NJ: Princeton University Press, 2014), xviii.

19. Cassin, "Introduction," xix.

20. Maria Tymoczko, *Enlarging Translation, Empowering Translators* (New York: Routledge, 2014), 265. See esp. chap. 7, "Liberating Meaning, Legitimating Translation" (265–309), for just such an extended polyphonic meditation on the history, theory, and praxis (including pedagogical praxis) of rethinking the location and production of meaning via the activity of translation. For work also theorizing translation's modes of power through rigorous contextualization, see Tejaswini Niranjana, *Siting Translation: History, Post-Structuralism, and the Colonial Context* (Berkeley: University of California Press, 1992); Maria Tymoczko, *Translation in a Postcolonial Context* (Manchester: Saint Jerome Press, 1999); Sandra Bermann and Michael Wood, eds., *Nation, Language, and the Ethics of Translation* (Princeton, NJ: Princeton University Press, 2005); Mona Baker, *Translation and Conflict: A Narrative Account* (New York: Routledge, 2006); Paul F. Bandia, *Translation as Reparation: Writing and Translation in Postcolonial Africa* (Manchester: Saint Jerome Press, 2008); Vicente Rafael, *Motherless Tongues: The Insurgency of Language amid Wars of Translation* (Durham, NC: Duke University Press, 2016). See also the essays collected in Mona Baker, ed., *Translating Dissent: Voices from and with the Egyptian Revolution* (New York: Routledge, 2005); Maria Tymoczko, ed., *Translation, Resistance, Activism* (Amherst: University of Massachusetts Press, 2010).

21. I do not suggest that translating for semantic accuracy is impossible or naive; indeed, my own translations in this book aim to do just that. My argument is that—for good or ill—an emphasis on meaning entails an inherently restrictive understanding of

what translation *can* do and *how* it does its work. The same idea motivates my interest in abstraction.
  22. Spivak, "Politics of Translation," 183.
  23. Haun Saussy, *Translation as Citation: Zhuangzi Inside Out* (New York: Oxford University Press, 2017), 22.
  24. Yunte Huang, *Transpacific Displacement: Ethnography, Translation, and Intertextual Travel in Twentieth-Century American Literature* (Berkeley: University of California Press, 2002); Steven Yao, *Translation and the Languages of Modernism: Gender, Politics, Language* (New York: Palgrave Macmillan, 2002); Daniel Katz, *American Modernism's Expatriate Scene: The Labour of Translation* (Edinburgh: Edinburgh University Press, 2007); Michael Gibbs Hill, *Lin Shu Inc.: Translation and the Making of Modern Chinese Culture* (New York: Oxford University Press, 2013). For how this historical moment has inflected later poetic relationships to translation, see Lucas Klein, "Silences, Whispers, and the Figure of China: Translation Anxiety in Contemporary American Poetry," *Genre* 51, no. 3 (2018): 267–93. The recent interest in the politics of untranslatability in comparative literature has also led to a rethinking of translation in European modernism, as seen in Jason Harding and John Nash, eds., *Modernism and Non-Translation* (Oxford: Oxford University Press, 2019).
  25. Janet Hoskins and Viet Thanh Nguyen, "Introduction—Transpacific Studies: Critical Perspectives on an Emerging Field," in *Transpacific Studies: Framing an Emerging Field*, ed. Janet Hoskins and Viet Thanh Nguyen (Honolulu: University of Hawai'i Press, 2014), 33.
  26. David Palumbo-Liu, *Asian/America: Historical Crossings of a Racial Frontier* (Stanford: Stanford University Press, 1999); Rob Wilson, *Reimagining the American Pacific: From South Pacific to Bamboo Ridge and Beyond* (Durham, NC: Duke University Press, 2000); Jodi Kim, *Ends of Empire: Asian American Critique and the Cold War* (Minneapolis: University of Minnesota Press, 2010); Christopher Lee, *The Semblance of Identity: Aesthetic Mediation in Asian American Literature* (Stanford: Stanford University Press, 2012); Josephine Park, *Cold War Friendships: Korea, Vietnam, and Asian American Literature* (New York: Oxford University Press, 2016); Richard Jean So, *Transpacific Community: America, China, and the Rise and Fall of a Cultural Network* (New York: Columbia University Press, 2016); Jinah Kim, *Postcolonial Grief: The Afterlives of the Pacific Wars in the Americas* (Durham, NC: Duke University Press, 2019); Aimee Bahng, *Migrant Futures: Decolonizing Speculation in Financial Times* (Durham, NC: Duke University Press, 2018).
  27. See the work in the special issue by Andrea Bachner and Pedro Erber, "Remapping the Transpacific: Critical Approaches between Asia and Latin America," *Verge: Studies in Global Asias* 3, no. 2 (Fall 2017): vi–xii. Shu-mei Shih, *Visuality and Identity: Sinophone Articulations across the Pacific* (Berkeley: University of California Press, 2007); Kuan-hsing Chen, *Asia as Method: Toward Deimperialization* (Durham, NC: Duke University Press, 2010); Jodi Byrd, *The Transit of Empire: Indigenous Critiques of Colonialism* (Minneapolis: University of Minnesota Press, 2011); Jeehyun Lim, *Bilingual Brokers: Race, Literature, and Language as Human Capital* (New York: Fordham University Press, 2017); Lily Wong, *Transpacific Attachments: Sex Work, Media Networks, and Affective Histories of Chineseness* (New York: Columbia University Press, 2018); Ana Paulina Lee, *Mandarin Brazil: Race, Representation, and Memory* (Stanford: Stanford University Press, 2018); Annmaria Shimabuku, *Alegal: Biopolitics and the Unintelligibility of Okinawan Life* (New York:

Fordham University Press, 2018); Sarah Dowling, *Translingual Poetics: Writing Personhood under Settler Colonialism* (Iowa City: University of Iowa Press, 2018).

28. Lydia Liu, *Translingual Practice: Literature, National Culture, and Translated Modernity—China, 1900–1937* (Stanford: Stanford University Press, 1995); Shengqing Wu, *Modern Archaics: Continuity and Innovation in the Chinese Lyric Tradition, 1900–1937* (Cambridge, MA: Harvard University Press, 2014); Wang Pu, *The Translatability of Revolution: Guo Moruo and Twentieth-Century Chinese Culture* (Cambridge, MA: Harvard University Press, 2018); Hu Ying, *Tales of Translation: Composing the New Woman in China, 1898–1918* (Stanford: Stanford University Press, 2000).

29. Hill, *Lin Shu Inc.*, 48. Hill's reflections on legitimizing the wide range of practices that constituted translation in the Chinese context have been particularly helpful for my attempts to articulate the stakes of abstraction via my readings of translation theory (which tends to traffic largely in European and American contexts). See too Hill's concluding argument that "the historical problems built into translation into Chinese—those questions of language and cultural legitimacy—must be read thematically with and against the literary experimentation found in the works of Lin Shu, his collaborators, and the many other Chinese-speaking writers and intellectuals who devoted large parts of their professional lives to translation" (238). For my own work on a few instances of such literary experimentation, I have been especially indebted to Hill's careful historical reconstructions and parsing of translation's wide-ranging conceptual and political labors.

30. In earlier periods of Chinese literary production, the notion of authorship was flexible and translation was collaborative by default, akin to the work of editing. "Original" texts were taken to be open-ended invitations to ongoing and cumulative commentary and active interpretation. This ethos of literary production as a distributive writing and reading is sometimes claimed to have fallen away with the growing interest in notions of a gathered self in lyric subjectivity (via European Romanticism) during the New Culture Movement. See the careful reconstruction of "tandem translation" and how translation functioned as an institution and infrastructure for late Qing Chinese modernity in Hill, *Lin Shu Inc.*, 25–49; as well as the powerful account of feminist subjectivity and its discontents in Hu, *Tales*.

31. The modern Chinese writer Eileen Chang (the subject of chap. 2) has a more pessimistic view of this moment in the history of Chinese translation, casting it as superficial appropriation rather than deep and transformational change: to be "basically Chinese with western technology . . . didn't work. The tremendous inertia that comes with the weight of history and the size of the population in a country that's almost a continent in itself—a complacency and sense of superiority so great [that] make[s] it impossible to absorb anything but the most superficial." In this analysis delivered to US academic audiences in the sixties, Chang casts doubt on the very changeability of China at all—and by that token its ability to be foreignized in any meaningful way. Eileen Chang, "Chinese Translation: A Vehicle of Cultural Influence," ed. Christopher Lee, *PMLA* 130, no. 2 (March 2015): 492.

32. For the locus classicus of Chinese cosmopolitanism, see Joseph R. Levenson, *Revolution and Cosmopolitanism: The Western Stage and the Chinese Stages* (Berkeley: University of California Press, 1971); for an account of Shanghai as a cosmopolitan city par excellence in a slightly later period, see Leo Ou-fan Lee, *Shanghai Modern: The Flowering of a New Urban Culture in China, 1930–1945* (Cambridge, MA: Harvard University Press,

1999); for the use of English as an index of cosmopolitical ambition, see Shuang Shen, *Cosmopolitan Publics: Anglophone Print Culture in Semi-Colonial Shanghai* (Piscataway, NJ: Rutgers University Press, 2009). A useful resource is the recent volume, Minghui Hu and Johan Elverskog, eds., *Cosmopolitanism in China, 1600–1950* (Amherst, NY: Cambria Press, 2016). A longer genealogy of cosmopolitanism would include Nikolai Volland's study of socialist internationalism and Aihwa Ong's examination of diasporic cultural flexibility in the era of globalization.

33. Bruce Robbins, "Introduction Part I: Actually Existing Cosmopolitanism," in *Cosmopolitics: Thinking and Feeling Beyond the Nation*, ed. Pheng Cheah and Bruce Robbins (Minneapolis: University of Minnesota Press, 1998), 2–3.

34. *Domestication*: to assimilate a translated or source text into the prevailing norms of the translating or target culture and language. This is at times understood in dichotomous opposition to *foreignization*, the strategy of allowing the translated or source text to exert pressure on the norms of the translating culture. Each paradigm is predicated on a conceptual integrity on the part of both the source and translating languages. Domestication and foreignization may also be understood as existing on a spectrum or as flexible categories available for description rather than prescription, which conceptual loosening provides a greater latitude for thinking about the politics and possibilities of translation. For examples of this perspective, see the discussions of foreignization—responding to Lawrence Venuti's championing of them—in Tymoczko, *Translation, Resistance, Activism*.

35. A version of this point arises in Shuang Shen's study of Anglophone writing and print culture, which served as an index of the cosmopolitical aspirations driving Chinese modernity. Indeed, Shen opens the book with the provocative question of whether English can be regarded as a Chinese language, arguing that it played a crucial role in the formation of Chineseness thanks to thinkers like Hu Shi and Lin Yutang whose studies abroad allowed Western ideas to be circulated back to China. *Cosmopolitan Publics*, 95–134.

36. Hu Shi is also a subject of chapter 1 and an important interlocutor for Eileen Chang in chapter 2. He retained a lifelong association with the United States: when his star in China began to wane, Hu rose to a short stint as China's ambassador to the United States during a particularly tumultuous period of World War II (1938–42). Shortly after the rise of the Communist Party forced him into exile in Taiwan, his long-held views on Chinese democracy made him a sought-after speaker and writer in US academic and diplomatic spaces.

37. For helpful discussions, see Bachner, *Beyond Sinology*; Thomas Mullaney, *The Chinese Typewriter: A History* (Boston: MIT Press, 2018); Yurou Zhong, *Chinese Grammatology: Script Revolution and Literary Modernity, 1916–1958* (New York: Columbia University Press, 2019). These studies collectively demonstrate that the pragmatist push for linguistic reform (undertaken in response to the changing global order and intensified commerce with the Western world) precipitated fundamental inquiries into the nature of language and translation itself; for further discussion, see chap. 1.

38. As modified from the typology of intralingual translation (paraphrase), interlingual translation, and intersemiotic translation developed in Jakobson, "Linguistic Aspects."

39. Qian Zhaoming, *Orientalism and Modernism: The Legacy of China in Pound and Williams* (Durham, NC: Duke University Press, 1995); Ming Xie, *Ezra Pound and the Appropriation of Chinese Poetry: Cathay, Translation, and Imagism* (New York: Routledge, 1999); Robert Kern, *Orientalism, Modernism, and the American Poem* (New York:

Cambridge University Press, 1996); Yao, *Translation and the Languages of Modernism*; Eric Hayot, *Chinese Dreams: Pound, Brecht, Tel Quel* (Ann Arbor: University of Michigan Press, 2004); Eric Hayot, Haun Saussy, and Steven Yao, eds., *Sinographies: Writing China* (Minneapolis: University of Minnesota Press, 2007); Josephine Park, *Apparitions of Asia: Modernist Form and Asian American Poetics* (New York: Oxford University Press, 2008); Christopher Bush, *Ideographic Modernism: China, Writing, Media* (New York: Oxford University Press, 2010); Timothy Billings, "Editor's Introduction: Cracking the Crib," in Ezra Pound, *Cathay: A Critical Edition*, ed. Timothy Billings (New York: Fordham University Press, 2019), 15–32.

40. Hugh Kenner, *The Pound Era* (Berkeley: University of California Press, 1973), 195.

41. Eric Hayot, *Chinese Dreams*, 20; see also Huang, *Transpacific Displacement*; Park, *Apparitions*; Jonathan Stalling, *Poetics of Emptiness: Transformations of Asian Thought in American Poetry* (New York: Fordham University Press, 2010).

42. See especially Timothy Yu, *Race and the Avant-Garde: Experimental and Asian American Poetry since 1965* (Stanford: Stanford University Press, 2009); Myung Mi Kim's reflections on translation across her poetry; and more recently, the pamphlet by Don Mee Choi, *Translation Is a Mode = Translation Is an Anti-Neocolonial Mode* (Brooklyn: Ugly Duckling Press, 2020).

43. In readings of T. S. Eliot's well-known pronouncement that Pound was "the inventor of Chinese poetry for our time," commentators have typically stressed the historically contingent nature of this well-trodden claim: Pound's achievement was *only* for "our time" because after all, as Eliot himself goes on to close the very same paragraph still about Pound, "every generation must translate for itself." T.S. Eliot, Introduction to Ezra Pound, *Selected Poems*, ed. T. S. Eliot (London: Faber & Gwyer, 1928), 14–15.

44. Shu-mei Shih, *The Lure of the Modern: Writing Modernism in Semicolonial China, 1917–1937* (Berkeley: University of California Press, 2001), 50–51.

45. Shaden Tageldin, *Disarming Words: Empire and the Seductions of Translation in Egypt* (Berkeley: University of California Press, 2011), uncovers a similar anxiety in the context of French- and British-colonized Egypt, wherein strains of colonized Arabic subjectivity take up a coercive invitation to translate themselves, via an imaginary identifying equivalence, into the colonizing European (pseudo-universal) powers. The dynamic structures a oppositional desire on the part of the colonized subject for whom "affect complicates resistance" (4). That complication is then conscripted in the ideological service of empire in ways that we must learn to detect; as Tageldin argues, in reading translation as an instrument of colonial power without attending to the affective striations that mediate the in-between of colonized response, we then unwittingly "mystify the *exchange*-value of literature in colonial contexts as *use*-value" (7) (original emphasis). Yet for Tageldin this will always only be an entrapment, a naive counter-instrumentalism: "a politics that lures the colonized to seek power *through* empire rather than against it, to translate their cultures into an empowered "equivalence" with those of their dominators and thereby repress the inequalities between those dominators and themselves" (10), that is, choosing power without choosing equality and liberation. For the semicolonial context of China, that colonial hierarchization of power has developed in an unexpected way, complicated by (partially Western narratives of) China's "ancient" civilizational power, the turn to communism, and the postsocialist "rise" in the capitalist world order across the twentieth century. What began as a proleptic desire of equivalence was realized through

the accumulation of capital and has been firmly consolidated as neocolonial power (as I write this in 2021). In short, the seductive lure is less to seek power via Western empire but via its fraternal twin, global capital—and as those fantasies of equivalence begin to obtain, I would argue that such a desire should also be assumed to take a mutated structure and development, hence my focus on abstraction. These and related questions motivate my close intellectual debts to Tageldin and Lydia Liu, as well as my extended look at the unequal structures of value in equivalence.

46. For a much less reductive development of this idea and a provocative critique of Japanese exceptionalism, see Masao Miyoshi, *Off Center: Power and Culture Relations between Japan and the United States* (Cambridge, MA: Harvard University Press, 1998).

47. Rey Chow, *The Protestant Ethnic and the Spirit of Capitalism* (New York: Columbia University Press, 2002), 34.

48. Aihwa Ong, *Flexible Citizenship: The Cultural Logics of Transnationality* (Durham, NC: Duke University Press, 1999); Aihwa Ong, *Neoliberalism as Exception: Mutations in Citizenship and Sovereignty* (Durham, NC: Duke University Press, 2006); Pheng Cheah, *Inhuman Conditions: On Cosmopolitanism and Human Rights* (Cambridge, MA: Harvard University Press, 2007).

49. Eric Hayot, *The Hypothetical Mandarin: Sympathy, Modernity, and Chinese Pain* (New York: Oxford University Press, 2009), 35; emphasis in the original.

50. Dipesh Chakrabarty, *Provincializing Europe: Postcolonial Thought and Historical Difference* (Princeton, NJ: Princeton University Press, 2000), 8.

51. Rey Chow, "Introduction: On Chineseness as a Theoretical Problem," in *Modern Chinese Literary and Cultural Studies in the Age of Theory*, ed. Rey Chow (Durham, NC: Duke University Press, 2000), 5. Relatedly, Lily Wong refigures the chauvinism of Chineseness in the gendered and sexed trope of the Chinese sex worker, who exemplifies a political structure of feeling reaching across transpacific migration: see *Transpacific Attachments: Sex Work, Media Networks, and Affective Histories of Chineseness* (New York: Columbia University Press, 2018).

52. Shu-mei Shih, "The Concept of the Sinophone," *PMLA* 123, no. 3 (May 2011): 717. Shih makes a related argument in the earlier "Against Diaspora: The Sinophone as Places of Cultural Production," in *Global Chinese Literature: Critical Essays*, ed. Jing Tsu and David Der-wei Wang (Leiden: Brill, 2010), 29–48.

53. Lydia Liu, "The Question of Meaning-Value in the Political Economy of the Sign," in *Tokens of Exchange: The Problem of Translation in Global Circulations*, ed. Lydia Liu (Durham, NC: Duke University Press, 2000), 19.

54. Harry Harootunian, *History's Disquiet: Modernity, Cultural Practice, and the Question of Everyday Life* (New York: Columbia University Press, 2002), 25. Harootunian iterates the argument in earlier and later essays as well; this is the locus classicus.

55. Kuan-Hsing Chen, *Asia as Method: Toward Deimperialization* (Durham, NC: Duke University Press, 2010), 212.

56. Wang Hui, "The Politics of Imagining Asia: A Genealogical Analysis," trans. Matthew Hale, *Inter-Asia Cultural Studies* 8, no. 1 (2007): 27.

57. Colleen Lye, *America's Asia: Racial Form and American Literature, 1893–1945* (Princeton, NJ: Princeton University Press, 2005), 9.

58. R. John Williams draws a sharp line from modernist translation practices to the Chinese Exclusion Act in his contrapuntal readings of Pound's Chinese translations and

the Angel Island poems written by anonymous immigrant detainees off the coast of San Francisco; see his "Decolonizing *Cathay*: Teaching the Scandals of Translation through Angel Island Poetry," *Transformations* 7, no. 2 (2007): 15–30. Park's *Apparitions* draws the locus classicus connection between modernist aesthetics and Asian American formal experimentation. The origins and afterlives of Asian disposability are explored in, among others: Chow, *The Protestant Ethnic*; Lye, *America's Asia*; Hayot, *Hypothetical Mandarin*; Iyko Day, *Alien Capital: Asian Racialization and the Logic of Settler Colonial Capitalism* (Durham, NC: Duke University Press, 2016); Lim, *Bilingual Brokers*.

59. Colleen Lye, "Racial Form," *Representations* 104, no. 1 (Fall 2008): 99.

60. Yao, *Foreign Accents*, 16.

61. "It is therefore essential to be rigorous and draw the conclusion that *the transition from Volume One to Volume Three of Capital has nothing to do with the transition from the abstract-in-thought to the real-concrete, with the transition from the abstractions of thought necessary in order to know it to the empitical concrete.* . . . We simply pass within the abstraction of knowledge from the concept of the structure and of its most general effects, to the concepts of the structure's particular effects—never for an instant do we set foot beyond the absolutely impassable frontier which separates the 'development' or specification of the concept from the development and particularity of things—and for a very good reason: *this frontier is impassable in principle because it cannot be a frontier, because there is no common homogeneous space (spirit or real) between the abstract of the concept of a thing and the empirical concrete of this thing which could justify the use of the concept of a frontier.*" Louis Althusser, *Reading* Capital, trans. Ben Brewster (London: New Left Books, 1977), 190; emphases Althusser's.

62. Day, *Alien Capital*, 10.

63. Lisa Lowe, *The Intimacies of Four Continents* (Durham, NC: Duke University Press, 2015), 174.

64. As Christine Mok and Aimee Bahng write, "Imagining an Asian futurist movement can be particularly tricky, as Asians have not so much inhabited or been excluded from the future, but served as the backdrop to it and, more recently, have become not only futurity's most invested stakeholders but also its most beholden underclass." The authors are alluding to the financialization of "futures" in the context of the supposedly hyper-developed Asian economy; the trope of techno-Orientalism following the economic rise of Japan in the 1980s (simply the obverse gesture of historical Orientalism which, instead of casting the East in a primitive light, insistently places it in the future to intensify economic anxieties on the part of the United States); and last, the ways in which futurity and economic development have been deeply involved in the work of decolonization across the region. Moving from the Asian to a transpacific paradigm, they invite readers to consider "how the transpacific and futurity dwell on each other." "Transpacific Overtures: An Introduction," *Journal of Asian American Studies* 20, no. 1 (February 2017): 1–9.

65. Hoskins and Nguyen, "Introduction—Transpacific Studies," 12.

66. Homi Bhabha's influential work on cultural translation avows his use of the term as a catachresis, translation improper: see *The Location of Culture* (New York: Routledge, 2004), 347.

67. The general point here complements Maria Tymoczko's argument by way of Gideon Toury, which calls for a radically inclusionary and activist sense of translation in which the very character of what we take to be "translation" is a posteriori and malleable—always to

be identified and determined by the target culture, language, and readers and demanding nonprescriptive, antinormative heuristics for defining translation to begin with. In this sense, it invites a methodologically reflexive and thoroughly theorized approach to descriptive translation studies (not to be understood in the simple empirical sense). What I am calling abstraction is then one way of deepening this claim. See *Enlarging Translation, Empowering Translators*.

68. For a careful and theoretically sophisticated account of the central role of textual editing in destabilizing (and reconstructing) the notion of the original for translation studies, see Karen Emmerich, *Literary Translation and the Making of Originals* (New York: Bloomsbury, 2017). As my invented list of examples may suggest, the political and philosophical stakes of reassessing the ontology of the original or source are higher than the book itself may suggest; I am indebted to Emmerich's work for enabling me to think through this point.

69. Ezra Pound, "I gather the limbs of Osiris," in Ezra Pound, *Selected Prose, 1909–1965*, ed. William Cookson (New York: New Directions, 1975), 21.

70. Walkowitz, *Born Translated*, 90.

71. Ernest Fenollosa and Ezra Pound, *The Chinese Written Character as a Medium for Poetry*, ed. Haun Saussy, Jonathan Stalling, and Lucas Klein (New York: Fordham University Press, 2008), 85–86.

72. See the discussion of concrete poetry and its connection to the visual misreadings of Chinese writing in Bachner, *Beyond Sinology*, 57–92; for an account of how modernist imagism paved the way and was translated into concrete poetry, see Infante, *After Translation*, 117–45. A recent volume on the political critiques effected by concretism in Brazil has also inflected my account here; see Antonio Sergio Bessa, ed., *Form and Feeling: The Making of Concretism in Brazil* (New York: Fordham University Press, 2021).

73. As influentially coined in Anne Anlin Cheng, "Memory and Anti-Documentary Desire in Theresa Hak Kyung Cha's *Dictée*," *MELUS* 23, no. 4 (Winter 1998): 119–33.

74. Yang Lian, "Moved Once Again by an Ancient Betrayal—by way of a Preface to *Concentric Circles*," in *Concentric Circles*, trans. Brian Holton and Agnes Chan (London: Bloodaxe, 2005), 9; trans. modified.

1. Transpacific Abstraction

1. What is, in Rey Chow's formulation, "the fantasy of an essentialized ethnicity, a standardized language, and a coercive equivalence between literary writing and Chineseness per se." "Introduction: On Chineseness as a Theoretical Problem," *boundary 2* 25, no. 3 (Autumn 1988): 22.

2. Fredric Jameson, *A Singular Modernity: Essay on the Ontology of the Present* (London: Verso, 2013), 141.

3. Clement Greenberg developed his ideas on abstract expressionism over a series of early essays. Arguably the first to historicize and theorize its defining features was "Towards a Newer Laocoön" (1940), followed by "Abstract Art" (1944) and "The Crisis of the Easel Picture" (1948). "Towards a Newer Laocoön" is to be found in volume 1 and the others in volume 2 of Clement Greenberg, *The Collected Essays and Criticism* (Chicago: University of Chicago Press, 1988). For a helpful overview and bracing critique of the early wartime Greenberg essays, see T. J. Clark, "Clement Greenberg's Theory of Art," *Critical Inquiry* 9 (September 1982): 139–56. For insights into the place of abstract art in literary

modernism, see also Charles Altieri, *Painterly Abstraction in Modernist American Poetry: The Contemporaneity of Modernism* (University Park: Pennsylvania State University Press, 1995); and a critical take on whiteness in abstraction by Charles Bernstein, "Disfiguring Abstraction," *Critical Inquiry* 39, no. 3 (Spring 2013): 486–89.

4. Fred Moten, *In the Break: The Aesthetics of the Black Radical Tradition* (Minneapolis: University of Minnesota Press, 2003); Stephen Best, *None Like Us: Blackness, Belonging, Aesthetic Life* (Durham, NC: Duke University Press, 2018); Darby English, *1971: A Year in the Life of Color* (Chicago: University of Chicago Press, 2016). In turning to abstraction, I have been indebted to work in Black studies—while vigilantly attending to the fact that the operations of abstraction fall differentially on the transpacific Asian nexus, compelling a related *and* distinct set of questions helpfully parsed by Iyko Day's comparative treatment (discussed in the introduction). Two key differences are indeed the distinctively *linguistic* apparatus of the ideograph as well as the weaponized sense of equivalence that comes under scrutiny across this book. Adopting a longer historical view, a very recent "performative lecture" by the Portland-based artist manuel arturo abreu highlights the non-European history of abstraction, understanding it "not as sublimation away from the concrete/market/functionality, but as fundamental to mundane daily life, expression, and function." "An Alternative History of Abstraction" (digital Zoom, Atlanta Contemporary, Atlanta, GA, May 16, 2020), https://atlantacontemporary.org/events/discrit-5-16 (accessed June 20, 2020). See also the introduction's discussion of experimentalism: Park, Yu, Huang, Yao, Jeon, et. al.

5. Marjorie Perloff, *Unoriginal Genius: Poetry by Other Means in the New Century* (Chicago: University of Chicago Press, 2010); Rebecca Walkowitz, *Born Translated: The Contemporary Novel in an Age of World Literature* (New York: Columbia University Press, 2015); Jacob Edmond, *Make it the Same: Poetry in the Age of Global Media* (New York: Columbia University Press, 2019).

6. Walkowitz, *Born Translated*, 4.

7. Edmond, *Make It the Same*, 10.

8. Ibid., 11.

9. Fredric Jameson, "Modernism and Imperialism," in *Nationalism, Colonialism, and Literature* (Minneapolis: University of Minnesota Press, 1986), 44.

10. Andrea Bachner, *Beyond Sinology: Chinese Writing and the Scripts of Culture* (New York: Columbia University Press, 2014), 68.

11. In Shu-mei Shih's argument, many Chinese modernists remained willfully blinded to the ideological assumptions they inherited wholesale from the West, so that what cultural power they appropriated was limited in its emancipatory promise and instead should be understood as "destabiliz[ing] facile determinations of agency and alert[ing] us to tensions and contradictions in its constitution" (16). Furthermore, by following Western thought in temporalizing the difference between East and West as an abstract linear development, Chinese intellectuals fell prey to the titular lure of the modern: "If time was the only measure of difference between China and the West, China could become an equal partner in a world dominated by the West by simply catching up as fast as it could" (50). *The Lure of the Modern: Writing Modernism in Semicolonial China, 1917–1937* (Berkeley: University of California Press, 2001). For a similarly bracing study that accordingly looks at the contradictions at work in this dynamic (and which is directly centered on translation), see chap. 2, on the late Qing translator Yan Fu, of Theodore Huters, *Bringing the World Home:*

Appropriating the West in Late Qing and Early Republican China (Honolulu: University of Hawai'i Press, 2005), 43–72.

12. A helpful account of Fenollosa's interest in Emerson and pragmatism may be found in Robert Kern, *Orientalism, Modernism, and the American Poem* (New York: Cambridge University Press, 1996), 115–39.

13. For an account of Fenollosa's aural poetics blending his Buddhist reading with classical Chinese prosody, see chap. 2 of Jonathan Stalling, *Poetics of Emptiness: Transformations of Asian Thought in American Poetry* (New York: Fordham University Press, 2010), 59–95. Fenollosa's understudied interest in sound is especially important as it was not only excised by Pound in his editing, but further provides insight into Fenollosa's particular transformations of those ideas. Relatedly, see also Haun Saussy's discussion of Tendai Buddhism's ascetic-aesthetic influence on Fenollosa in "Fenollosa Compounded: A Discrimination," in Ernest Fenollosa and Ezra Pound, *The Chinese Written Character as a Medium for Poetry*, ed. Haun Saussy, Jonathan Stalling, and Lucas Klein (New York: Fordham University Press, 2008), 20–23.

14. Hu's writing on Buddhism is complex insofar as it charts a triangulating anxiety of semicolonial influence between two major cultural (and translational) coordinates for China. His xenophobic disdain for Buddhism stemmed from his thinking that Buddhism posed such obstacles to the flourishing of China's indigenous thinking that it was as though "India conquered and dominated China culturally for twenty centuries without ever having to send a single soldier across her border." His quasi-scholastic— and ideologically charged—remarks were published as part of the Harvard conference proceedings cited here. Hu Shi, "The Indianization of China: A Case Study in Cultural Borrowing," in *Independence, Convergence, and Borrowing in Institutions, Thought, and Art* (Cambridge, MA: Harvard University Press, 1937), 219–47. Many years later, Hu's understanding of Buddhism took a turn when he became interested in Chan (Zen) Buddhism via a Japanese interlocutor. Chan Buddhism, in Hu's thinking, was the result of Chinese thought transforming the tenets of Buddhism: to borrow his earlier formulation, one might even call it the Sinicization of Buddhism. In Chan Buddhism, Hu saw the principles of teaching oneself and intellectual transformation so appealing to his political sensibilities and desired historical narrative for the development of China. His thoughts are most pronounced in a disagreement with Daisetsu Teitaro Suzuki, a leading Japanese scholar of Chan (Zen) Buddhism, in which Hu defends its philosophical integrity and interest by way of a long and also quasi-scholastic narrative of its development over the course of Chinese intellectual history. "Ch'an (Zen) Buddhism in China Its History and Method," *Philosophy East and West* 3, no. 1 (1953): 3–24.

15. For discussions of the fraught trans/cultural constitutions of nature in this time period, see Kern, *Orientalism, Modernism, and the American Poem*; Zhaoming Qian, *Orientalism and Modernism: The Legacy of China in Pound and Williams* (Durham, NC: Duke University Press, 1995); Zong-qi Cai, "Poundian and Chinese Aesthetics of Dynamic Force: A Re-Discovery of Fenollosa and Pound's Theory of the Chinese Written Character," *Comparative Literature Studies* 30, no. 2 (1993): 170–87; Robin G. Schulze, *The Degenerate Muse: American Nature, Modernist Poetry, and the Problem of Cultural Hygiene* (New York: Oxford University Press, 2013).

16. *Hu Shi wencun* [Anthology of Hu Shi's Writing], (Beijing: Huaxia chubanshe, 2000), 246–47. Hu's interest in empiricism is likely a debt to the American philosopher

John Dewey, with whom he studied at Columbia University. Largely thanks to Hu's efforts, Dewey's ideas on liberalism and skeptical empiricism were popular in the process of modernizing China.

17. Christopher Bush, *Ideographic Modernism: China, Writing, Media* (New York: Oxford University Press, 2010), xxvii.

18. Bachner, *Beyond Sinology*, 26. Bachner generalizes this argument with an emphasis on the materiality of signification in the later *Mark of Theory: Inscriptive Figures, Poststructuralist Prehistories* (New York: Fordham University Press, 2017).

19. Christopher Bush, *Ideographic Modernism: China, Writing, Media* (New York: Oxford University Press, 2010), 3.

20. Writing on the translingual constitution of the Poundian ideogram, John Cayley notes that "these are not the ideograms of any one language; they are the 'transletters' of an irreducible verbal art." John Cayley with Yang Lian, "Hallucination and Coherence," *positions: east asia cultures critique* 10, no. 3 (Winter 2002): 780. Of course, suggesting that something is translingual and hybrid does not void it of political charge (and this does not seem to be Cayley's intent); my goal in this chapter might be usefully understood as an attempt to understand the politics of that "transletter" and its transfigured modalities of power.

21. Bachner, *Beyond Sinology*, 14.

22. Ibid., 60, 199.

23. Kitasono's avant-garde theoretical leanings owed much to Pound's notion of the ideogram, leading him also to incorporate foreign words and script in his own poetry. The Japanese language has *katakana*, a specialized phonetic script that is used primarily for the incorporation of foreign loanwords. Kitasono used *katakana* as well as alphabetic scripts of European languages like English and French.

24. Christopher Bush provides a helpful account of the Pound-Japan-China triangulation and especially the textual relays of reading, interpretation, and translation that produced Pound's earlier translingual adventures in *Cathay* (predating his encounter with Fenollosa's work): see "Introduction: 'From the Decipherings,'" in Ezra Pound, *Cathay: A Critical Edition*, ed. Timothy Billings (New York: Fordham University Press, 2019), 5–11.

25. Ezra Pound, *The Letters of Ezra Pound 1907–1941*, ed. D. D. Paige (New York: Haskell House Publishers, 1974), 449. *VOU* (rhymes with 'wow') was an avant-garde journal founded by Kitasono.

26. Pound's English translation of Canto LXXII was published for the first time late in 1993 in the *Paris Review*. The Italian Cantos were published in their present form only in 1993, which as New Directions notes was the thirteenth printing of the text. Ezra Pound, *The Cantos* (New York: New Directions, 1996).

27. Pound, *Letters*, 449. From our historical perspective, it is certainly known that many writers and artists in the Italian and Japanese milieus had in common a turn toward fascist totalitarianism—along with long-held interests in modernist aesthetics and cosmopolitan modernization at the time of Pound's writing. Yet given the relatively minute literalism of Pound's inquiries to Kitasono, this wider geopolitical connection does not seem to be on his mind. Instead, Pound does seem to be engaged in a quasi-ethnography here, whence perhaps Yunte Huang's unexpected strong claim that "Pound [with Fenollosa] was never merely an ideographer. . . . [H]e had always been an ethnographer." Yunte Huang,

Transpacific Displacement: Ethnography, Translation, and Intertextual Travel in Twentieth-Century American Literature (Berkeley: University of California Press, 2002), 70.

28. Pound, *Letters*, 449. The fragment is also published as paratext in the standard New Directions text of the *Cantos* under the title "Addendum for C" (presumably Canto C), dated ca. 1941, 820. Due to the disjointed nature of Pound's writing, it is difficult to ascertain what the effect of including this additional fragment might be and how it may have fit in the larger picture for Pound.

29. The favored line about the water-bug's mittens does make it into Canto XCI of the main text, its image a little changed and bearing traces of Pound's attempts to "ideograph it": "The water-bug's mittens / petal the rock beneath, / The natrix glides sapphire into the rock-pool." *Cantos*, 636.

30. Pound, *Letters*, 149.

31. For a careful account of Pound's misreadings of Marx in his later economic theory paired with a reading of the two Italian *Cantos*, see Peter Nicholls, *Ezra Pound, Politics, Economics and Writing: A Study of the Cantos* (London: Macmillan, 1984), 138–60. Nicholls's book is also a helpful overview of Pound's economic theory and intellectual coordinates more generally.

32. Alec Marsh, *Money and Modernity: Pound, Williams, and the Spirit of Jefferson* (Tuscaloosa: University of Alabama Press, 1998), 68–110; Meghnad Desai, *The Route of All Evil: The Political Economy of Ezra Pound* (London: Faber and Faber, 2006).

33. Nicholls, *Ezra Pound, Politics, Economics and Writing*, 154–60.

34. Indeed, the unlikely intersection of Pound's anti-Semitic reading of money and capital with his Sinophiliac interest in Confucius is an intriguing complement to Iyko Day's argument of how Asianness comes to be aligned with global capital and triangulated against Black and Indigenous lives as "the new Jew" (discussed in the introduction), such that his political aesthetics may well be legible as a form of romantic anticapitalism.

35. Paul Morrison, *The Poetics of Fascism: Ezra Pound, T. S. Eliot, Paul de Man* (Oxford: Oxford University Press, 1996), 18.

36. Jonathan Stalling has undertaken heroic attempts at such experimental translations: see his *Yingelishi: Sinophonic English Poetry and Poetics* (Denver, CO: Counterpath, 2011).

37. Jameson, "Modernism and Imperialism," 54.

38. By this point it should not come as a surprise that the Japanese expression for the reality of "language" is connected to the image of petals that emerge from the sky. Yet even in moments where translation—"ideographing"—is a manipulation of material and visible script, here we have still remained in a figural domain of language. This fact is of particular interest to philosophical scholars of Martin Heidegger: in his "Dialogue on Language" with an unnamed Japanese friend, the friend makes this very point in an extended discussion articulating the "Saying" of petals through its relation with the sky. This relation is the reality in and through which language emerges. Martin Heidegger, "Dialogue on Language," in *On the Way to Language*, trans. Peter D. Hertz (New York: HarperCollins, 1982), 47–53.

39. On the politics of *wen* and *wenxue*, as well as its use as a translating term for the English "education," see Theodore Huters, *Bringing the World Home: Appropriating the West in Late Qing and Early Republican China* (Honolulu: University of Hawai'i Press, 2005), 78–79. For an account of the attractions of *wen* for the Western imagination and an example of how to rethink its precepts in a comparative frame, see Haun Saussy, "The Prestige of

Writing: *Wen*, Letter, Picture, Image, Ideography," in *Great Walls of Discourse and Other Adventures in Cultural China* (Cambridge, MA: Harvard University Asia Center, 2001), 35–74; as well as the introduction to Bush, *Ideographic Modernism*, 3–29. For a discussion of how this has been mobilized toward an entrenched sense of cultural difference between East and West, see Zhang Longxi, "What Is Wen and Why Is It Made So Terribly Strange?" *College Literature* 23, no. 1 (1996): 15–35. *Wenhua* also has a rich life in Japanese translation as *bun-gaku*, a translated sense of "literature" that came into prominence during the Meiji era of increasing Westernization and syncretism, thickening its related pre-Meiji sense: Naoki Sakai (one among many critics working on Japanese literary history) offers a helpful account of the former in Sakai, *Translation as Subjectivity: On "Japan" and Cultural Nationalism* (Minneapolis: University of Minnesota Press, 1997), 21–24.

40. For the history and more recent (postsocialist) complications of this line of thinking, see Leo Ou-fan Lee, *The Romantic Generation of Modern Chinese Writers* (Cambridge, MA: Harvard University Press, 1973); Shih, *Lure of the Modern*; Wang Ban, *The Sublime Figure of History: Aesthetics and Politics in Twentieth-Century China* (Stanford: Stanford University Press, 1997); Ari Heinrich, *The Afterlife of Images: Translating the Pathological Body between China and the West* (Durham, NC: Duke University Press, 2008); Bonnie MacDougall, *Translation Zones in Modern China: Authoritarian Command versus Gift Exchange* (Amherst, NY: Cambria Press, 2011); Belinda Kong, *Tiananmen Fictions Outside the Square: The Chinese Literary Diaspora and the Politics of Global Culture* (Philadelphia: Temple University Press, 2012); Lucas Klein, *The Organization of Distance: Poetry, Translation, Chineseness* (Leiden: Brill, 2018).

41. I have relied on Yunte Huang's translation in his recent anthology, making silent changes only to highlight aspects of the poem important to my argument. Yunte Huang, ed., *The Big Red Book of Modern Chinese Literature: Writings from the Mainland in the Long Twentieth Century* (New York: Norton, 2016), 28.

42. *Hu Shi wencun* [Hu Shi Anthology] (Beijing: Huaxia chubanshe, 2000), 246–47.

43. See especially chapter 2's discussion of pronouns and translation.

44. *Hu Shi wencun*, 246 (my trans.). Hu provides the neologistic English translation in his original Chinese text.

45. Critics working on American Transcendentalism have identified some pathways of influence of Hegelian philosophy on the Transcendentalists, primarily filtered through Goethe. See Henry A. Pochmann, *New England Transcendentalism and St. Louis Hegelianism: Phases in the History of American Idealism* (Philadelphia: Carl Schurz Memorial Foundation, 1948); Gustav van Croumphout, *Emerson's Modernity and the Example of Goethe* (Columbia: University of Missouri Press, 1990).

46. In this regard, Christopher Bush notes, with tongue somewhat in cheek, that "the ideograph-stricken 'Oriental' prefigures the benighted victim of media" that Benjamin writes about in "The Work of Art in the Age of Mechanical Reproduction." Following this observation, Bush considers the ideograph as a problem of proto-technological media and mediation. See Bush, *Ideographic Modernism*, 22.

47. Stalling, *Poetics of Emptiness*, 55.

48. Kern, *Orientalism, Modernism, and the American Poem*, 38.

49. Here and throughout the chapter, I have preserved the editorial markers used in the critical edition of Fenollosa's original manuscript established by Saussy et al.: Pound's deletions are [in square brackets], and his additions are in **bold type**.

50. The text of the manuscript links the asterisk to Fenollosa's marginalia: "So a nerve, a wire, a roadway and a clearing house are only varying channels which communication forces for itself. This is more than analogy: it is identity of structure. Laws of structure are the same in the spiritual and the material world. Human character grows with the same stresses and knots as mountain pines." Moving from analogy to structure suggests also a move from an epistemological register to one of universal immanence, which parallels the later claim of moving from subjectivity to "objective lines of relation." The analogy and/ or structural identity between the knots of human character and the mountain pines echo also the imagery of Immanuel Kant's well-known observation on the regulative ideal, an important point of reference for Hu Shi and where the project is not at all dissimilar from Fenollosa's: "Nothing straight can be constructed from such warped wood as that which man is made of. Nature only requires of us that we should approximate to this idea." Immanuel Kant, "Idea for a Universal History with a Cosmopolitan Purpose," in *Political Writings*, trans. H. B. Nisbet (Cambridge: Cambridge University Press, 2002), 46–47.

51. Ernest Fenollosa and Ezra Pound, *The Chinese Written Character as a Medium for Poetry*, ed. Haun Saussy, Jonathan Stalling, and Lucas Klein (New York: Fordham University Press, 2008), 94–95. This critical edition makes widely available for the first time both the text of Fenollosa's own manuscript (with annotations by Pound) and Pound's prepared version, familiar to most readers over the years. Unless otherwise indicated, my references are to the text of Fenollosa's manuscript. My quotes throughout this chapter are consistent with the (at times idiosyncratic) grammar, spelling, punctuation, etc., given in the critical edition.

52. It is debatable if Hegel indeed condemned the faculty of imagination, although it seems fair to suggest that the imagination does not seem to occupy much of his thought. See Jennifer Ann Bates, *Hegel's Theory of Imagination* (Albany: State University of New York Press, 2004), for a reading that develops Hegel's underwritten thoughts on the imagination in a way that is more nuanced than Fenollosa's dismissal.

53. To my ear, it is difficult not to hear a slight agitation of Percy Bysshe Shelley's *A Defense of Poetry* here, for whom the poets' language "is vitally metaphorical; that is, it marks the before unapprehended relations of things and perpetuates their apprehension, until the words which represent them, become, through time, signs for portions or classes of thoughts instead of pictures of integral thoughts." It is unknown if Fenollosa read Shelley directly, but it is possible that he received a diluted understanding of Shelley via the American Transcendentalists, primarily Emerson.

54. The Cubist painter Georges Braque had spoken in 1950 of painting the relations between things as a specifically "poetic" endeavor. See John Golding, *Braque: The Late Works* (New Haven, CT: Yale University Press, 1997), 23.

55. Kern, *Orientalism, Modernism, and the American Poem*, 126.

56. See also Donald M. Murray, "Emerson's 'Language as Fossil Poetry': An Analogy from Chinese," *New England Quarterly* 29, no. 1 (1956): 204–15. For Emerson, language is fossilized not in medias res, as it might have been for Fenollosa, but in such a way that words are static representations of natural "facts."

57. *Hu Shi liuxue riji* [Diaries from Studying Abroad], (Tai bei shi: Taiwan shangwu, 1977), 1071–73.

58. Tangentially, one may well detect the aesthetic influence of Browning's dramatic monologues in Hu Shi's *Experimental Verses* (*Changshi ji*), his collection of vernacular

poetry, although Hu does not make the connection himself. Later in this chapter I examine an instance of such optimism and self-determination.

59. *Hu Shi liuxue riji*, 1071.

60. Hu Shi, "Some Modest Proposals for the Reform of Literature," in *Modern Chinese Literary Thought: Writings on Literature 1893–1945*, trans. and ed. Kirk A. Denton (Stanford: Stanford University Press, 1996), 139. I generally follow the Denton translation; my only modifications have been to interpolate lexical detail from the Chinese source to help my argument. For a comparison of Hu's proposals with Pound's (with a greater conceptual emphasis on Pound's work), see John J. Nolde, "The Literary Revolutions of Hu Shih and Ezra Pound," *Paideuma* 9, no. 2 (Fall 1980): 235–48.

61. See Yurou Zhang, *Chinese Grammatology: Script Revolution and Literary Modernity, 1916–1958*, for a useful account of the complex mutual constitutions of speech and literary writing in this moment of Chinese history.

62. Hu, "Modest Proposals," 130.

63. Ibid., 132.

64. Ibid., 133.

65. Hu takes this from the *I Ching* or *Book of Changes*: "the gentleman must have substance in his words to have stability in his actions," as cited by Denton, in Hu, "Modest Proposals," 124.

66. Also as cited by Denton from the *Zuozhuan*: *yanzhi wuwen, xingzhi buyuan*. Hu, "Modest Proposals," 124.

67. Hu, "Modest Proposals."

68. Ibid., 125.

69. Ibid., 124.

70. Ibid., 125.

71. Fenollosa and Pound, *Chinese Written Character*, 89.

72. Ibid., 89–90; original emphasis.

73. Ibid., 75.

74. Ibid., 75–76.

75. Ibid., 75.

76. Ibid., 77.

77. With a similar prolepsis and in the same passage, Fenollosa also calls on "American Education" (76) to do its part in developing Chinese studies and singles out the University of California "appropriately on the Pacific Coast" (76) as well as a professor of comparative literature at Columbia, a "Professor Woodberry" (77), for his work and attentiveness to contemporary historical and geopolitical realities. Ibid., 76–77. The reference is to George Edward Woodberry (1855–1930), who also complemented his work as a literary critic by writing poetry. Woodberry specialized in American literature (Edgar Allan Poe and the American Transcendentalists) and notably edited *The Complete Poetical Works of Percy Bysshe Shelley* (1892).

78. The overall drift of Fenollosa's argument enters into elliptical conversation with the story of Balzac's mandarin that provides the anecdotal germ of Eric Hayot's *The Hypothetical Mandarin*: entering the parlance as *tuer le mandarin* ("to kill the mandarin," an evil that can be done without detection), Balzac's hypothetical question, attributed in his text to Rousseau, forces the question of responsibility and sympathy with others who may be faraway or invisible, mediated by a space of hypothesis and imagination.

The Hypothetical Mandarin: Sympathy, Modernity, and Chinese Pain (New York: Oxford University Press, 2009). On Balzac's mandarin, see Samuel Weber's discussion of Freud's iteration, *tuer son mandarin*, 'to kill his mandarin': for Weber, the mandarin's narrative is "transformed through its circulation," encompassing the globe before ending up as a self-estrangement closest to home, a murderous affront to the sovereignty of the subject. "The proverbial expression *Tuer son Mandarin* is not just directed at a distant other; it is also directed at the self.... [I]t reveals that the 'secret readiness' of the self to kill the other also turns out to be a threat to its own property. *Tuer son Mandarin* can be read as designating not just the fantasy of enriching oneself by doing away with the other, but also that of doing away with one's own property and provenance. To kill *one's* Mandarin would then be to do away with everything required for the one to be a proper and property-owning subject." Samuel Weber, "Wartime," in *Violence, Identity, and Self-Determination*, ed. Hent de Vries and Samuel Weber (Stanford: Stanford University Press, 1997), 104–5; original emphasis.

79. Fenollosa and Pound, *Chinese Written Character*, 84–85.
80. Ibid., 84.
81. Ibid., 85–86.
82. Nicolai Volland, "All the Literature That's Fit to Print: A Print Culture Perspective on Modern Chinese Literature," in *A Companion to Modern Chinese Literature*, ed. Yingjin Zhang (West Sussex: Wiley Blackwell, 2015), 368–70; see also Volland's note on 376. Volland reads the fact of multilingual publication as an important transnational nexus in Hu's ambitious literary reform, manifest in the print culture of *New Youth*. To this, I add that reading Hu's poem qua *translation* also turns up crucial differences indicative of Hu's praxis and poetics of translation.
83. *Hu Shi wencun*, 258. In a note accompanying the poem, Hu writes that his source is the English translation of the Persian poet Omar Khayyam's *Rubaiyat* (which Hu glosses for his readers as *jueju*) as presented by the English translator "Fitzgerald." (Hu did not know Persian and does not seem to have otherwise demonstrated any interest in the systematic study of Persian thought and literature. I have not been able to find out how and where Hu first encountered this text, though given the date and provenance it is likely when he encountered English literature for the first time as a student in the United States, especially given his interest in Browning, as discussed above. His student diaries reveal him to be an intellectual magpie.) Edward Fitzgerald's 1859 translation of the *Rubaiyat* was itself a controversial instance of "free" poetic translation that had an important afterlife for the Victorian Orientalist philological tradition, being responsible for (among other things) making Khayyam a cult figure of the Pre-Raphaelites. Questions remain about the stability and authenticity of the corpus from which Fitzgerald was working, which primarily consisted of transcripts of two manuscripts given to him by a former teacher. These may well have been forged, possibly due to a tradition of attributing poetry to Khayyam even when not written by him, suggesting that he was more of a figurehead. As well, scholars are divided on the philosophy of skepticism that Fitzgerald sought to attribute to Khayyam and worked to highlight in his translation. (Khayyam was largely known as a medieval scientist working on mathematics and astronomy.) On one level, then, Hu's translation represents another step in a similarly free direction. More subtly, however, it also represents a certain blindness (or blitheness) to the constitutive function of Orientalism for his source. That *his* translation was published with a partial opacity and

unknowability for his readership (as I discuss below) is perhaps a subtle cultural translation of the historical and epistemic conditions that attended the Fitzgerald translation (more subtle than Hu himself likely intended). My argument should not be taken as an attempt to circumvent the Orientalism of either Hu's source text or his own unthinking inheritance of it (or indeed an attempt to position Hu as an anticolonial thinker, which would be disingenuous and clumsy); it is rather an attempt to think through the politics of this unusual conjunction in order to consider what Hu achieves in relation to—and in excess of—the text he translates and how that may reflect on the conditions of knowing and unknowing in which his translational literary reform functions.

84. For a discussion of the English advertisements published with this poem, see Volland, "All the Literature That's Fit to Print," 367.

85. Volland, "All the Literature That's Fit to Print," 369.

86. The *shijie* or *world* that Hu installs is a fraught term: while serving as a retranslation of the sense of worldhood inherited from European cosmopolitanism (which, from context, is most likely what Hu intended), it also calls to the historical use of *shijie* as a standard translating term from Buddhist philosophy: what is *worldly* or *lokadhatu* in Sanskrit is the imbrication of space and time. It is not clear if Hu knew of this function, though he was derisive of Buddhist philosophy and its importation into China across his career; nevertheless, his choice is suggestive in itself.

87. Steven G. Yao, *Translation and the Languages of Modernism: Gender, Politics, Language* (New York: Palgrave Macmillan, 2002), 185.

2. Sound Translation

1. Chang, "Yi Hushi zhi" [Remembering Hu Shi], in *Zhangkan* [Chang Sees] (Taibei shi: Huangguan chubanshe, 1997), 16–27. *Dream of the Red Chamber* is also the subject of Chang's only work of literary criticism, a contribution to the vast critical energy surrounding *Dream* known as *Hongxue* or *Redology*. The work on *Dream* was also undertaken during her time in the United States.

2. Language reform in China generally took place in three waves: (i) around and after the May Fourth Movement; (ii) a second Mao-era wave in the 1950s after the Communist Party rose to power and then after the long hiatus of the Cultural Revolution and the period led by the Gang of Four; (iii) a third wave in the 1970s, the period in which Chang makes her "small observations" on modern Chinese (1978) as treated later in this chapter. For a classic examination of May Fourth reform, see John deFrancis, *Nationalism and Language Reform in China* (Princeton, NJ: Princeton University Press, 1950). For a deeply researched account of the first two stages, see Yurou Zhong, *Chinese Grammatology: Script Revolution and Literary Modernity, 1916–1958* (New York: Columbia University Press, 2019). For a useful historical overview of the later years, I have relied on Peter J. Seybolt and Gregory Kuei-ke Chiang, eds., *Language Reform in China: Documents and Commentary* (New York: M.E. Sharpe, 1978); as well as commentary in Bachner, *Beyond Sinology*; and Tsu, *Sound and Script*.

3. Han Bangqing, *Haishanghua kai* [Shanghai Flowers—Opening] (Taibei shi: Huangguan chubanshe, 1981), 38. Chang's Mandarin translation of Han's *Flowers* was published in two volumes titled "Opening" and "Falling," respectively.

4. "sing-song girl, n." OED Online, October 2019, https://www-oed-com.libproxy.uoregon.edu/view/Entry/180169?rskey=rWxqkW&result=1&isAdvanced=false#eid (accessed October 4,

2019). The *Oxford English Dictionary* credits the first use of "sing-song girl" as a compound term to a novel titled *The Ginger Griffin* (1934) by the then-popular middlebrow British novelist Ann Bridge (pen name, Mary Ann Dolling Sanders). Sanders had lived in Beijing with her diplomat husband in 1925–27 and began writing upon her return to Britain, eventually authoring fourteen novels (mainly travelogues and mysteries). The other sources cited in the *OED* are ethnographic and uniformly colonial, ending with a journalistic account from 1978. It is, however, impossible to verify *or* falsify Chang's quasi-philological account, and it is not my intention to do so; the unverifiability of origin—an existence forged only through hearsay—is closer to the point here.

5. "Shanghai Flowers—Opening," 47.

6. In the Columbia edition, the social hierarchy of courtesans is discussed qua historical contextualization in the editorial apparatus of the text with no reference to Chang; the mishearing that Chang describes is not discussed. Eva Hung, "The World of the Shanghai Courtesans," in *The Sing-song Girls of Shanghai*, ed. Eva Hung (New York: Columbia University Press, 2007), 540.

7. Eileen Chang, "Chinese Translation: A Vehicle of Cultural Influence," ed. Christopher Lee, *PMLA* 130, no. 2 (March 2015): 488–98. Unpublished until recently, Chang's lecture was written in English and delivered to several academic audiences between 1966 and 1969, a period of itinerancy in her life before settling in Los Angeles; see Lee's introduction, 488.

8. *Zhang Ailing geiwo de xinjian* [Letters from Eileen Chang], ed. C. T. Hsia (Taibei shi: Lianhe wenxue chubanshe, 2013), 26.

9. Tsu Jing, *Sound and Script in Chinese Diaspora* (Cambridge, MA: Harvard University Press, 2010), 97. For an account of self-translation as feminist praxis in Chang, see two articles by Jessica Tsui Yan Li: "Politics of Self-Translation: Eileen Chang," *Perspectives* 14, no. 2 (2006): 99–106; and "Self-Translation/Rewriting: The Female Body in Eileen Chang's *Jinsuo ji*, *The Rouge of the North*, *Yuannü* and *The Golden Cangue*," *Neohelicon* 37, no. 2 (2010): 391–403.

10. Wang Xiaojue goes so far as to consider Chang's Mandarin translation of *Shanghai Flowers* a kind of dubbing over of the vernacular: see *Modernity with a Cold War Face: Reimagining the Nation in Chinese Literature Across the 1949 Divide* (Cambridge, MA: Harvard University Press, 2013), 143; the same book offers a helpful overview of Chang's turn to the *Dream of the Red Chamber* in the Cold War context. Wang extends the argument into a consideration of translation's historical dimension in a later article: see "Creation and Transmission: Eileen Chang and *Sing-song Girls of Shanghai*," *Chinese Literature: Essays, Articles, Reviews* 36 (December 2014): 125–48.

11. These tend to orbit questions of personhood, performativity, and the impersonality of Chang as translator and mediator. See, e.g., Shuang Shen, "Betrayal, Impersonation, and Bilingualism: Eileen Chang's Self-Translation," in *Eileen Chang: Romancing Languages, Cultures and Genres*, ed. Louie Kam (Hong Kong: Hong Kong University Press, 2012), 91–111; Luo Xuanmin and Wang Jing, "Cultural Mediation: On Eileen Chang's English Translation of *Jinsuo ji*," *Amerasia Journal* 38, no. 2 (2012): 123–35; Richard Jean So, "Literary Information Warfare: Eileen Chang, the US State Department, and Cold War Media Aesthetics," *American Literature* 85, no. 4 (2013): 719–44. Adopting a different angle, David Der-wei Wang examines the question of betrayal via the writing of Chang's first husband, Hu Lancheng, a collaborator with the Japanese during the Japanese Occupation: see *The Lyrical in Epic Time: Modern Chinese Intellectuals and Artists through the 1949 Crisis* (New York: Columbia University Press, 2015). Most recently, Christopher Lee has sought

to extend the critical consensus on the negative effacements of translation in Chang's work as itself a performative gesture of escape: "Instead of declaring the emergence of a global cosmopolitan culture, what Chang seems to be performing is a distracted relationship to geopolitical divisions, that is, the ability to hold onto ethno-cultural identities, or at least to recognize their inescapability, through frequent moments of escape as well as escapism." "Translation in Distraction: On Eileen Chang's 'Chinese Translation: A Vehicle of Cultural Influence,'" *Journal of Modern Literature in Chinese* 14, no. 1 (Summer 2017): 84; for an earlier iteration of the argument in which Lee suggests that, "combining the roles of author and translator, Chang articulated a phantasmatic sense of cultural identity that she kept returning to even as her migrations took her to different surroundings," see *The Semblance of Identity: Aesthetic Mediation in Asian American Literature* (Stanford: Stanford University Press, 2012), 31.

12. Tze-lan Sang argues that Chang's later work—and especially *Little Reunions*—evinces a growing interest in factuality and quasi-documentation, as well as an uncredited maintenance of literary technique: "*Little Reunions* is constructed like a maze, with multiple temporal and dramatic lines weaving in and out of one another. Its language is cryptic and understated, deliberately requiring laborious decoding rather than easily ingested and consumed. It is not, as some critics claim, a shoddy, unfinished work. It is, rather, one of the last formal experiments Chang undertook." "Romancing Rhetoricity and Historicity: The Representational Politics and Poetics of *Little Reunion*," in *Eileen Chang: Romancing Languages, Cultures and Genres*, ed. Kam Louie (Hong Kong: Hong Kong University Press, 2012), 212. Sang's account resonates with Chang's and Hu's descriptions of *Dream of the Red Chamber* and *Shanghai Flowers* as discussed in this chapter. In a book review of the English translation, Carlos Rojas similarly speculates on an intertextual resonance between *Little Reunions* and Chang's translation work on *Shanghai Flowers*. www.shanghailiterary.com/tslr-online/2019/3/21/review-of-eileen-changs-little-reunions (accessed May 27, 2019).

13. Jonathan Stalling, *Yingelishi: Sinophonic English Poetry and Poetics* (Denver, CO: Counterpath, 2011). For a thoughtful and convincing reading of how Stalling's approach may unseat hegemonic expectations surrounding the English language, see also Tara Fickle, "English before Engrish: Asian American Poetry's Unruly Tongue," *Comparative Literature Studies* 51, no. 1 (2014): 84–89.

14. Yunte Huang, "Chinese Whispers," in *The Sound of Poetry/The Poetry of Sound*, ed. Marjorie Perloff and Craig Dworkin (Chicago: University of Chicago Press, 2009), 55.

15. Myung Mi Kim, *Commons* (Berkeley: University of California Press, 2002), 109–10. For readings of Kim's take on translation and how its abstractions proliferate meaning and testify to historical violence, see especially Kathy Lou Schultz, "The Process of Meaning and the Meaning of Process," in *Building Is a Process, Light Is an Element: Essays and Excursions for Myung Mi Kim*, ed. Michael Cross and Andrew Rippeon (Buffalo, NY: Queue Books, 2008), 61–69.

16. David Bellos, *Is That a Fish in Your Ear? Translation and the Meaning of Everything* (New York: Farrar, Straus and Giroux, 2011), 34–36; original emphasis.

17. Charles Bernstein, "Breaking the Translation Curtain: The Homophonic Sublime," *L'Esprit Créateur* 38, no. 4 (Winter 1998): 66.

18. Eileen Chang, *Zhang Ailing geiwo de xinjian*, 114. Like Chang, Hsia had made a new life in the United States after leaving Communist China, eventually becoming a professor of Chinese literature at Columbia University. His support was important to Chang in both

material and intellectual ways: in addition to being an influential patron who promoted and anthologized Chang's work in order to position her as one of China's great moderns to a Western academic audience, Hsia recommended her to various host institutions and often served as a sounding board for matters of Chinese-English translation.

19. Chloe Starr, *Red-light Novels of the Late Qing* (Leiden: Brill, 2007), 244.

20. Alexander des Forges, "Building Shanghai, One Page at a Time: The Aesthetics of Installment Fiction at the Turn of the Century," *Journal of Asian Studies* 62, no. 3 (2003): 788.

21. Stephen Cheng, "*Sing-song Girls of Shanghai* and Its Narrative Methods," *Renditions* 17–18 (Spring and Autumn 1982): 112.

22. Starr, *Red-light Novels*, 187.

23. David Der-wei Wang, *Fin-de-Siècle Splendor: Repressed Modernities of Late Qing Fiction, 1848–1911* (Stanford: Stanford University Press, 1997), 91.

24. Hu was in turn influenced by fellow May Fourth intellectual Lu Xun's genealogy of so-called *xiaxie xiaoshuo*, literally, *wayward fiction*, his term for the increasingly popular and often sensationalist vernacular novels about prostitution. *Xiaxie* refers partly to the literally winding alleys of red-light districts but (like the English) heavily connotes a normative judgment of moral deviance. The genre is today translated in descriptive terms, typically "courtesan," "brothel," or "red-light" novels; because these works are typically focused on wider social and structural conditions rather than courtesans per se, and in deference to the term's etymological origins in those streets, I follow the last here. In Lu Xun's account, *Shanghai Flowers* belongs to the second of three stages of the genre's development, from (i) idealized representation of courtesans to (ii) realistic representation and (iii) denigration. For Lu Xun, its muted naturalism made *Flowers* the best instance of the genre, offering an element of disappointment that functions as a cautionary tale to the reader—a sedate aesthetic that is *pingdan er jinziran*, a *calm blandness that still edges close to nature*. Hu echoes and extends Lu Xun's positive appraisal, focusing especially on that very sedate quality. For instructive complications of Lu Xun's schema in relation to *Shanghai Flowers*, see Patrick Hanan, "*Illusion of Romance [Fengyue meng]* and the Courtesan Novel," in *Chinese Fiction of the Nineteenth and Early Twentieth Centuries* (New York: Columbia University Press, 2004), 33–57; D. Wang, *Fin-de-Siècle Splendor*, 53–116; Starr, *Red-light Novels*, 19–23; Paola Zamperini, *Lost Bodies: Prostitution and Masculinity in Chinese Fiction* (Leiden: Brill, 2010), 9–11.

25. X. Wang, "Creation and Transmission," 145.

26. Chang's Mandarin translation of *Shanghai Flowers* was published in 1981, ninety-nine years after its first publication.

27. Eileen Chang (Zhang Ailing), "Guoyuben haishanghua yihouji [Translator's Afterword to the Mandarin Translation of *Shanghai Flowers*]," in *Haishanghua luo* [Shanghai Flowers—Falling] (Taibei shi: Huangguan chubanshe, 1981), 722. My translation here and henceforth.

28. In this chapter, I follow Chang's habit elsewhere of translating idiomatic Chinese more or less literally and word for word, resulting in what reads like an excessively figural (and estranging) translation in English; this is especially visible in Chang's translations of her own work. Second, and because the deixis of the subject-position "I" is a fraught matter for translation between modern Chinese and English—also as discussed in this chapter—I have departed from convention by refraining from silently supplying the

pronouns denoting subject-position in my translations. Instead, I have used "I" (and "me," "myself," etc.) *only* where Chang uses the Chinese *wo* or *ziji*. If this reads as informal and fragmented to the average English-speaking ear, then that is also felicitously suited to the conversational and intimate—yet still impersonal—effect that Chang creates in her essays. Last, I have sought to re-create the cadences of Chang's sentences—particularly the variations between lengths of clauses—and their alternately agglutinating, sudden, sinuous, elegant, and awkward movements. This aspect of Chang's prose style often betrays her reading in the tradition and is an important aspect of her thinking and self-performance as rendered in prose. The reader may judge that this produces grammatically incorrect, syntactically awkward, or inelegantly punctuated English: this also broadly accords with those of Chang's translations that take liberties with the English language, which I would rather present as a matter of style on Chang's terms than a lack that is measured against an invisible norm of English-language fluency.

29. Hu Shi, "Haishanghua liezhuan xu" [Preface to Shanghai Flowers], in *Haishanghua kai* [Shanghai Flowers—Opening] (Taibeishi: Huangguan chubanshe, 1981), 9, 12. My translations henceforth.

30. As cited and translated in X. Wang, "Creation and Transmission," 148.

31. See especially the account of May Fourth grapplings with realism or naturalism [*xieshi*] and the debates over the didactic import of literature for cultivating a national readership in Marston Anderson, *The Limits of Realism: Chinese Fiction in the Revolutionary Period* (Berkeley: University of California Press, 1990), 27–75; as well as the high level of attention to translation in Edward Gunn, *Rewriting Chinese: Style and Innovation in Twentieth-Century Chinese Prose* (Stanford: Stanford University Press, 1991).

32. Lydia Liu, *Translingual Practice: Literature, National Culture, and Translated Modernity—China, 1900–1937* (Stanford: Stanford University Press, 1995), 81 passim.

33. Chang, "Afterword," 723.

34. Ibid., 722.

35. Ibid., 724.

36. *Guoyü*, lit., *nation language*, is the term for Mandarin Chinese in Taiwan. On the mainland, Mandarin is known as *putonghua*, lit., *ordinary or common speech*.

37. Chang, "Afterword," 722.

38. Xiaojue Wang also pauses on this couplet but focuses on its first part: Chang's self-positioning as a transmitter of the literary tradition through her act of translation. By calling attention to the second part of the couplet, I seek to highlight the precarious nature of that transmission. "Creation and Transmission," 128.

39. This moment recalls what David Der-wei Wang has called an involutory (rather than *re*volutionary) approach to history and aesthetics in Chang's work: an inward etiolation that eschews the ethos of dialectical dynamism so crucial to political change and that keeps Chang at a remove from the political imperatives of the time. Yet to conjugate this insight with the politics of translation in Chang's context then invites a question of the involutionary *reader* or readership whose aesthetic anti-practice of abandonment is—as Chang implies throughout her commentary—covalent with that of the author and translator. "Madame White, *The Book of Change*, and Eileen Chang: On a Poetics of Involution and Derivation," in *Eileen Chang: Romancing Languages, Cultures and Genres*, ed. Kam Louie (Hong Kong: Hong Kong University Press, 2012), 215–41.

40. I have only been able to locate it in my edition published by a mainland house.

41. Eileen Chang, "Dui xiandai zhongwen de yidian xiaoyijian" [A Few Small Observations on Modern Chinese], in *Chongfang biancheng* [A Return to the Frontier], ed. Zhi An (Beijing: Beijing shiyue wenyi chubanshe, 2012), 107.

42. Ibid., 115.

43. Haun Saussy, "Always Multiple Translation, Or, How the Chinese Language Lost Its Grammar," in *Tokens of Exchange: The Problem of Translation in Global Circulations*, ed. Lydia Liu (Durham, NC: Duke University Press, 1999), 108.

44. One might speculatively note that Chang's subtlety on this point can be attributed to her lifelong bilingualism, though it is of course difficult to prove through evidentiary means. I would also be wary of valorizing or fetishizing bi- or multilingualism from a straightforwardly Western-liberal perspective, and this is far from my intent here.

45. Liu, *Translingual Practice*, 155–56.

46. Chang's little joke is accessible only to someone who reads *both* Chinese and English. It is likely derived from an English idiom: to "speak baldly" is to speak plainly and without restraint, in a way that might be excessively blunt. When writing her text in the Chinese, Chang translates the English idiom quite literally and humorously recalls the image of a bald *head* specifically, so in translating it back into the English I have re-created her humorously literal image. Her admiration of "bald speech" resonates also with Hu's admiration of plainspokenness as discussed in chapter 1.

47. Chang, "Small Observations," 114.

48. Ibid., 109.

49. For Liu's discussion of neologisms as a trope of translingual practice, see *Translingual Practice*, 27–42. Of special interest to the argument here is the claim that "because it [neologistic construction] has been invented simultaneously to represent and to replace foreign words, . . . it identifies itself as Chinese and foreign locked in linguistic tension. One does not translate between equivalents; rather, one creates tropes of equivalence in the middle zone of interlinear translation between the host and the guest languages. This middle zone of hypothetical equivalence, which is occupied by neologistic imagination, becomes the very ground for change" (40).

50. Ten years before this essay was published, in a 1968 letter to her mentor, C. T. Hsia, Chang complains that an overly zealous copyeditor had corrected her use of the second-person pronoun in her translation of her USIS Anglophone novel *The Rouge of the North* (into Chinese as *Yuannü*, lit., *vengeful, plaintive woman*). In her account, the copyeditor had changed her use of the universal (formerly masculine) second-person pronoun to its feminine iteration, possibly in a misguided attempt to make a feminist point. Chang then parenthetically jokes—part seriously—that if there is a feminine *you* then there should also be a feminine *I*. *Letters*, 104. This level of attention to copyediting is not limited to questions of pronouns and address; the essay treated in the next section is also catalyzed by her attention to copyediting mistakes.

51. I use the term "philology" advisedly, guided by two important critical arguments. Benjamin Elman's work on *kaozheng xue*, literally translated as *evidential scholarship* and translated as *philology* by Elman among others, in late imperial China points to a new skeptical empiricism in reading and interpreting literary writing and its pragmatics, eschewing the a priori and rule-bound generalizations of old. *From Philosophy to Philology: Intellectual and Social Aspects of Change in Late Imperial China* (Los Angeles: UCLA Asia Institute Monograph Series, 2001). Too, I have in mind Sheldon Pollock's engagement

with Michel Foucault's idea that language becomes historical—that is, philological—in (European) Enlightenment modernity. As Pollock notes, for Foucault "philology in the modern era began with the transformed understanding of the nature of language itself at the end of the eighteenth century. . . . For the first time in history all languages acquired an equal value, they merely had different internal structures; language came to be treated as a totality of phonetic, not graphic, elements." Pollock reconsiders the Foucauldian gesture of a radical break in European modernity by tracing this philological dynamic into premodern texts and practices, arguing therefore for a universalizable potential for philological practice qua reading the historicity of language. "Future Philology? The Fate of a Soft Science in a Hard World," *Critical Inquiry* 35 (Summer 2009): 936. (In the interest of compression, I will not rehearse the arguments from a long list of European-theoretical touchstones on philology: Erich Auerbach, Edward Said, Paul de Man, Werner Hamacher.) I am not arguing that Chang *intentionally* engages in the modes of philology described by Elman, Pollock, or Foucault—only that her attitude toward her found words and phrases from the Shanghai of the past and the United States of her present adopts—while playfully skewing—the principles of scholastic philology. By tracing their translingual substitutions in a mock-historical analysis, Chang exposes the fictive and imaginary dimension of historicity—and the kinetic quality of language and translation qua objects of knowledge *and* historical promissories of that knowledge.

52. Such as was played upon by Hu Shi in his story "Mr. Not So Different" (among many other related instances, the most famous of which is Zhao Yuanren's *Shishishishishi*, a poem entirely written with words that sound like *shi* and that had to be visually read to make sense).

53. For an incisive account of anti-African sentiment and colorism as it intersected with the question of class- and ethnically-based revolution in China (a strain of history to which Chang was clearly not immune), see Shu-mei Shih, "Race and Revolution: Blackness in China's Long Twentieth Century," *PMLA* 128, no. 1 (January 2013): 156–62.

54. "Caolubing" [Grass Flatbread], in *Chongfang biancheng* [A Return to the Frontier], ed. Zhi An (Beijing: Beijing shiyue wenyi chubanshe, 2012), 164. My translations henceforth. "Sound of Shanghai" [*Shanghai zhiyin*] was a highly popular radio station.

55. Chang calls this type of word a *yuzhuci* or *yuqici*: auxiliary utterance particles—a class of "empty word" (*xuzi*), the general term for words that served grammatical and nonsemantic functions in Chinese—and understood in contradistinction to *shizi*—"full or real word." For helpful accounts of how "empty words" take on new dimension in modernization and Chinese-English translation, see Tommaso Pellin, "Inventing a Modern Lexicon for Grammar in Chinese: The Experience of Wang Fengzao, Ma Jianzhong and Yan Fu," *Language Sciences* 30, no. 5 (September 2008): 529–45; David E. Pollard, "Empty Words: Modal Adverbs," in *An Encyclopaedia of Translation: Chinese-English English-Chinese*, ed. Chan Sin-wai and David E. Pollard (Hong Kong: Chinese University Press, 1995), 216–22.

56. "嗄," in *Chongfang biancheng* [A Return to the Frontier], 168. My translations henceforth.

57. Ibid.

58. Ibid., 169–70.

3. Concrete Translation

1. Theresa Hak Kyung Cha, *Dictée* (Berkeley: University of California Press, 2001), 1.

2. In an analysis of *Dictée* and its early critical recovery via the edited volume devoted to her work, *Writing Self, Writing Nation* (ed. Elaine H. Kim and Norma Alarcón), Anne Anlin Cheng seeks to "complicate and add to the idea of 'difference-as-intervention' foregrounded in Alarcón and Kim's collection by introducing the concept of fantasy and mimesis as the other two logics equally at work in Cha's text" (142). Elsewhere in the same text, in a reading of a short video piece titled "Re Dis Appearing" also thematizing translation, Cheng adds that "Cha's aesthetics thus insist as much on the principle of sameness as on the principle of difference. Sameness can be at once fascistic *and* a strategy of intervention (that is, correspondences that enact unauthorized forms of reproduction)" (160). By insisting on the process of *identification* in identity formation, Cheng's is an important touchstone for my complication of difference and differentiation in the realm of translation studies. *The Melancholy of Race: Psychoanalysis, Assimilation, and Hidden Grief* (New York: Oxford University Press, 2000).

3. "The notion of translation in which the same message is transferred from one linguistic medium to another is feasible only after the enunciation of translation has taken place, and the symmetrical equivalence implied in the correctness of translation between the original and its translation is necessarily a retrospective construction," which in Cha is fictionalized as the activity of the reader—and which I am staging here. Naoki Sakai, *Translation as Subjectivity: On "Japan" and Cultural Nationalism* (Minneapolis: University of Minnesota Press, 1997), 54.

4. Theresa Cha, "Paths" (MFA thesis statement, unpublished typescript, Berkeley Art Museum and Pacific Film Archive, May 1978), 2.

5. Ibid., 3. See too the discussion of a collective consciousness, within which the audience is a crucial element, in Lawrence Rinder, "The Plurality of Entrances, the Opening of Networks, the Infinity of Languages," in *The Dream of the Audience: Theresa Hak Kyung Cha (1951–1982)*, ed. Constance M. Lewallen (Berkeley: University of California Press, 2001), 28–30.

6. Cha, *Dictée*, 1.

7. Sakai, *Translation and Subjectivity*, 26.

8. What David Palumbo-Liu, in a more general register, argues is the "constant transitivity" and "undecidability" that at once conjoins and differentiates "Asian" and "American" across the Pacific: *Asian/American: Historical Crossings of a Racial Frontier* (Stanford: Stanford University Press, 1999), 5.

9. Lisa Lowe, *Immigrant Acts: On Asian American Cultural Politics* (Durham, NC: Duke University Press, 1996), 151. See also Cheng, *The Melancholy of Race*.

10. Shelley Sunn Wong, "Unnaming the Same: Theresa Hak Kyung Cha's *Dictée*," in *Writing Self, Writing Nation*, ed. Elaine H. Kim and Norma Alarcón (Berkeley: Third Woman Press, 1994), 120.

11. Despite significant uptake in Asian American and, increasingly, modernist studies, Cha's work thematizing the problems and material conditions of translation has received little to no traction with scholars self-identified as working in translation studies (who most often have a foot in comparative literature and national literatures/languages). Naoki

Sakai and Jonathan Stalling, both engaged in this chapter, are exceptions rather than the norm.

12. Cha's aesthetic is visibly influenced by the concrete poetry movement founded in Brazil in the 1950s, even if she does not (as is typical for her) cite or document her sources or call them by the names they have outside of her world. For related readings, see the chapter on Cha in Joseph Jeon, *Racial Things, Racial Form: Objecthood in Avant-Garde Asian American Poetry* (Iowa City: University of Iowa Press, 2012). Importantly for this book's argument and corpus, the concrete movement developed in part from the Poundian-Fenollosan ideographic sensibility. For useful scholarly studies of concretism or concrete poetry, see Jamie Hilder, *Designed Words for a Designed World: The International Concrete Poetry Movement 1955–1971* (Montreal: McGill-Queen's University Press, 2016); Andrea Bachner, *Beyond Sinology: Chinese Writing and the Scripts of Culture* (New York: Columbia University Press, 2014), 74–91; Antonio Sergio Bessa, ed., *Form and Feeling: The Making of Concretism in Brazil* (New York: Fordham University Press, 2021). For discussions of how concrete poetry has been translated in several linguistic and cultural contexts, see John Corbett and Ting Huang, eds., *The Translation and Transmission of Concrete Poetry* (New York: Routledge, 2019). My interest is less the translation or cultural drift of concretism, insofar as I do take for granted a general integrity in its aesthetic principles as they function in Cha's work. By adopting concretism as a guiding thought for this chapter, I am especially interested in how its formal principles lead Cha to theorize and formalize her sense of a critical translation—excavating the critical potential in abstraction—in ways that have not previously been grappled with. A term like "concrete translation" thus seeks to define not a genre or a movement but an *activity* of arrangement marking the "active social relation" of racial form—here molding new shapes of translation. Colleen Lye, "Racial Form," *Representations* 104, no. 1 (Fall 2008): 99.

13. Cha, "Paths," 2.

14. I have in mind Kandice Chuh's call for imagining a "subjectless discourse," i.e., one that understands the subject as a formation intelligible *only* through the matrices of violence that precede it (and no less of a social fact for that). Kandice Chuh, *Imagine Otherwise: On Asian Americanist Critique* (Durham, NC: Duke University Press, 2003), 9. As well, Chuh's argument is traceable to the insights of queer-of-color critique.

15. Trinh T. Minh-Ha, "White Spring," in Lewallen, *The Dream of the Audience*, 35.

16. Cheng, *Melancholy of Race*, 139. I do not however position mine as an anti-identitarian or "post-identity" argument; rather, working with arguments that Cha's theme of translation illuminates the contradictions and limits of identity, I am interested in how that structure also invites a reconsideration of equivalence in the field of translation studies. In speaking of flexibility, I especially have in mind two works that deal with the questions of transpacific capital and abstraction as discussed in the introduction: Aihwa Ong, *Flexible Citizenship: The Cultural Logics of Transnationality* (Durham, NC: Duke University Press, 1999); Iyko Day, *Alien Capital: Asian Racialization and the Logic of Settler Colonial Capitalism* (Durham, NC: Duke University Press, 2016).

17. In the early history of photography and cinema, superimposition was generally used to render (i) the impression of movement and (ii) ghosts, spirits, and other dreamlike elements of the fantastic and uncanny. Steeped in French film theory and herself an editor of a volume on apparatus theory, Cha (though without directly citing her sources as is habitual for her) is almost certainly calling upon those associations

in her own work. The film theorist André Bazin's essay "The Life and Death of Superimposition" (1946) offers an account of these uses. Even as he criticizes its reductive effects, superimposition remains for Bazin the locus of a tension between realism and the fantastic: "If you think about it, such supernatural phenomena are essential to verisimilitude. There is no reason why a ghost should not occupy an exact place in space, nor why it should blend mindlessly into its surroundings." André Bazin, "The Life and Death of Superimposition (1946)," trans. Bert Cardullo, *Film-Philosophy* 6, no. 1 (February 2002).

18. Augusto de Campos, Haroldo de Campos, and Décio Pignatari, "Pilot Plan for Concrete Poetry," in *Novas: Selected Writings*, ed. Antonio Sergio Bessa and Odile Cisneros, trans. Jon Tolman (Evanston, IL: Northwestern University Press, 2007), 218.

19. Cha, *Dictée*, 140.

20. Theresa Cha, *White Dust from Mongolia*, in *Exilée/Temps Morts: Selected Works*, ed. Constance M. Lewallen (Berkeley: University of California Press, 2009), 153.

21. The cultural translation took the form of a desire to "bring forth in this book, all the elements that are historical to lessen the physical geographical distance as well as the psychological distance of the Asian people from other ethnic cultures. The causes for the Korean War, and the reasons for the division of Korea into North and South, and the perpetuating conditions of Cold War will contribute to the understanding of Korea and Asia as whole cultures, not merely state their economic and political status as nations." Here already Cha speaks of this tacit translation as a lessening and reduction of distance, a telling echo of the moment in *Temps Morts* I examine in the next section. Typewritten text of "Statement of Plans" for *White Dust from Mongolia*, 1980, 1992.4.91, Theresa Hak Kyung Cha Collection, 1971–1991, Berkeley Art Museum and Pacific Film Archive, Berkeley, California, USA [hereafter BAMPFA].

22. Theresa Cha, *Temps Morts*, in Lewallen, *Exilée/Temps Morts*, 69.

23. Ed Park, "This is the writing you have been waiting for," in Lewallen, *Exilée/Temps Mort* 13.

24. Cha, *Temps Morts*, 70.

25. Cha, "Statement of Plans," BAMPFA.

26. Cha, *White Dust*, 148.

27. Ibid.

28. Ibid., 149.

29. Ibid.

30. Cha, "Statement of Plans," BAMPFA.

31. Cha, *White Dust*, 153.

32. Ibid., 151.

33. Ibid., 154.

34. Ibid., 150.

35. Ibid.

36. Ibid., 165.

37. To list a few key readers: Juliana Spahr, *Everybody's Autonomy: Connective Reading and Collective Identity* (Tuscaloosa: University of Alabama Press, 2001); Amie Parry, *Interventions into Modernist Cultures: Poetry from Beyond the Empty Screen* (Durham, NC: Duke University Press, 2007); Susan Stanford Friedman, *Planetary Modernisms: Provocations on Modernity across Time* (New York: Columbia University Press, 2015).

38. Jonathan Stalling notes that Cha had also studied *taiji* and Daoist thought when at Berkeley in the mid-1970s and identifies Chang Chung-yuan as an important source for her thinking. Chang's book discusses important principles of Daoism but is not a direct (copied) source for the English translation presented here. I discuss Stalling's argument in further detail later in this chapter. Jonathan Stalling, *A Poetics of Emptiness: Transformations of Asian Thought in American Poetry* (New York: Fordham University Press, 2001), 228. See also Chang Chung-yuan, *Creativity and Daoism: A Study of Chinese Philosophy, Art and Poetry* (Philadelphia: Singing Dragon Press, 2011).

39. Stalling, *A Poetics of Emptiness*, 29.

40. Cha, *Dictée*, 159, 161–62.

41. Ibid., 170.

42. Timothy Yu, *Race and the Avant-Garde: Experimental and Asian American Poetry since 1965* (Stanford: Stanford University Press, 2009), 107.

43. Cha, *Dictée*, 173.

44. Ibid., 175.

45. Ibid., 169–70.

46. Ibid., 170.

47. For a reading of the color white and "the *twohold* (Cha's multilingual hold) of black and red in which infinite shades of white exist," see Trinh, "White Spring," 40. Black and red are consistently connected to ink and blood in the system of leitmotifs that is Cha's work; Trinh moreover suggests that these color metaphors represent a way "by which the creative potential of a new relationship is kept alive between strategic nationality and transnational political alliance," drawing a connection to another color line of anticolonial struggle and coalitionist politics that have always been read closely with Cha's work.

48. Trinh Minh-ha reads a similar moment of pronominal ambiguity earlier in *Dictée* as summoning "a whole generation of Asian women in their relation to silence and language." "White Spring," 49.

4. Translingual Erasure

1. Yang Lian, "Watermint Narrative 5—Elegies, after Li Shangyin," in *Narrative Poem*, trans. Brian Holton (Eastburn, UK: Bloodaxe Books, 2017), 192–93. The original reads: "寫下一首詩 世界也可以消失" My translation is modified from Holton's: "write down a poem for the world to disappear."

2. Translations of Yang's poetry are my own unless otherwise indicated, with debts to the prior translators Brian Holton and Agnes Chan (working in collaboration) acknowledged here. Translations of Yang's prose and spoken commentary are reproduced and occasionally adapted from existing translations where available and translated by me where no translations exist. A note about the translations in this chapter: translating Yang's poetry into English becomes even less simple if one accepts the critical accounts of his poetry's inherently translated and translingual status. It is a task fraught with decision and intervention, perhaps even a little more than is usual for translations, given that his poetry works through nonrepresentational processes that do not so much *make* meaning but simply *observe*—in both the watching and complying senses of the term, done with a kind of light melancholy—its signifying limits. As much of my argument hinges on the idiomatic or untranslatable aspects of his work, I have instead conceived of my translation as an analytic prism, refracting and parsing the object of translation into more than one

possible English translation. This approach abandons as impossible the quest that tacitly drives most works of translation to produce only *one* formal translated text—indeed, that very model of an older equivalence that this book has stubbornly sought to unlearn. It also has the advantage of ameliorating the need for extreme inventiveness within the English language, as Yang's existing translators are at such pains to perform; their works are, in the strongest possible sense of the term, *new* texts, but despite my admiration, I have found that my own modes of reading and argumentation demand the closest possible embeddedness in the poetic resourcefulness of Yang's text. In this closeness resides the big picture I am seeking to paint about the transpacific.

3. Yang Lian, "Moved Once Again by an Ancient Betrayal—by way of a Preface to *Concentric Circles*," in *Concentric Circles*, trans. Brian Holton and Agnes Chan (London: Bloodaxe, 2005), 12; Yang Lian, "Zai bei gulao de beipan suo gandong" [Moved Once Again by an Ancient Betrayal], in *Yizuo xiangxia xiujian de ta* [A Tower Built Downward] (Nanjing: Fenghuang chubanshe, 2009), 156–57.

4. Writing about contemporary Chinese prose poetry and thinking thoroughly about his own English translations of them, Nick Admussen considers an aesthetics of prose recitation—a sense of *re*-citation reminiscent of the deconstructive reading of citationality—as a way of foregrounding a prose poem's transformative intervention into its vernacular genre. For Admussen, "Recitation summons the voices of others into the present, and into the present speaker: when prose poetry recites prose that is socialist, nationalist, capitalist, scientific, or religious, any forms assumed to contain or deliver truths, those claims are brought into a new laboratory in which they can be tested, transformed, or used for new purposes." Where Admussen broadly thinks through repetition as an act of renewal and generic growth (informed by extant paradigms in translation studies), I seek to think about repetition as a paradoxical activity of disappearance in translation. *Recite and Refuse: Contemporary Chinese Prose Poetry* (Honolulu: University of Hawai'i Press, 2016), 8.

5. Yang, "Moved Once Again by an Ancient Betrayal—by way of a Preface to *Concentric Circles*," 9, trans. modified.

6. Andrea Bachner, *Beyond Sinology: Chinese Writing and the Scripts of Culture* (New York: Columbia University Press, 2014), 216.

7. John Cayley with Yang Lian, "Hallucination and Coherence," *positions: east asia cultures critique* 10, no. 3 (Winter 2002): 779–80.

8. See especially John deFrancis, *Visible Speech: The Diverse Oneness of Writing Systems* (Honolulu: University of Hawai'i Press, 1989); John deFrancis, *The Chinese Language: Fact and Fantasy* (Honolulu: University of Hawai'i Press, 1984); Tsu Jing, *Sound and Script in Chinese Diaspora* (Cambridge, MA: Harvard University Press, 2010); Bachner, *Beyond Sinology*.

9. Lydia Liu, *Translingual Practice: Literature, National Culture, and Translated Modernity—China, 1900–1937* (Stanford: Stanford University Press, 1995), 26.

10. Sarah Dowling, *Translingual Poetics: Writing Personhood under Settler Colonialism* (Iowa City: University of Iowa Press, 2018), 7–8.

11. Yang Lian, *Concentric Circles*, trans. Brian Holton and Agnes Chan (London: Bloodaxe, 2005). For rendering the title, I have followed the existing published translation by Brian Holton and Agnes Chan. Notable however is an untranslatable play on the notion of the center. In Chinese, this word *xin* can mean both *center* and *heart*: the image

of concentric circles should therefore be read as also having a figural heart grounding their orbits, so that they are simultaneously *circles, spheres with the same heart*. The same character, with similar metaphysical implications, is also used when Yang writes about the "changeless core of existence" below. Yet these should not be taken at face value; if anything, Yang writes in the wake of the Yeatsian aphorism about a center that cannot hold. In addition, Yang sometimes renders the concentric circles in the singular: *yige tongxinyuan—one concentric circle/s*. The geometric impossibility is the poetic insight.

12. This may certainly be understood as an accommodation to censorship on the mainland—and indeed Edmond's account would support that claim. However, my argument is less interested in asking what Yang's work would look like with or without censorship than with the poetic and epistemic effects of writing under such conditions—one of which is then the question of how to mourn within the Chinese language, here understood with a greater capaciousness. For the account of Yang and his experiences with censorship post-Tiananmen, see Jacob Edmond, "Dissidence and Accommodation: The Publishing History of Yang Lian from 'Today' to Today," *China Quarterly*, no. 185 (March 2006): 111–27.

13. Jacob Edmond, *Make It the Same: Poetry in the Age of Global Media* (New York: Columbia University Press, 2020), 98.

14. For versions of this idea from the early reception, see (among others) Chuan Xiang, "Differing Views on Yang Lian's Recent Works," *Renditions* 23 (Spring 1985): 164–65. Ironically, the best-known version of this critique comes from the western Sinologist Stephen Owen, for whom the writing of poets like Yang and fellow Misty poet Bei Dao loses lyric authenticity within the frame of world poetry—ironic because one imagines that the version of Chineseness that Owen mourns is only pandering to Western appetites in a different way. Notably, one of Owen's complaints is that such poems are lesser in aesthetic integrity because they rely on imagery—therefore more translatable, even translating themselves—rather than the technical or formal aspects of Chinese lyric, which are untranslatable in his account. Owen rehearses his original argument from 1990 and responds to his critics—notable examples are Rey Chow, Michelle Yeh, and Yunte Huang—in "Stepping Forward and Back: Issues and Possibilities for 'World' Poetry," *Modern Philology* vol. 100 no. 4 (May 2003): 532–548.

15. Jacob Edmond, "Modernist Waves: Yang Lian, John Cayley, and the Location of Global Modernism in the Digital Age," in *Chinese Poetic Modernisms*, ed. Paul Manfredi and Christopher Lupke (Leiden: Brill, 2019), 283–303; an iteration of the argument also appears in Edmond's *Make It the Same*. Edmond is particularly interested in how the dynamism of media theory is anticipated and remade by Yang's master trope of the sea and its waves. This perhaps stems from the image of *drifting* or *piaobo*, Yang's word for the condition of exile: whence a long poetic sequence titled *Where the Sea Stands Still* [*dahai tingzhi zhichu*] that is the main subject of Edmond's piece.

16. Hence Cosima Bruno adopts Yang's work and its copious translations into English as a case study for thinking about the problems and possibilities of a literary criticism that works via translations of poetry, examining translation as both a creative process and a critical instrument. *Between the Lines: Yang Lian's Poetry through Translation* (Leiden: Brill, 2012). While the astringent experiments of Yang's work can hardly be said to correspond to the kinds of homogenizing "translatese" often attributed to translations intended for the circuits of world literature, one may plausibly argue that they are experimental and even "difficult" in

a manner that is largely familiar to the English-speaking literati world (so that it is a question of *order* of difficulty). See Rebecca Walkowitz, *Born Translated: The Contemporary Novel in the Age of World Literature* (New York: Columbia University Press, 2015), for helpful nuances on the aesthetics of world literature beyond the conventions of "translatese," including visual and other modes of nonlingual semiotics akin to Yang's plays on ideographic thinking.

17. Tony Barnstone, "Introduction: Chinese Poetry through the Looking Glass," in *Out of the Howling Storm: The New Chinese Poetry* (Hanover, NH: Wesleyan University Press, 1993), 2–3.

18. Jacob Edmond, "Dissidence and Accommodation," 111–27.

19. Lucas Klein, *The Organization of Distance: Poetry, Translation, Chineseness* (Leiden: Brill, 2018), 77.

20. Cayley and Yang, "Hallucination and Coherence," 780–81.

21. See Klein's discussion of the Western epic tradition as routed between Hegel, Pound, Yang, and the ideogrammic method: *The Organization of Distance*, 72–74.

22. Yang Lian, "Moved Once Again," 9, trans. modified. The original Chinese passage may be found in "Zai bei gulao de beipan suo gandong," 153–54.

23. As also cited in Yunte Huang, "Ezra Pound, Made in China," *Paideuma* 42 (2015): 39; and Cayley and Yang, "Hallucination and Coherence," 773. The point about completion is especially important to Cayley as well, who takes it seriously as a reading of both Pound and Yang. The *Cantos* was textually incomplete as a work in that Pound never finished it, but in all likelihood this was not Yang's intended sense.

24. It should go without saying (but perhaps is worth saying still) that I do not endorse on the level of factuality Yang's comments about the static linguistic properties of the Chinese language, nor am I interested in extending the content of his commentary and poetry into a speculative or ethnographic discussion about Chinese epistemology, Chinese people as a group, etc. These are not the objects on which my claims bear, nor are they the subject-positions that I assume or inhabit as a reader. Further, I do not suggest that Chinese literature has no history or bears no relation to history and cultural conditions on a factual level; indeed, I take this for granted and instead wish to nuance the point by considering the epistemological conditions of such claims through a test case of literary reading (Yang's). In all cases, my aim is not to draw generalizing and essentializing conclusions. Instead, my claims center on the multiple modes of signification in Yang's poetry and metatextual commentary, moving carefully from this instance to a consideration of its theoretical implications. Such a gesture emerges from the understanding that literary reading, via its engagement with language as a medium of thought, is itself already theoretical in the sense of being able to engage with the epistemological and material conditions that make it possible to begin with. What is at issue here is the modality of that engagement.

25. Yang Lian, "Moved Once Again," 9, trans. modified.

26. Klein, *Organization of Distance*, 75.

27. 活 這個字 [*huo zhegezi*]. Holton and Chan translate this as "Life This Word." I have modified their translation in order to mark the ambiguity I discuss: it is unclear if the first word functions as a noun or a verb, and my reading seeks to affirm and interrogate the transitivity of the verb.

28. The Constitution of the PRC was officially adopted in 1954. This means that it too "turned forty" sometime during the conceptualization or writing of *Concentric Circles*. It is difficult to determine if this historical detail is at play in the poem.

29. Yang Lian, "Tongxinyuan" [Concentric Circles], in *Dahai tingzhi zhi chu: Yang lian zuopin 1982–1997 shigejuan* [Where the Sea Stands Still: Poetry by Yang Lian 1982–1997] (Shanghai: shanghai wenyi chubanshe, 1998), 558.

30. Huang, "Ezra Pound," 39.

31. Klein helpfully contextualizes Yang's ethnocentrism within the postsocialist Roots-Seeking (*xungen*) movement, which mobilizes a nativist and traditionalist discourse against normative conceptions of modern Chinese cultural identity after the Cultural Revolution. With his amalgamated and internationalist roots, Yang's claim may then be seen as part of this complex rootedness. *Organization of Distance*, 82–84.

32. Huang, "Ezra Pound," 40; original emphasis.

33. Ibid., 53.

34. Yang, "Tongxinyuan" [Concentric Circles], 642–43.

35. Holton and Chan translate this as "vanishing." In the interest of communicating a bifurcating sense of active loss and negativity that I will locate in this and further instances of the same word elsewhere, I have opted for a somewhat more philosophically freighted formulation that attaches a negative prefix to an active verb: hence "dis-appearance." Also, as Yang's earlier comments note, translating all verb forms in Chinese necessitates something of an active decision, in the sense that one has to interpretively identify a tense every time one translates a verb. My decisions have been to choose grammatical accuracy in the context of his work while striving to retain any ambiguity that I have identified and that my argument dwells on.

36. "Tongxinyuan," 643. 消失進親愛的 / 詩 [*xiaoshi jin qinai de / shi*].

37. "Tongxinyuan," 642. 死後 美麗的情節 [*si hou /meili de qingjie*].

38. "Tongxinyuan," 631. [*weiyi mei beipan zhe shou shi de shi sizhe*].

39. "Tongxinyuan," 605. 消失的形式 [*xiaoshi de xingshi*].

40. "Tongxinyuan," 619–20.

41. "Tongxinyuan," 620. 日期停在危險的一刻 [*riqi tingzai weixian de yike*].

42. Tongxinyuan," 620. 躺在海底/作為行型樂隊的讀者 [*tangzai haidi / zuowei hangxing yuedui de duzhe*].

43. Tongxinyuan," 620. 此刻 什麼不是詩 [*cike / shenme bu shi shi*].

44. Holton and Chan translate 比喻歷史 *biyu lishi* as "likened to history," but I have elected to use "parable" and "comparable" for the opportunity to register the related possibilities in this line.

45. Holton and Chan translate 風和風的間隙, *feng he feng de jianxi* as "gap between the winds." I have modified this in order to note the structural symmetry in the original, which draws the two moments very close together. I also wished to register the compoundedness in the phrase 間隙, wherein pairing 隙 (*fissure*) with 間 (*between or inter*) suggests fissuring an existing fissure. In this way, Yang allows his compound phrase to resonate with the doubled syntax and images. 風和風的間隙 / 紅色大理石切成薄片 [*feng he feng de jianxi / hongse dalishi qiecheng baopian*].

46. 語言學 / 容納現實 [*yuyanxue / rongna xianshi*].

47. Holton and Chan translate 譯成, *yicheng* as *translates as*. I have chosen *translated into* in the past tense because *cheng* also suggests a completed action, as well as a transforming translation into or *as* something else. My choice of *little heart-organ* in lieu of *tiny heart* (Holton and Chan) is likewise aimed at conveying the dissonance in Yang's original: it is part term of conventional endearment and infantilization and part surprisingly corporeal

and technical image. Notably, the character for "heart," *xin*, is also used in the title *Concentric Circles*, as in its literal translation "circles with the same heart." [譯成／小小心臟失血的藝術, *yi cheng / xiao xiao xinzang shīxue de yishu*].

48. "Tongxinyuan," 613.

Conclusion

1. Genesis 11:7 as translated in the King James Bible. On the matter of communication and understanding, the verse is consistently translated by the major sources: in the New International Version, it reads, "Come, let us go down and confuse their language so they will not understand each other."

2. Jacques Derrida, "Des tours de Babel," trans. Joseph F. Graham, in *Psyche: Inventions of the Other*, vol. 1, ed. Peggy Kamuf and Elizabeth Rottenberg (Stanford: Stanford University Press, 2007): 191.

3. "Des tours de Babel" has in its title another homophonic pun that Graham declines to translate: *des tours* also sounds like *détour/s* or the *detour/s* that may lead one astray. The pun is audible only in the plural: to speak of plural Babels—the title implies—will lead inevitably to detours from meaning.

4. Jacques Lezra's formalization of value with un/translatability in his contribution "Translation" to the Political Concepts series offers a subtle account of the point I state bluntly here; I extend his thought to a thinking of equivalence. www.politicalconcepts.org/translation-jacques-lezra/.

5. Naoki Sakai, *Translation and Subjectivity: On "Japan" and Cultural Nationalism* (Minneapolis: University of Minnesota, 1997), 51.

6. Lydia Liu, "The Question of Meaning-Value in the Political Economy of the Sign," in *Tokens of Exchange: The Problem of Translation in Global Circulations*, ed. Lydia H. Liu (Durham, NC: Duke University Press, 2000), 13–41. On this point, Liu is close to Sakai's theory of equivalence and co-figuration. Her argument on the construction of equivalent meanings is taken from the Jakobsonian paradigm.

7. Gayatri Spivak, "The Politics of Translation," in *Outside in the Teaching Machine* (New York: Routledge, 1993), 180.

8. Sakai, *Translation and Subjectivity*, 54.

9. Homi Bhabha, *The Location of Culture* (New York: Routledge, 2004), 346; original emphasis.

10. Antoine Berman, *The Experience of the Foreign: Culture and Translation in Romantic Germany*, trans. S. Heyvaert (Albany: State University of New York Press, 1992), 180. Considering this idea in its historical context, Emily Apter notes via her reading of Barbara Cassin that even the received word-concept "translation" is marked by a Germanic ethnonationalism—however vigorously disavowed. *Against World Literature: On the Politics of Untranslatability* (London: Verso, 2013), 36.

11. Lawrence Venuti, *The Translator's Invisibility: A History of Translation* (New York: Routledge, 2012), 15–16. I am using the second edition; the first edition, making the same and now-classic intervention, was published in 1995.

12. Ibid., 15.

13. Talal Asad, "The Concept of Cultural Translation in British Social Anthropology," in *Writing Culture: The Poetics and Politics of Ethnography*, ed. James Clifford and George E. Marcus (Berkeley: University of California Press, 1986), 157–58.

14. Venuti, *The Translator's Invisibility*, 15.
15. Liu, "Meaning-Value," 24.
16. Mona Baker, "Editorial: Translation and the Production of Knowledge(s)," *Alif: Journal of Comparative Poetics*, no. 38 (2018): 8.
17. Liu, "Meaning-Value," 15–16; original emphasis.
18. Elsewhere and in the same special issue edited by Baker, Liu is the subject of an interview wherein she schematizes her notion of a "super-sign" as "a hetero-linguistic signifying chain that cuts across the semantic fields of two or several languages through translation[,] . . . leav[ing] behind the metaphysical obsession with semantic equivalences across languages . . . [and] allow[ing] the analyst to identify the bonding of heterolinguistic elements through a mobile process of translation that typically renders that process invisible." Lydia H. Liu, "The Battleground of Translation: Making Equal in a Global Structure of Inequality," interview by James St. Andre, *Alif: Journal of Comparative Poetics*, no. 38, "Translation and the Production of Knowledges" (2018): 377. The schematic argument is filled out in Lydia Liu, *The Clash of Empires: The Invention of China in Modern World Making* (Cambridge, MA: Harvard University Press, 2004); see esp. chaps. 1, 2, 6.
19. Naoki Sakai, *Translation and Subjectivity: On "Japan" and Cultural Nationalism* (Minneapolis: University of Minnesota, 1997), 25. Sakai routes this argument through a reading of Theresa Cha's *Dictée*, the subject of chap. 3.
20. Ibid., 25–26.
21. Vicente Rafael, *Motherless Tongues: The Insurgency of Language amid Wars of Translation* (Durham, NC: Duke University Press, 2016), 18.
22. I have in mind a recent movement toward Marxian and leftist articulations of translation studies—generally coinciding with a rising interest in the Global South and decolonial studies and motivated by the ways in which translation may de-provincialize Marxist thought. These developmental narratives, elucidated by special issue editors Nergis Ertürk and Özge Serin, may well trace their roots to an Ur text of translation studies—Walter Benjamin's "The Task of the Translator"—yet they also eschew the *uncertain* potential Benjamin imputes to translational afterlives by arguing that Marx's call to revolution is *already* answered by the translators who (still unevenly) inherit and fulfill his promise in their own times and in their own lives. Translating Marxism—that thought most seeking to be translatable, premised on universalism as the field of action within which thought becomes praxis—across an internationalist life of communism is then not an act of copying but, in the strongest possible way, realizes the potential of Marx's original as history—a "redemption of the hopes of the past." In that way, and precarious as this developmental and redemptive narrative may seem, translation may be a means of organizing "the event of the revolution." Nergis Ertürk and Özge Serin, "Marxism, Communism, and Translation: An Introduction," *boundary 2* 43, no. 3 (2016): 26.
23. I especially have in mind the interventions of Rebecca Walkowitz, *Born Translated: The Contemporary Novel in the Age of World Literature* (New York: Columbia University Press, 2015); Pheng Cheah, *What Is a World? On Postcolonial Literature as World Literature* (Durham, NC: Duke University Press, 2016); Michael Allan, *In the Shadow of World Literature: Sites of Reading in Colonial Egypt* (Princeton, NJ: Princeton University Press, 2016); and Gloria Fisk, *Orhan Pamuk and the Good of World Literature* (New York: Columbia University Press, 2018). In these hands, the unevenness of world literature emerges as an invitation for further and ongoing critical receptivity and reparation.

24. Axiomatic perhaps due to the now-classic work in which Dipesh Chakrabarty argues for translation as a mediation between the two forms of history that he locates in globalized capitalism: the first beholden to its analytic and the second (which he wishes to bring out and affirm), "more affective narratives of human belonging where life forms, although porous to one another, do not seem exchangeable through a third term of equivalence such as abstract labor." In analytically distinguishing abstract analysis from nonabstract affect, and in allowing them to unevenly "interrupt each other's narrative," Chakrabarty in effect engages in a kind of abstracting translation as I describe it in this section. One way to state my broad project in this book is to discuss what Chakrabarty calls the "porous" as itself a mode of translational equivalence: a porosity I locate in poetics, which occupies a difficult status between "life-form" and a still perpetual dying. *Provincializing Europe: Postcolonial Thought and Historical Difference* (Princeton, NJ: Princeton University Press, 2007), 71–72. I use the second edition; the book was first published in 2000.

25. Emily Apter, *Against World Literature: On The Politics of Untranslatability* (New York: Verso, 2013), 34, 138. Apter is by no means the originator of untranslatability as a concept, but her argument bringing it to the field's collective attention—as well as the closely identified work of Barbara Cassin—has become something of a flashpoint, as indicated by the responses and contributions to the recent volume, Duncan Large, Motoko Akashi, Wanda Józwikowska, and Emily Rose, eds., *Untranslatability: Interdisciplinary Perspectives* (New York: Routledge, 2018); as well as a polemical rebuttal by Lawrence Venuti, "Hijacking Translation: How Comp Lit Continues to Suppress Translated Texts," *boundary 2* 43, no. 2 (2016): 179–204. Jacques Lezra also offers a bracing defense of the concept's potential for resisting the forces of global capitalism; see *Untranslating Machines: A Genealogy for the Ends of Global Thought* (Lanham, MD: Rowman & Littlefield, 2017).

26. Caesura is raised as a "time-lag" of modernity in Bhabha's *Location of Culture*, 360.

27. "Non que je cultive l'intraduisible. Rien n'est intraduisible pour peu qu'on se donne le temps de la dépense ou l'expansion d'un discours compétent qui se mesure à la puissance de l'original. Mais «intraduisible» demeure—doit rester, me dit ma loi—l'économie poétique de l'idiome, celui qui m'importe, car je mourrais encore plus vite sans lui, et qui m'importe, moi-même à moi-même, là où une « quantité » formelle donnée échoue toujours à restituer l'événement singulier de l'original, c'est-à-dire à le faire oublier, une fois enregistré, à emporter son nombre, l'ombre prosodique de son quantum. Un mot pour un mot, si tu veux, syllabe par syllabe. Dès lors qu'on renonce à cette équivalence économique, d'ailleurs strictement impossible, on peut tout traduire, mais dans une traduction lâche au sens lâche du mot « traduction ». Je ne parle même pas de poésie, seulement de prosodie, de métrique (l'accent et la quantité dans le temps de la prononciation). Rien n'est intraduisible en un sens, mais en un autre sens tout est intraduisible, la traduction est un autre nom de l'impossible. En un autre sens du mot « traduction », bien sûr, et d'un sens à l'autre il m'est facile de tenir toujours ferme entre ces deux hyperboles qui sont au fond la même et se traduisent encore l'une l'autre." Jacques Derrida, *Le monolinguisme de l'autre* (Paris: Galilée, 1996), 100–103; translated as Jacques Derrida, *Monolingualism of the Other; or, The Prosthesis of Origin*, trans. Patrick Mensah (Stanford: Stanford University Press, 1998), 56–57. I have silently modified a few moments in the published English translation. Thanks are due to Geoffrey Bennington for verifying my changes in the translation; any remaining errors are my own.

28. See Lezra, *Untranslating Machines*, 16–17, for a discussion of this conjunction.

29. Karl Marx, *Capital Volume 1: A Critique of Political Economy*, trans. Ben Fowkes (London: Penguin, 1990), 256.

30. Ibid., 164–65.

31. Ibid., 256.

32. Aihwa Ong, *Neoliberalism as Exception: Mutations in Citizenship and Sovereignty* (Durham, NC: Duke University Press, 2006). For a discussion of a similar argument in regard to the contested morphology of human rights, see also Pheng Cheah, *Inhuman Conditions: On Cosmopolitanism and Human Rights* (Cambridge, MA: Harvard University Press, 2007).

33. I am indebted to Apter's conceptualization of the "translation zone" and Sherry Simon's longtime interest in the cities and sites of translation as locations from which to inflect the very grounds of translation theory; both trace their arguments as well to Niranjana, *Siting Translation*. See Sherry Simon's *Translating Montréal: Episodes in the Life of a Divided City* (Montreal: McGill-Queen's University Press, 2006); *Cities in Translation: Intersections of Language and Memory* (New York: Routledge, 2013); *Translation Sites: A Field Guide* (New York: Routledge, 2019).

Works Cited

Admussen, Nick. *Recite and Refuse: Contemporary Chinese Prose Poetry*. Honolulu: University of Hawai'i Press, 2016.
Allan, Michael. *In the Shadow of World Literature: Sites of Reading in Colonial Egypt*. Princeton, NJ: Princeton University Press, 2016.
Althusser, Louis. *Reading* Capital. Translated by Ben Brewster. London: New Left Books, 1977.
Altieri, Charles. *Painterly Abstraction in Modernist American Poetry: The Contemporaneity of Modernism*. University Park: Pennsylvania State University Press, 1995.
Anderson, Marston. *The Limits of Realism: Chinese Fiction in the Revolutionary Period*. Berkeley: University of California Press, 1990.
Apter, Emily. *Against World Literature: On the Politics of Untranslatability*. New York: Verso, 2013.
———. *The Translation Zone: A New Comparative Literature*. Princeton, NJ: Princeton University Press, 2006.
Asad, Talal. "The Concept of Cultural Translation in British Social Anthropology." In *Writing Culture: The Poetics and Politics of Ethnography*, edited by James Clifford and George E. Marcus, 141–64. Berkeley: University of California Press, 1986.
Bachner, Andrea. *Beyond Sinology: Chinese Writing and the Scripts of Culture*. New York: Columbia University Press, 2014.
———. *The Mark of Theory: Inscriptive Figures, Poststructuralist Prehistories*. New York: Fordham University Press, 2017.
Bachner, Andrea, and Pedro Erber. "Remapping the Transpacific: Critical Approaches between Asia and Latin America." *Verge: Studies in Global Asias* 3, no. 2 (Fall 2017): vi–xii.
Bahng, Aimee. *Migrant Futures: Decolonizing Speculation in Financial Times*. Durham, NC: Duke University Press, 2018.
Baker, Mona. "Editorial: Translation and the Production of Knowledge(s)." *Alif: Journal of Comparative Poetics*, no. 38 (2018): 8–10.
———. *In Other Words: A Coursebook on Translation*. New York: Routledge, 2018.
———, ed. *Translating Dissent: Voices from and with the Egyptian Revolution*. New York: Routledge, 2005.
———. *Translation and Conflict: A Narrative Account*. New York: Routledge, 2006.
Bandia, Paul F. *Translation as Reparation: Writing and Translation in Postcolonial Africa*. Manchester: Saint Jerome Press, 2008.

Barnstone, Tony. Introduction to *Out of the Howling Storm: The New Chinese Poetry*, edited by Tony Barnstone, 1–40. Hanover, NH: Wesleyan University Press, 1993.

Bates, Jennifer Ann. *Hegel's Theory of Imagination*. Albany: State University of New York Press, 2004.

Bazin, André. "The Life and Death of Superimposition (1946)." Translated by Bert Cardullo. *Film-Philosophy* 6, no. 1 (February 2002), https://doi.org/10.3366/film.2002.0001.

Bellos, David. *Is That a Fish in Your Ear? Translation and the Meaning of Everything*. New York: Farrar, Straus and Giroux, 2011.

Benjamin, Walter. "The Translator's Task—Walter Benjamin." Translated by Steven Rendall. *TTR: traduction, terminologie, rédaction* 10, no. 2 (1997): 151–65.

Berman, Antoine. *The Experience of the Foreign: Culture and Translation in Romantic Germany*. Translated by S. Heyvaert. Albany: State University of New York Press, 1992.

Bermann, Sandra, and Michael Wood, eds. *Nation, Language, and the Ethics of Translation*. Princeton, NJ: Princeton University Press, 2005.

Bernstein, Charles. "Breaking the Translation Curtain: The Homophonic Sublime." *L'Esprit Créateur* 38, no. 4 (Winter 1998): 64–70.

———. "Disfiguring Abstraction." *Critical Inquiry* 39, no. 3 (Spring 2013): 486–97.

Bessa, Antonio Sergio, ed. *Form and Feeling: The Making of Concretism in Brazil*. New York: Fordham University Press, 2021.

Best, Stephen. *None Like Us: Blackness, Belonging, Aesthetic Life*. Durham, NC: Duke University Press, 2018.

Bhabha, Homi. *The Location of Culture*. New York: Routledge, 2004.

Billings, Timothy. Introduction to Ezra Pound, *Cathay: A Critical Edition*, edited by Timothy Billings, 15–32. New York: Fordham University Press, 2019.

Bruno, Cosima. *Between the Lines: Yang Lian's Poetry through Translation*. Leiden: Brill, 2012.

Bush, Christopher. *Ideographic Modernism: China, Writing, Media*. New York: Oxford University Press, 2010.

———. Introduction to Ezra Pound, *Cathay: A Critical Edition*, edited by Timothy Billings, 5–11. New York: Fordham University Press, 2019.

Byrd, Jodi. *The Transit of Empire: Indigenous Critiques of Colonialism*. Minneapolis: University of Minnesota Press, 2011.

Cai, Zong-qi. "Poundian and Chinese Aesthetics of Dynamic Force: A Re-Discovery of Fenollosa and Pound's Theory of the Chinese Written Character." *Comparative Literature Studies* 30, no. 2 (1993): 170–87.

de Campos, Augusto, Haroldo de Campos, and Décio Pignatari. "Pilot Plan for Concrete Poetry." In *Novas: Selected Writings*, edited by Antonio Sergio Bessa and Odile Cisneros, translated by Jon Tolman, 217–19. Evanston, IL: Northwestern University Press, 2007.

Cassin, Barbara. Introduction to *Dictionary of Untranslatables: A Philosophical Lexicon*, edited by Barbara Cassin, translated by Michael Wood, xvii–xx. Princeton, NJ: Princeton University Press, 2014.
Cayley, John, and Yang Lian. "Hallucination and Coherence." *positions: east asia cultures critique* 10, no. 3 (Winter 2002): 773–84.
Cha, Theresa Hak-Kyung. *Dictée*. Berkeley: University of California Press, 2001.
———. "Paths." MFA thesis statement, unpublished typescript dated May 1978. Theresa Hak Kyung Cha Collection 1971–91, Berkeley Art Museum and Pacific Film Archive, Berkeley CA.
———. *Temps Morts*. In Theresa Hak Kyung Cha, *Exilée/Temps Morts: Selected Works*, edited by Constance M. Lewallen, 61–85. Berkeley: University of California Press, 2009.
———. Typewritten text of "Statement of Plans" for *White Dust from Mongolia*, dated 1980. Theresa Hak Kyung Cha Collection, 1971–91, Berkeley Art Museum and Pacific Film Archive, Berkeley, CA.
———. *White Dust from Mongolia*. In Theresa Hak Kyung Cha, *Exilée/Temps Morts: Selected Works*, edited by Constance M. Lewallen, 148–71. Berkeley: University of California Press, 2009.
Chakrabarty, Dipesh. *Provincializing Europe: Postcolonial Thought and Historical Difference*. Princeton, NJ: Princeton University Press, 2000.
Chang, Chung-yuan. *Creativity and Daoism: A Study of Chinese Philosophy, Art and Poetry*. Philadelphia: Singing Dragon Press, 2011.
Chang, Eileen (Zhang Ailing). " ." In *Chongfang biancheng* [A Return to the Frontier], edited by Zhi An, 166–71. Beijing: Beijing shiyue wenyi chubanshe, 2012.
———. "Caolubing" [Grass Flatbread]. In *Chongfang biancheng* [A Return to the Frontier], edited by Zhi An, 162–64. Beijing: Beijing shiyue wenyi chubanshe, 2012.
———. "Chinese Translation: A Vehicle of Cultural Influence." Edited by Christopher Lee. *PMLA* 130, no. 2 (March 2015): 488–99.
———. "Dui xiandai zhongwen de yidian xiaoyijian" [A Few Small Observations on Modern Chinese]. In *Chongfang biancheng* [A Return to the Frontier], edited by Zhi An, 107–15. Beijing: Beijing shiyue wenyi chubanshe, 2012.
———. "Guoyuben haishanghua yihouji" [Translator's Afterword to the Mandarin Translation of *Shanghai Flowers*]. In *Haishanghua luo* [Shanghai Flowers—Falling], 706–24. Taibei shi: Huangguan chubanshe, 1981.
———. "Yi Hushi zhi" [Remembering Hu Shi]. In *Zhangkan* [Chang Sees], 16–27. Taibei shi: Huangguan chubanshe, 1997.
———. *Zhang Ailing geiwo de xinjian* [Letters from Zhang Ailing]. Edited by C. T. Hsia. Taibei shi: Lianhe wenxue chubanshe, 2013.
Cheah, Pheng. *Inhuman Conditions: On Cosmopolitanism and Human Rights*. Cambridge, MA: Harvard University Press, 2007.

———. *What Is a World? On Postcolonial Literature as World Literature*. Durham, NC: Duke University Press, 2016.

Chen, Kuan-hsing. *Asia as Method: Toward Deimperialization*. Durham, NC: Duke University Press, 2010.

Cheng, Anne Anlin. *The Melancholy of Race: Psychoanalysis, Assimilation, and Hidden Grief.* New York: Oxford University Press, 2000.

———. "Memory and Anti-Documentary Desire in Theresa Hak Kyung Cha's *Dictée*." *MELUS* 23, no. 4 (Winter 1998): 119–33.

Cheng, Stephen. "*Sing-song Girls of Shanghai* and Its Narrative Methods." *Renditions* 17–18 (Spring and Autumn 1982): 111–36.

Choi, Don Mee. *Translation Is a Mode = Translation Is an Anti-Neocolonial Mode*. Brooklyn, NY: Ugly Duckling Press, 2020.

Chow, Rey. *The Age of the World Target: Self-Referentiality in War, Theory, and Comparative Work*. Durham, NC: Duke University Press, 2006.

———. "Introduction: On Chineseness as a Theoretical Problem." In *Modern Chinese Literary and Cultural Studies in the Age of Theory*, edited by Rey Chow, 1–25. Durham, NC: Duke University Press, 2000.

———. *Not Like a Native Speaker: On Languaging as a Postcolonial Experience*. New York: Columbia University Press, 2014.

———. *The Protestant Ethnic and the Spirit of Capitalism*. New York: Columbia University Press, 2002.

Chuh, Kandice. *Imagine Otherwise: On Asian Americanist Critique*. Durham, NC: Duke University Press, 2003.

Clark, T. J. "Clement Greenberg's Theory of Art." *Critical Inquiry* 9 (September 1982): 139–56.

Corbett, John, and Ting Huang, eds. *The Translation and Transmission of Concrete Poetry*. New York: Routledge, 2019.

van Croumphout, Gustav. *Emerson's Modernity and the Example of Goethe*. Columbia: University of Missouri Press, 1990.

Damrosch, David. *What Is World Literature?* Princeton, NJ: Princeton University Press, 2003.

Day, Iyko. *Alien Capital: Asian Racialization and the Logic of Settler Colonial Capitalism*. Durham, NC: Duke University Press, 2016.

DeFrancis, John. *The Chinese Language: Fact and Fantasy*. Honolulu: University of Hawai'i Press, 1984.

———. *Nationalism and Language Reform in China*. Princeton, NJ: Princeton University Press, 1950.

———. *Visible Speech: The Diverse Oneness of Writing Systems*. Honolulu: University of Hawai'i Press, 1989.

Derrida, Jacques. "Des tours de Babel." In *Psyche: Inventions of the Other*, vol. 1, 191–225. Translated by Joseph F. Graham, edited by Peggy Kamuf and Elizabeth Rottenberg. Stanford: Stanford University Press, 2007.

———. *Le monolinguisme de l'autre*. Paris: Galilée, 1996.

———. *Monolingualism of the Other; or, The Prosthesis of Origin*. Translated by Patrick Mensah. Stanford: Stanford University Press, 1998.

Desai, Meghnad. *The Route of All Evil: The Political Economy of Ezra Pound*. London: Faber and Faber, 2006.

Dowling, Sarah. *Translingual Poetics: Writing Personhood under Settler Colonialism*. Iowa City: University of Iowa Press, 2018.

Edmond, Jacob. "Dissidence and Accommodation: The Publishing History of Yang Lian from 'Today' to Today." *China Quarterly*, no. 185 (March 2006): 111–27.

———. *Make It the Same: Poetry in the Age of Global Media*. New York: Columbia University Press, 2019.

———. "Modernist Waves: Yang Lian, John Cayley, and the Location of Global Modernism in the Digital Age." In *Chinese Poetic Modernisms*, edited by Paul Manfredi and Christopher Lupke, 283–303. Leiden: Brill, 2019.

Eliot, T. S. Introduction to Ezra Pound, *Selected Poems*. Edited by T. S. Eliot. London: Faber & Gwyer, 1928.

Elman, Benjamin. *From Philosophy to Philology: Intellectual and Social Aspects of Change in Late Imperial China*. Los Angeles: UCLA Asia Institute Monograph Series, 2001.

Emmerich, Karen. *Literary Translation and the Making of Originals*. New York: Bloomsbury, 2017.

English, Darby. *1971: A Year in the Life of Color*. Chicago: University of Chicago Press, 2016.

Ertürk, Nergis, and Özge Serin. "Marxism, Communism, and Translation: An Introduction." *boundary 2* 43, no. 3 (2016): 1–26.

Fenollosa, Ernest, and Ezra Pound. *The Chinese Written Character as a Medium for Poetry*. Edited by Haun Saussy, Jonathan Stalling, and Lucas Klein. New York: Fordham University Press, 2008.

Fickle, Tara. "English before Engrish: Asian American Poetry's Unruly Tongue." *Comparative Literature Studies* 51, no. 1 (2014): 78–105.

Fisk, Gloria. *Orhan Pamuk and the Good of World Literature*. New York: Columbia University Press, 2018.

Friedman, Susan Stanford. *Planetary Modernisms: Provocations on Modernity across Time*. New York: Columbia University Press, 2015.

des Forges, Alexander. "Building Shanghai, One Page at a Time: The Aesthetics of Installment Fiction at the Turn of the Century." *Journal of Asian Studies* 62, no. 3 (2003): 781–810.

Golding, John. *Braque: The Late Works*. New Haven, CT: Yale University Press, 1997.

Greenberg, Clement. *The Collected Essays and Criticism*. Chicago: University of Chicago Press, 1988.

Gunn, Edward. *Rewriting Chinese: Style and Innovation in Twentieth-Century Chinese Prose*. Stanford: Stanford University Press, 1991.

Hanan, Patrick. "*Illusion of Romance* [*Fengyue meng*] and the Courtesan Novel." In *Chinese Fiction of the Nineteenth and Early Twentieth Centuries*, 33–57. New York: Columbia University Press, 2004.

Harding, Jason, and John Nash, eds. *Modernism and Non-Translation*. Oxford: Oxford University Press, 2019.

Harootunian, Harry. *History's Disquiet: Modernity, Cultural Practice, and the Question of Everyday Life*. New York: Columbia University Press, 2002.

Hayot, Eric. *Chinese Dreams: Pound, Brecht, Tel Quel*. Ann Arbor: University of Michigan Press, 2004.

———. *The Hypothetical Mandarin: Sympathy, Modernity, and Chinese Pain*. New York: Oxford University Press, 2009.

Hayot, Eric, Haun Saussy, and Steven Yao, eds. *Sinographies: Writing China*. Minneapolis: University of Minnesota Press, 2007.

Heidegger, Martin. "Dialogue on Language." In *On the Way to Language*, 47–53. Translated by Peter D. Hertz. New York: HarperCollins, 1982.

Heinrich, Ari. *The Afterlife of Images: Translating the Pathological Body between China and the West*. Durham, NC: Duke University Press, 2008.

Hilder, Jamie. *Designed Words for a Designed World: The International Concrete Poetry Movement 1955–1971*. Montreal: McGill-Queen's University Press, 2016.

Hill, Michael Gibbs. *Lin Shu Inc.: Translation and the Making of Modern Chinese Culture*. New York: Oxford University Press, 2013.

Hoskins, Janet, and Viet Thanh Nguyen. "Introduction—Transpacific Studies: Critical Perspectives on an Emerging Field." In *Transpacific Studies: Framing an Emerging Field*, edited by Janet Hoskins and Viet Thanh Nguyen, 1–38. Honolulu: University of Hawai'i Press, 2014.

Hu, Minghui, and Johan Elverskog, eds. *Cosmopolitanism in China, 1600–1950*. Amherst, NY: Cambria Press, 2016.

Hu Shi. "Chabuduo xiansheng zhuan" [The Story of Mr. Close Enough]. In *Hushi sanwen xuanji* [Selected Writings by Hu Shi], 123–25. Tianjin: Baihua wenyi chubanshe, 1995.

———. "Ch'an (Zen) Buddhism in China: Its History and Method." *Philosophy East and West* 3, no. 1 (1953): 3–24.

———. "Haishanghua liezhuan xu" [Preface to *Shanghai Flowers*]. In *Haishanghua kai* [Shanghai Flowers—Opening], 3–17. Taibeishi: Huangguan chubanshe, 1981.

———. "The Indianization of China: A Case Study in Cultural Borrowing." In *Independence, Convergence, and Borrowing in Institutions, Thought, and Art*, 219–47. Cambridge, MA: Harvard University Press, 1937.

---. "Some Modest Proposals for the Reform of Literature." In *Modern Chinese Literary Thought: Writings on Literature 1893–1945*, translated and edited by Kirk A. Denton, 123–39. Stanford: Stanford University Press, 1996.
Hu Shi liuxue riji [Hu Shi's Diaries from Studying Abroad]. Tai bei shi: Taiwan shangwu, 1977.
Hu Shi wencun [Anthology of Hu Shi's Writing]. Beijing: Huaxia chubanshe, 2000.
Hu Ying. *Tales of Translation: Composing the New Woman in China, 1898–1918*. Stanford: Stanford University Press, 2000.
Huang, Yunte, ed. *The Big Red Book of Modern Chinese Literature: Writings from the Mainland in the Long Twentieth Century*. New York: Norton, 2016.
---. "Chinese Whispers." In *The Sound of Poetry / The Poetry of Sound*, edited by Marjorie Perloff and Craig Dworkin, 53–59. Chicago: University of Chicago Press, 2009.
---. "Ezra Pound, Made in China." *Paideuma* 42 (2015): 39–55.
---. *Transpacific Displacement: Ethnography, Translation, and Intertextual Travel in Twentieth-Century American Literature*. Berkeley: University of California Press, 2002.
Hung, Eva. "The World of the Shanghai Courtesans." In *The Sing-song Girls of Shanghai*, edited by Eva Hung, 535–54. New York: Columbia University Press, 2007.
Huters, Theodore. *Bringing the World Home: Appropriating the West in Late Qing and Early Republican China*. Honolulu: University of Hawai'i Press, 2005.
Infante, Ignacio. *After Translation: The Transfer and Circulation of Modern Poetics across the Atlantic*. New York: Fordham University Press, 2013.
Jakobson, Roman. "On Linguistic Aspects of Translation." In *On Translation*, edited by Reuben A. Brower, 232–39. Cambridge, MA: Harvard University Press, 1959.
Jameson, Fredric. "Modernism and Imperialism." In *Nationalism, Colonialism, and Literature*, 43–66. Minneapolis: University of Minnesota Press, 1986.
---. *A Singular Modernity: Essay on the Ontology of the Present*. London: Verso, 2013.
Jeon, Joseph. *Racial Things, Racial Form: Objecthood in Avant-Garde Asian American Poetry*. Iowa City: University of Iowa Press, 2012.
Kant, Immanuel. "Idea for a Universal History with a Cosmopolitan Purpose." In Immanuel Kant, *Political Writings*, edited by H. S. Reiss, translated by H. B. Nisbet, 41–53. Cambridge: Cambridge University Press, 2002.
Katz, Daniel. *American Modernism's Expatriate Scene: The Labour of Translation*. Edinburgh: Edinburgh University Press, 2007.
Kenner, Hugh. *The Pound Era*. Berkeley: University of California Press, 1973.
Kern, Robert. *Orientalism, Modernism, and the American Poem*. New York: Cambridge University Press, 1996.

Kim, Jinah. *Postcolonial Grief: The Afterlives of the Pacific Wars in the Americas.* Durham, NC: Duke University Press, 2019.

Kim, Jodi. *Ends of Empire: Asian American Critique and the Cold War.* Minneapolis: University of Minnesota Press, 2010.

Kim, Myung Mi. *Commons.* Berkeley: University of California Press, 2002.

Klein, Lucas. *The Organization of Distance: Poetry, Translation, Chineseness.* Leiden: Brill, 2018.

———. "Silences, Whispers, and the Figure of China: Translation Anxiety in Contemporary American Poetry." *Genre* 51, no. 3 (2018): 267–93.

Kong, Belinda. *Tiananmen Fictions Outside the Square: The Chinese Literary Diaspora and the Politics of Global Culture.* Philadelphia: Temple University Press, 2012.

Large, Duncan, Motoko Akashi, Wanda Józwikowska, and Emily Rose, eds. *Untranslatability: Interdisciplinary Perspectives.* New York: Routledge, 2018.

Lee, Ana Paulina. *Mandarin Brazil: Race, Representation, and Memory.* Stanford: Stanford University Press, 2018.

Lee, Christopher. *The Semblance of Identity: Aesthetic Mediation in Asian American Literature.* Stanford: Stanford University Press, 2012.

———. "Translation in Distraction: On Eileen Chang's 'Chinese Translation: A Vehicle of Cultural Influence.'" *Journal of Modern Literature in Chinese* 14, no. 1 (Summer 2017): 65–87.

Lee, Leo Ou-fan. *The Romantic Generation of Modern Chinese Writers.* Cambridge, MA: Harvard University Press, 1973.

———. *Shanghai Modern: The Flowering of a New Urban Culture in China, 1930–1945.* Cambridge, MA: Harvard University Press, 1999.

Levenson, Joseph R. *Revolution and Cosmopolitanism: The Western Stage and the Chinese Stages.* Berkeley: University of California Press, 1971.

Lezra, Jacques. *On the Nature of Marx's Things: Translation as Necrophilology.* New York: Fordham University Press, 2018.

———. *Untranslating Machines: A Genealogy for the Ends of Global Thought.* Lanham, MD: Rowman & Littlefield, 2017.

Li, Jessica Tsui Yan. "Politics of Self-Translation: Eileen Chang." *Perspectives* 14, no. 2 (2006): 99–106.

———. "Self-Translation/Rewriting: The Female Body in Eileen Chang's 'Jinsuo ji,' *The Rouge of the North, Yuannü* and *The Golden Cangue*." *Neohelicon* 37, no. 2 (2010): 391–403.

Lim, Jeehyun. *Bilingual Brokers: Race, Literature, and Language as Human Capital.* New York: Fordham University Press, 2017.

Liu, Lydia. *The Clash of Empires: The Invention of China in Modern World Making.* Cambridge, MA: Harvard University Press, 2004.

———. "The Question of Meaning-Value in the Political Economy of the Sign." In *Tokens of Exchange: The Problem of Translation in Global Circulations*, edited by Lydia Liu, 13–42. Durham, NC: Duke University Press, 2000.

———. *Translingual Practice: Literature, National Culture, and Translated Modernity—China, 1900–1937.* Stanford: Stanford University Press, 1995.
Liu, Lydia, interviewed by James St. Andre. "The Battleground of Translation: Making Equal in a Global Structure of Inequality." *Alif: Journal of Comparative Poetics*, no. 38 (2018): 368–87.
Lowe, Lisa. *Immigrant Acts: On Asian American Cultural Politics.* Durham, NC: Duke University Press, 1996.
———. *The Intimacies of Four Continents.* Durham, NC: Duke University Press, 2015.
Luo, Xuanmin, and Wang Jing. "Cultural Mediation: On Eileen Chang's English Translation of *Jinsuo ji.*" *Amerasia* 38, no. 2 (2012): 123–35.
Lye, Colleen. *America's Asia: Racial Form and American Literature, 1893–1945.* Princeton, NJ: Princeton University Press, 2005.
———. "Racial Form." *Representations* 104, no. 1 (Fall 2008): 92–101.
MacDougall, Bonnie. *Translation Zones in Modern China: Authoritarian Command versus Gift Exchange.* Amherst, NY: Cambria Press, 2011.
Marsh, Alec. *Money and Modernity: Pound, Williams, and the Spirit of Jefferson.* Tuscaloosa: University of Alabama Press, 1998.
Marx, Karl. *Capital. Volume 1: A Critique of Political Economy.* Translated by Ben Fowkes. London: Penguin, 1990.
Miyoshi, Masao. *Off Center: Power and Culture Relations between Japan and the United States.* Cambridge, MA: Harvard University Press, 1998.
Mok, Christine, and Aimee Bahng. "Transpacific Overtures: An Introduction." *Journal of Asian American Studies* 20, no. 1 (February 2017): 1–9.
Morrison, Paul. *The Poetics of Fascism: Ezra Pound, T. S. Eliot, Paul de Man.* Oxford: Oxford University Press, 1996.
Moten, Fred. *In the Break: The Aesthetics of the Black Radical Tradition.* Minneapolis: University of Minnesota Press, 2003.
Mullaney, Thomas. *The Chinese Typewriter: A History.* Boston: MIT Press, 2018.
Murray, Donald M. "Emerson's 'Language as Fossil Poetry': An Analogy from Chinese." *New England Quarterly* 29, no. 1 (1956): 204–15.
Nancy, Jean Luc. *After Fukushima: The Equivalence of Catastrophes.* Translated by Charlotte Mandell. New York: Fordham University Press, 2014.
Nicholls, Peter. *Ezra Pound, Politics, Economics and Writing: A Study of the Cantos.* London: Macmillan, 1984.
Nida, Eugene A. *Toward a Science of Translating.* Leiden: Brill, 1964.
Nida, Eugene A., and Charles R. Taber. *The Theory and Practice of Translation.* Leiden: Brill, 1969.
Niranjana, Tejaswini. *Siting Translation: History, Post-Structuralism, and the Colonial Context.* Berkeley: University of California Press, 1992.
Nolde, John J. "The Literary Revolutions of Hu Shih and Ezra Pound." *Paideuma* 9, no. 2 (Fall 1980): 235–48.

Ong, Aihwa. *Flexible Citizenship: The Cultural Logics of Transnationality.* Durham, NC: Duke University Press, 1999.

———. *Neoliberalism as Exception: Mutations in Citizenship and Sovereignty.* Durham, NC: Duke University Press, 2006.

Owen, Stephen. "Stepping Forward and Back: Issues and Possibilities for 'World' Poetry." *Modern Philology* 100, no. 4 (May 2003): 532–48.

Palumbo-Liu, David. *Asian/America: Historical Crossings of a Racial Frontier.* Stanford: Stanford University Press, 1999.

Park, Ed. "This is the writing you have been waiting for." In *Exilée/Temps Mort: Selected Works*, edited by Constance M. Lewallen, 9–15. Berkeley: University of California Press, 2009.

Park, Josephine. *Apparitions of Asia: Modernist Form and Asian American Poetics.* New York: Oxford University Press, 2008.

———. *Cold War Friendships: Korea, Vietnam, and Asian American Literature.* New York: Oxford University Press, 2016.

Parry, Amie. *Interventions into Modernist Cultures: Poetry from Beyond the Empty Screen.* Durham, NC: Duke University Press, 2007.

Pellin, Tommaso. "Inventing a Modern Lexicon for Grammar in Chinese: The Experience of Wang Fengzao, Ma Jianzhong and Yan Fu." *Language Sciences* 30, no. 5 (September 2008): 529–45.

Perloff, Marjorie. *Unoriginal Genius: Poetry by Other Means in the New Century.* Chicago: University of Chicago Press, 2010.

Pochmann, Henry A. *New England Transcendentalism and St. Louis Hegelianism: Phases in the History of American Idealism.* Philadelphia: Carl Schurz Memorial Foundation, 1948.

Pollard, David E. "Empty Words: Modal Adverbs." In *An Encyclopaedia of Translation: Chinese-English English-Chinese*, edited by Chan Sin-wai and David E. Pollard, 216–22. Hong Kong: Chinese University Press, 1995.

Pollock, Sheldon. "Future Philology? The Fate of a Soft Science in a Hard World." *Critical Inquiry* 35 (Summer 2009): 931–61.

Pound, Ezra. *The Cantos.* New York: New Directions, 1996.

———. "I gather the limbs of Osiris." In Ezra Pound, *Selected Prose, 1909–1965*, edited by William Cookson, 21–43. New York: New Directions, 1975.

———. *The Letters of Ezra Pound 1907–1941.* Edited by D. D. Paige. New York: Haskell House Publishers, 1974.

Qian, Zhaoming. *Orientalism and Modernism: The Legacy of China in Pound and Williams.* Durham, NC: Duke University Press, 1995.

Rafael, Vicente. *Motherless Tongues: The Insurgency of Language amid Wars of Translation.* Durham, NC: Duke University Press, 2016.

Rinder, Lawrence. "The Plurality of Entrances, the Opening of Networks, the Infinity of Languages." In *The Dream of the Audience: Theresa Hak Kyung Cha*

(1951–1982), edited by Constance M. Lewallen, 15–31. Berkeley: University of California Press, 2001.

Robbins, Bruce. "Introduction Part I: Actually Existing Cosmopolitanism." In *Cosmopolitics: Thinking and Feeling Beyond the Nation*, edited by Pheng Cheah and Bruce Robbins, 1–19. Minneapolis: University of Minnesota Press, 1998.

Sakai, Naoki. *Translation as Subjectivity: On "Japan" and Cultural Nationalism*. Minneapolis: University of Minnesota Press, 1997.

Sang, Tze-lan. "Romancing Rhetoricity and Historicity: The Representational Politics and Poetics of *Little Reunion*." In *Eileen Chang: Romancing Languages, Cultures and Genres*, edited by Kam Louie, 194–214. Hong Kong: Hong Kong University Press, 2012.

de Saussure, Ferdinand. *Course in General Linguistics*. Translated by Wade Baskin, edited by Perry Meisel and Haun Saussy. New York: Columbia University Press, 2011.

Saussy, Haun. "Always Multiple Translation, Or, How the Chinese Language Lost Its Grammar." In *Tokens of Exchange: The Problem of Translation in Global Circulations*, edited by Lydia Liu, 107–24. Durham, NC: Duke University Press, 1999.

———. "Fenollosa Compounded: A Discrimination." In Ernest Fenollosa and Ezra Pound, *The Chinese Written Character as a Medium for Poetry*, edited by Haun Saussy, Jonathan Stalling, and Lucas Klein, 1–40. New York: Fordham University Press, 2008.

———. "The Prestige of Writing: *Wen*, Letter, Picture, Image, Ideography." In *Great Walls of Discourse and Other Adventures in Cultural China*, 35–74. Cambridge, MA: Harvard University Asia Center, 2001.

———. *Translation as Citation: Zhuangzi Inside Out*. New York: Oxford University Press, 2017.

Schultz, Kathy Lou. "The Process of Meaning and the Meaning of Process." In *Building Is a Process, Light Is an Element: Essays and Excursions for Myung Mi Kim*, edited by Michael Cross and Andrew Rippeon, 61–69. Buffalo, NY: Queue Books, 2008.

Schulze, Robin G. *The Degenerate Muse: American Nature, Modernist Poetry, and the Problem of Cultural Hygiene*. New York: Oxford University Press, 2013.

Seybolt, Peter J., and Gregory Kuei-ke Chiang, eds. *Language Reform in China: Documents and Commentary*. New York: M. E. Sharpe, 1978.

Shen, Shuang. "Betrayal, Impersonation, and Bilingualism: Eileen Chang's Self-Translation." In *Eileen Chang: Romancing Languages, Cultures and Genres*, edited by Louie Kam, 91–111. Hong Kong: Hong Kong University Press, 2012.

———. *Cosmopolitan Publics: Anglophone Print Culture in Semi-Colonial Shanghai*. Piscataway, NJ: Rutgers University Press, 2009.

Shih, Shu-mei. "Against Diaspora: The Sinophone as Places of Cultural Production." In *Global Chinese Literature: Critical Essays*, edited by Jing Tsu and David Derwei Wang, 29–48. Leiden: Brill, 2010.

———. "The Concept of the Sinophone." *PMLA* 123, no. 3 (May 2011): 709–18.

———. *The Lure of the Modern: Writing Modernism in Semicolonial China, 1917–1937.* Berkeley: University of California Press, 2001.

———. "Race and Revolution: Blackness in China's Long Twentieth Century." *PMLA* 128, no. 1 (January 2013): 156–62.

———. *Visuality and Identity: Sinophone Articulations across the Pacific.* Berkeley: University of California Press, 2007.

Shimabuku, Annmaria. *Alegal: Biopolitics and the Unintelligibility of Okinawan Life.* New York: Fordham University Press, 2018.

Simon, Sherry. *Cities in Translation: Intersections of Language and Memory.* New York: Routledge, 2013.

———. *Translating Montréal: Episodes in the Life of a Divided City.* Montreal: McGill-Queen's University Press, 2006.

———. *Translation Sites: A Field Guide.* New York: Routledge, 2019.

So, Richard Jean. "Literary Information Warfare: Eileen Chang, the US State Department, and Cold War Media Aesthetics." *American Literature* 85, no. 4 (2013): 719–44.

———. *Transpacific Community: America, China, and the Rise and Fall of a Cultural Network.* New York: Columbia University Press, 2016.

Spahr, Juliana. *Everybody's Autonomy: Connective Reading and Collective Identity.* Tuscaloosa: University of Alabama Press, 2001.

Spivak, Gayatri. "The Politics of Translation." In *Outside in the Teaching Machine*, 179–200. New York: Routledge, 1993.

———. "Rethinking Comparativism." *New Literary History* 40, no. 3 (Summer 2009): 609–26.

Stalling, Jonathan. *Poetics of Emptiness: Transformations of Asian Thought in American Poetry.* New York: Fordham University Press, 2010.

———. *Yingelishi: Sinophonic English Poetry and Poetics.* Denver, CO: Counterpath, 2011.

Starr, Chloe. *Red-light Novels of the Late Qing.* Leiden: Brill, 2007.

Steiner, George. *After Babel: Aspects of Language and Translation.* Oxford: Oxford University Press, 1998.

Tageldin, Shaden. *Disarming Words: Empire and the Seductions of Translation in Egypt.* Berkeley: University of California Press, 2011. Trinh, T. Minh-Ha. "White Spring." In *The Dream of the Audience: Theresa Hak Kyung Cha (1951–1982)*, edited by Constance M. Lewallen, 33–50. Berkeley: University of California Press, 2001.

Tsu, Jing. *Sound and Script in Chinese Diaspora.* Cambridge, MA: Harvard University Press, 2010.

Tymoczko, Maria. *Enlarging Translation, Empowering Translators*. New York: Routledge, 2014.
———. *Translation in a Postcolonial Context*. Manchester: St. Jerome, 1999.
———, ed. *Translation, Resistance, Activism*. Amherst: University of Massachusetts Press, 2010.
Venuti, Lawrence. "Hijacking Translation: How Comp Lit Continues to Suppress Translated Texts." *boundary 2* 43, no. 2 (2016): 179–204.
———. *The Translator's Invisibility: A History of Translation*. New York: Routledge, 2008.
Volland, Nicolai. "All the Literature That's Fit to Print: A Print Culture Perspective on Modern Chinese Literature." In *A Companion to Modern Chinese Literature*, edited by Yingjin Zhang, 360–78. West Sussex: Wiley Blackwell, 2015.
Walkowitz, Rebecca. *Born Translated: The Contemporary Novel in an Age of World Literature*. New York: Columbia University Press, 2017.
Wang, Ban. *The Sublime Figure of History: Aesthetics and Politics in Twentieth-Century China*. Stanford: Stanford University Press, 1997.
Wang, David Der-Wei. *Fin-de-Siècle Splendor: Repressed Modernities of Late Qing Fiction, 1848–1911*. Stanford: Stanford University Press, 1997.
———. *The Lyrical in Epic Time: Modern Chinese Intellectuals and Artists through the 1949 Crisis*. New York: Columbia University Press, 2015.
———. "Madame White, *The Book of Change*, and Eileen Chang: On a Poetics of Involution and Derivation." In *Eileen Chang: Romancing Languages, Cultures and Genres*, edited by Kam Louie, 215–41. Hong Kong: Hong Kong University Press, 2012.
Wang, Hui. "The Politics of Imagining Asia: A Genealogical Analysis." Translated by Matthew Hale. *Inter-Asia Cultural Studies* 8, no. 1 (2007): 1–33.
Wang, Pu. *The Translatability of Revolution: Guo Moruo and Twentieth-Century Chinese Culture*. Cambridge, MA: Harvard University Press, 2018.
Wang, Xiaojue. "Creation and Transmission: Eileen Chang and *Sing-song Girls of Shanghai*." *Chinese Literature: Essays, Articles, Reviews* 36 (December 2014): 125–48.
———. *Modernity with a Cold War Face: Reimagining the Nation in Chinese Literature across the 1949 Divide*. Cambridge, MA: Harvard University Press, 2013.
Weber, Samuel. "Wartime." In *Violence, Identity, and Self-Determination*, edited by Hent de Vries and Samuel Weber, 80–105. Stanford: Stanford University Press, 1997.
Williams, R. John. "Decolonizing *Cathay*: Teaching the Scandals of Translation through Angel Island Poetry." *Transformations* 7, no. 2 (2007): 15–30.
Wilson, Rob. *Reimagining the American Pacific: From South Pacific to Bamboo Ridge and Beyond*. Durham, NC: Duke University Press, 2000.

Wong, Lily. *Transpacific Attachments: Sex Work, Media Networks, and Affective Histories of Chineseness*. New York: Columbia University Press, 2018.
Wong, Shelley Sunn. "Unnaming the Same: Theresa Hak Kyung Cha's *Dictée*." In *Writing Self, Writing Nation*, edited by Elaine H. Kim and Norma Alarcón, 103–40. Berkeley: Third Woman Press, 1994.
Wu, Shengqing. *Modern Archaics: Continuity and Innovation in the Chinese Lyric Tradition, 1900–1937*. Cambridge, MA: Harvard University Press, 2014.
Xiang, Chuan. "Differing Views on Yang Lian's Recent Works." *Renditions* 23 (Spring 1985): 164–65.
Xie, Ming. *Ezra Pound and the Appropriation of Chinese Poetry: Cathay, Translation, and Imagism*. New York: Routledge, 1999.
Yang, Lian. "Moved Once Again by an Ancient Betrayal—by way of a Preface to *Concentric Circles*." In *Concentric Circles*, translated by Brian Holton and Agnes Chan, 9–15. London: Bloodaxe, 2005.
———. "Tongxinyuan" [Concentric Circles]. In *Dahai tingzhi zhi chu: Yang lian zuopin 1982–1997 shigejuan* [Where the Sea Stands Still: Poetry by Yang Lian 1982–1997], 529–643. Shanghai: Shanghai wenyi chubanshe, 1998.
———. "Watermint Narrative 5—Elegies, after Li Shangyin." In *Narrative Poem*, translated by Brian Holton, 87–203. Eastburn, UK: Bloodaxe Books, 2017.
———. "Zai bei gulao de beipan suo gandong" [Moved Once Again by an Ancient Betrayal]. In *Yizuo xiangxia xiujian de ta* [A Tower Built Downward], 153–57. Nanjing: Fenghuang chubanshe, 2009.
Yao, Steven. *Foreign Accents: Chinese American Verse from Exclusion to Postethnicity*. New York: Oxford University Press, 2010.
———. *Translation and the Languages of Modernism: Gender, Politics, Language*. New York: Palgrave Macmillan, 2002.
Yu, Timothy. *Race and the Avant-Garde: Experimental and Asian American Poetry since 1965*. Stanford: Stanford University Press, 2009.
Zamperini, Paola. *Lost Bodies: Prostitution and Masculinity in Chinese Fiction*. Leiden: Brill, 2010.
Zhang, Longxi. "What Is Wen and Why Is It Made So Terribly Strange?" *College Literature* 23, no. 1 (1996): 15–35.
Zhong, Yurou. *Chinese Grammatology: Script Revolution and Literary Modernity, 1916–1958*. New York: Columbia University Press, 2019.

Index

abstraction, 13–24, 30; under capitalism in Marxian analytic, 8–9, 13, 17, 155–57, 161–64; concrete abstraction, 17, 19–20; ethnic abstraction (Yao), 16–17, 23, 32; Greenberg's theory, 177n3; in literary modernism, 32, 177n3; into money in Pound's anti-Semitic reading of Marx, 39–40; in non-European history, 178n4; nonrepresentational aesthetics, 4; as poetic erasure, 128–29, 133–34; race and aesthetics, 32, 177n3, 178n4, 196n47 (Cha); translation's character, 19–22; in transpacific context, 8, 31–33, 35–36, 41, 65–66. *See also* Marx; meaning; translation; value

Admussen, Nick, 197n4

alterity, Otherness, 151–55, 157, 164; as displacement into futurity, 176n64; as exclusion, 168n11. *See also* domestication; foreignization; immigration; untranslatability

American pragmatism, 52–53. *See also* Dewey

aporia, thinking with, 30, 157–64

Apter, Emily, 157–59, 164, 169n17, 201n10, 203n25, 204n33

Asad, Talal, 153–54, 169n15

Asia: as geopolitical situation, 18–19; as idea derived from West, 15–16; as object of decolonial thought, 16, 18–19

Asian American studies: alongside Asian studies, 13–19; centrality of labor as analytic, 13–14; on social and racial differentiation, 97–99; alongside translation studies, 98–99. *See also* Cha, Theresa; differentiation; equivalence, as anti-colonial critique; immigration; transpacific

Asian studies: as discursive formation, 13–16, 184n77. *See also* Asian American; transpacific

Babel myth, 151–52. *See also* meaning; translation; universalism

Bachner, Andrea, 3, 33–36 passim, 127

bad, or not-so-bad, habits of mind, 1–2, 4, 8, 94; about translation, 6, 81–82, 87–88, 93–96, 189n28

Baker, Mona, 155, 169n14, 169n17

Bellos, David, 73

Benjamin, Walter, 157–58, 167n1, 202n22; Derrida on, 151

Berman, Antoine, 153–54, 201n10

Bernstein, Charles, 32, 73, 177n3

Bhabha, Homi, 98, 153–54, 169n15, 176n66, 203n26

Browning, Robert: influence on Hu, 52, 183n58, 185n83

Bruno, Cosima, 132, 198n16

Buddhism, 34, 179n13–14, 186n86

Bush, Christopher, 35–36, 180n24

Cassin, Barbara, 5, 169n17, 201n10, 203n25

Cayley, John, 36, 128, 133–34, 180n20

Cha, Theresa, 26–28, 96–97, 101–2; anti-colonial and feminist critique, 95–101, 124–125, 196n47; "anti-documentary desire" (Cheng), 27, 99–100, 118, 194n12; cultural translation in documentary, 100–2, 108–9, 114–19; identity and racial formation, 97–99, 112–13, 114–19; ideographic opacity, 120, 123, 125; influence of concretism, 27, 100, 194n12; influence of Daoism, 120–123, 196n38; participatory aesthetics, 95–96, 99; politics of multilingualism, 119–120; translation, 95–101, 114–19, 119–25; superimposition as formal principle, 27–28, 100, 102, 108–113, 194n17; "trans-immigration of image and memory," 12, 112–13; visual and process art, 27; *Dictée*, 26–28, 95–101, 108, 112, 119–125; *Temps Mort*, 102–7; *White Dust from Mongolia*, 27, 100–2, 108–119, 195n21

Chang, Eileen (Zhang Ailing), 25–26, 70; colorism and racial inscription, 90–91; correspondence with Hsia, 67, 188n18; on Hu Shi, 67–68, 74, 76–79; narratological experimentation influenced by work

219

on late Qing novels, 67, 75–82, 188n12, 189n24; philologies of error and forgetfulness, 68–69, 89–94, 186n4, 191n51; relational pronouns in translation, 84–88, 191n50; translating ambivalently, 71–74, 187n11; on translation in China, 172n31, 187n7; translingual plays on sound in vernacular, 68–69, 71–72, 74, 82, 86–88, 89–95; on vernacular Shanghainese Wu, 67–68, 71–72, 74–82, 89–94; *Biographies of Shanghai Flowers* (*Haishanghua*), 25, 74–82, 187n10; "Caolubing," 90–91; *Dream of the Red Chamber* (*Hongloumeng*), 67, 77–82, 186n1, 187n10; "A Few Small Observations on Modern Chinese," 82–88; *Little Reunions* (*Xiaotuanyüan*), 71, 188n12; "Sha," 91–94; *Sing-song Girls of Shanghai* (English translation of *Haishanghua*), 25, 68–69, 89

Cheng, Anne Anlin, on anti-documentary poetics, 27, 99–100, 118, 193n2, 194n16

China: censorship, 198n2; colorism and anti-blackness in China, 90–91, 192n53; domesticating and appropriating strategies of translation, 10–11, 170n31, 178n11; false teleology of political equivalence, 12–13, 69; translation in Chinese context: 10–13, 172n30; as transpacific, 18–19; writing, script reform and simplification: 31–36, 48–51, 66, 69, 86–88, 93–94, 173n37, 186n2. *See also* Chineseness; Hu; modernism; New Culture Movement; vernacular

Chineseness as lived idea, 14–15, 177n1, 199n24; the language as political concept: 29, 69, 198n2; freedom from essentialism, 33; national character as fiction, 1–2; as marshaled and questioned by Yang, 132–133, 138–39, 141–2, 150; *xungen* or *Roots-seeking* movement, 200n31. *See also* Sinophone; Yang; translingual erasure; translingual practice

Chow, Rey, 14–15, 168n11, 169n15, 177n1, 198n14

close reading: as aesthetic education in abstract detail, 19, 21–22, 30; for immanent theory, 22, 29–30, 151–52, 164, 199n24; as translation, 2, 95–96, 196n2, 198n16

comparative literature: as field, 4–5, 29–30; as linked to translation studies, 169n17. *See also* equivalence; translation; translation studies

concrete poetry, 27, 36, 41, 177n72; afterlife of ideographic thinking, 27, 177n72. *See also* Cha; Fenollosa; ideograph; poetics of equivalence; Yang

concrete translation, useful definitions of, 9, 26–28, 96, 99–100, 121, 128, 194n12. *See also* Cha; Fenollosa; ideograph; poetics of equivalence; Yang

cosmopolitanism, *shijie zhuyi*, 11, 64, 186n86

Day, Iyko, 17–18, 163, 178n4, 181n34
decolonial thinking, 10, 15–16, 18–19, 155, 157–58, 202n22
Derrida, Jacques: *Des tours des Babel* (on Benjamin), 151–52, 201n3; with Marx on loss of value, 162–64; *Le monolinguisme de l'autre* (trans. Mensah, *Monolingualism of the Other*), 159–161
Derridean transcendental signifier, 48, 58–59
Dewey, John: influence on Hu, 11, 53, 180n16
"differencing" (Chow), 168n11
differentiation: as caesura, time-lag of modernity (Bhabha), 203n26; through caesura, 159, 193n2; linguistic differentiation in translation: 2, 5, 31, 66, 95–96, 153–154; social differentiation: 2, 4–5, 13–15, 23, 95–101; subsumption of in translation, 23, 99–101, 125. *See also* Cha; Chang; Chinese modernity; translation, as loss made impossible; value domestication, 173n34. *See also* China; equivalence; foreignization; translation
Dowling, Sarah, 129–30

Edmond, Jacob, 32–33, 131–33, 198n12, 198n15
Emerson, Ralph Waldo: influence on Fenollosa, 46–51 passim
Emmerich, Karen, 21, 177n68
empiricism: classical connection to nature, 46–51; as poetic and ideographic mediation, 23–25, 34–36, 54–57, 60–62, 66; "poeticempiricism" (Hu), 24, 34, 42–46, 56, 62
equivalence, 4–5; anti-colonial critique of, 4–5, 20, 26, 29–30, 152–53, 154–57, 169n15, 174n45, 193n45, 203n24; as coercive

Index

identification, 97–98, 174n45, 193n2; Derrida's unreading, 159–61; functional equivalence in translation theory (Nida): 164, 169n14; hypothetical and figurative (Liu): 3, 153–55, 191n49, 201n6; hypostatization of equivalence in contemporary China, 174n45; political equivalence of China in global order, 11–13, 31–33, 43–45, 58, 63–65, 69. *See also* poetics of equivalence; transpacific

Fenollosa, Ernest (*Chinese Written Character as a Medium of Poetry*), 23–25, 31–32; on ideograph, 34–36; on nature as metaphor, 45–46; on "like forms" of Chinese and English sentences, 36, 48, 57–62; influence of American Transcendentalism, 182n45; influence of Hegel, 183n52; influence of Percy Bysshe Shelley, 183n53, 184n77; compared to Yang, 127–29, 134, 138
foreignization: as literary praxis, 189n28; as problem of contingent value assignment, 154–55; on spectrum with domestication, 10–11, 173n34. *See also* domestication; equivalence; translation

Han Bangqing (*Haishanghua*), 75–76, 92–94. *See also* Chang
harmophone (translating neologism for *xieyin*), 1, 28, 167n4; in action, 127–29, 134–36, 142–50. *See also* sound translation
homophone. *See* sound translation
Hill, Michael Gibbs, 172n29–30
Hu Shi, 11, 23–25, 173n36; on Buddhism as ethno-nationalist threat and cultural translation, 1, 179n14; as read by Chang, 67–68, 74, 76–79; empiricism and "poeticempiricism," 24, 34, 42–46, 56, 62, 179n16; why compare with Fenollosa, 34–36; Kantian regulative ideal and categorical imperative, 43, 183n50; "Dream and Poetry," 42–46; "Experimental Verses," *Changshiji*, 42–46, 62–66; "Hope" as translated from the *Rubaiyat*, 62–66, 185n82; Orientalism and cultural translation, 185n83; "Some Modest Proposals for the Reform of Literature," 51–57; "The Story of Mr. Not so Different" (*Chabuduo xiansheng zhuan*), 1–5, 11, 19, 167n2

Huang, Yunte: as critic, 9, 72, 180n27, 198n14; as translator of *Cantos*, 28, 137, 141–42

ideograph: as aesthetic education, 46–47, 58, 65–66; as nature's sentence-forms, 46–52, 58–62; as translingual constitution, 12, 23–25, 180n20; as transpacific dialectical fabulation, 33–42, 178n4. *See also* Cha; concrete poetry; empiricism; Fenollosa; Pound; Yang
"ideographing" as transitive verb, 37–42, 61, 181n38
immigration, Asian: Angel Island poems, 175n58; Chinese Exclusion Act, 16–18; "Chinese problem" per Fenollosa, 58; in comparison with Black and Indigenous social death, 17–18; "trans-immigration of image and memory" (Cha), 112–13. *See also* abstraction; Asian American studies; Cha; racial form
inheritance as genealogical critique, 8, 30, 124–25, 202n22

Jakobson, Roman, 5, 11, 169n14, 173n38, 201n6
Jameson, Fredric, 32–33, 41

Kim, Myung Mi, 72–73, 188n15
Klein, Lucas, 133, 138, 200n31

Lezra, Jacques, 169n16, 201n4, 203n25
literature: as aesthetic or philosophical concept, 5 155, 159; as sociohistorical formation, 5, 8–9, 156. *See also* abstraction; poetics of equivalence; poetry; racial form; vernacular; *wen*
Liu, Lydia: on meaning value and critique of equivalence, 3, 153–56, 169n15, 174n45, 201n6, 202n18; on universalism, 15. *See also* neologisms; translingual practice
Lowe, Lisa, 18, 97–98
Lowell, Amy: influence on Hu Shi, 34, 51–53
Lye, Colleen. *See* racial form

Marx, Karl, 2, 3; in Althusser's eyes, 17, 176n61; on capital as translation, 158; in Liu's eyes, with Saussure, 155–57; in Pound's eyes, 39; realizing revolution in translation, 202n22; on vanishing of surplus value read with Derrida, 161–64. *See also* abstraction; value meaning: collapsed distinction between meaning and non-meaning, 3–4, 22, 35, 198n16; in equilibrium (Steiner), 168n12; location across levels of language and culture, 170n20; structuralist and post-structuralist accounts, 1, 3–4, 83, 156, 168n10; surrender of, when translating, 1–8, 20, 201n3; transformation in translation, 6, 167n11; as visible through etymology, 46–47. *See also* abstraction; ideograph; translation; value

media prototypes, of sorts: absence, 110–11; sinograph, 36; ideograph as proto-cinematic etymology, 46, 182n46; over-zealous scribes and copyeditors, 89–94, 95, 191n50; possible films of Cha's *White Dust*, 108–119; street cries of racial outsider, 90–91; vanishing inscriptions, 127–28; waves, 198n15

Misty school, *menglongpai*, 28, 132–34, 198n14

modernism, literary: and abstraction, 33; afterlives of, in ethnic American writing, 12, 175n58; Anglo-American, as subfield, 23–25; experimentation in China: 23–26, 32–33, 56, 172n29; translation, 12, 32–33, 175n58; transpacific and global, as subfield, 31–33, 51–53, 59, 193n11. *See also* Cha; Chang; Fenollosa; Jameson; Pound; translation

neoliberalism, 3, 13–14, 17–19, 163; in contemporary China, 174n45; in transpacific financialization, 176n64

neologisms in translation: as element of my translation practice, 167n4; as forging of equivalence, 191n49; as meaningless excess, 86–88. *See also* translingual practice

New Culture Movement, 10–13, 31, 34–36, 43–46, 51–54, 62–65, 167n2; May Fourth, 76, 190n31. *See also* Chang; China; Chineseness; equivalence; Hu; vernacular

New Youth, Xinqingnian, 43, 53, 62–64, 185n82

Nida, Eugene, 5, 169n14. *See also* equivalence

Orientalism: as Europe's distant mandarin, 184n78; as Hu's source or crib for translation: 62–64; ideographic, 35–37, 41–42, 46–47, 49–50, 58; Pound's, 66; in technocratic present and future, 176n64. *See also* alterity

paradox, thinking with, 7–8, 12–13, 22–24, 35–36, 151–52

particularity: as aspect of abstraction, 17; denial of universalism through particularism, 15, 191n50; as epistemic violence, 15, 90–91; radiant particularity, 29–30, 164. *See also* abstraction; close reading; differentiation; romantic anticapitalism; universalism; untranslatability

poetics of equivalence: defined generally, 8, 22–23,151–152, 164, 203n24; defined as grounded in untranslatability, 155–64, 169n17; defined as translator's craft, gestural force: 8, 22–23, 71–72, 178n4; fictional arrangements (Cha), 95, 99–100, 125; as grammatical tense (Yang), 126–7, 135–138; as ideographic, 34–36, 48–51, 57–64; as product of cultural equivalence, 31–34, 62–65; word-for-word across sound and script, 69, 71–72, 73–74, 89–94, 134, 142, 150. *See also* concrete translation; equivalence; sound translation; translingual erasure; value

poetry: as concept, 29; 160–161; 163–64; as theorized by Yang: 126–27, 142–50; vernacular, by Hu, 43–46, 52–53, 62–65. *See also* Fenollosa; Hu; poetics of equivalence; Yang

Pound, Ezra, 23–25, 28–29, 175n58; anti-Semitism and fascism, expressed in economic theory, 37–39, 66, 181n34; correspondence with Kitasono, 37–40, 180n23; and his Era of translations, 11–12; as ethnographer, 38, 180n27; "luminous detail," 21; as editor of Fenollosa, 31, 51, 57; influence on Hu Shi, 34, 52–53; "inventor of Chinese poetry for our time," 12, 174n43; reading someone other than, 41–42; unreadability or opacity, 65–66; Chinese translation of *Cantos*, 28–29; *Cantos*, 37–40, 66; *Cathay*, 37, 66, 175n58, 180n24; "A Few Don'ts by an Imagiste," 52. *See also* Fenollosa; ideograph; modernism

pronominal instability: in lyrical subject-formation, 45, 85, 124, 196n48; in translation, 84–88, 189n28, 191n50

Index

race, racialization, 2, 13–14, 17–18, 32; language as vector of, 99, 114–116, 118–19; in subject-formation and identification, 13–14, 193n2, 194n16. *See also* abstraction; Cha; differentiation; value
racial form, 16–17, 194n12
Rafael, Vicente, 157
romantic anticapitalism, 17–20, 181n34. *See also* abstraction; Day
Rubaiyat by Omar Khayyam, 62–63, 185n83; Victorian-era translation by Edward Fitzgerald, 62–65. *See also* Hu

Sakai, Naoki, 97, 153–54; 156, 169n15, 181n39, 193n3, 193n11, 201n6
Saussy, Haun, 7, 83–84
Shih, Shu-mei, 12–13, 15, 178n11, 192n53
Sinophone, Sinitic languages, 15, 69. *See also* China; Chineseness
sound translation, 3–4, 25–26; 28–29; genealogy of, 72–73; as poetry and prosody (Derrida), 160–161. *See also* Chang; harmophone; poetics of equivalence; translation; vernacular; Yang
Spivak, Gayatri, 7, 153, 169n15
Stalling, Jonathan, 48–50, 72, 121, 179n13, 181n36, 188n13, 193n11, 196n38
Steiner, George, 168n12

Tageldin, Shaden, 169n15, 174n45
transcription, 8–9, 25–26, 72–73, 87–94, 96–97, 129
translation: as afterlife, historical promise and transmission (*Fortleben*), 77–82, 157, 187n10, 191n51, 202n22; allegories of, 63–65, 101–6, 112, 122–25; as anti-hermeneutic gesture, 4, 5–7, 22, 25–27, 69–70, 73, 74–82, 96, 155; broadened understanding of, 6, 20–21, 40–42, 57–58, 71–74, 158–59, 172n29; as catachresis, 18, 176n66; contested ontology of original and derivative, 21, 32–33, 160–61, 177n68, 187n4; cultural: 3, 5, 19–22, 153–55, 176n66, 203n24; distinction between literary and cultural, 3, 19–22; as dynamic equilibrium, 107, 168n12; as identification and dis-identification, 187n11, 193n2, 194n16; intention and agency, 7–8, 98–100, 159, 178n11; internalizing of ideograph, 36; literary, 3, 19–22, 28,

189n28, 198n16; as lived power relations: 10–11, 32, 169n17, 188n15; as loss, 160–61; as loss made impossible in vanishing of difference, 27, 100, 106–107, 120, 125, 141, 149–50, 161–64; as palimpsest (Cha), 101–7, 121; as pedagogical gesture, 58 (Fenollosa), 64–66 (Hu), 95–96; thought through political economy, value-formation, 3, 22, 69, 153, 158, 160–64; postcolonial translation, 5, 96–99, 153–55, 159, 169n15, 169n17, 174n45, 193n3, 203n24; as praxis imbricated with theory, 6–8, 10–11, 23, 159, 189n28, 196n2; refusing fluency, 158, 189n28; as shared object, 164, 172n30, 202n22; word-for-word as impossible, 7, 30, 57–58 (*see also* Chang, translingual plays on sound). *See also* concrete translation; meaning; sound translation; transcription; translingual erasure; transliteration; value
translation studies: definition of field as discursive formation, 4–6, 20–22, 29–30, 42, 152–59, 169n17; as epistemology, complex agency, 19–22, 30, 98–99, 151–152, 155–56, 158–59; as taken up in Global South discourse, 155–56, 202n22; as heuristic or method, 18–19, 164; as reflexive empiricism in descriptive translation studies, 22, 176n67; as restitution, 20–22. *See also* domestication; equivalence; foreignization
translingual aesthetics and poetics (Dowling), 129–30. *See also* poetics of equivalence
translingual erasure, 28–29, 127–30, 134–38. *See also* Yang Lian
translingual practice (Liu), 28–29, 129–30; structures of signification, 84–88, 202n18. *See also* neologisms in translation
transliteration as phenomenon, 40–41, 69, 72–73, 89–94, 120–121
transpacific: definition as field and site of knowledge production, 8–10, 184n77 ; Sino-US as synecdoche of, 4–5, 8–9, 12–13, 18–19. *See also* abstraction; China; Chineseness; equivalence; US imperialism
Trinh Minh-ha, 124, 196n47–48
Tymoczko, Maria, 6, 169n17, 170n20, 173n34, 176n67

universalism: as Babel ideology, 151–52; concrete universalisms dialectically mediated through particular, 5, 15, 30, 164; as ideographic contradiction, 35–36; via Kantian regulative ideal, 43, 47; as field of action, 164, 202n22. *See also* abstraction; particularity; translation

unlearning as epistemic work, 3–8, 19–22, 152, 158–59. *See also* abstraction; translation; translingual erasure; untranslatability

untranslatability: as pendant to poetic equivalence, 157–64, 169n17; as poetic economy of idiom, 160–61; politics of: 5, 23–25, 29, 169n17, 152, 203n25; in pragmatic sense, 157; as praxis against exchange-value, 159, 169n17; as problem of value and incommensurability, 2, 5. *See also* Apter; Cassin; poetics of equivalence; translation; value

US imperialism, Cold War, 5, 9, 16–17, 33, 70–71, 96–98, 101–2, 107, 114–19, 125, 195n21; United States Information Service (USIS): 25–26, 70–71

value as theory of translation: as autopoetics, 161–64; contestation of, 7–8; definition, 2–8; in Enlightenment philology, 191n51; as epistemology of translation, 19–22; linguistic value (Saussure), 3–4, 83, 156; Marxian account of surplus and exchange-value in global political economy, 2–3, 13–14, 153, 155–56, 159, 174n45; meaning-value (Liu): 3, 5–8, 19, 156; value assignation, 2, 34, 154. *See also* meaning; Liu; translation

Venuti, Lawrence, 20–21, 154, 169n17, 173n34, 203n25

vernacular in Chinese context, *baihua*, 1–2, 11, 25–26, 31–32, 34–36; national formation of, 51–54, 167n2; *xiebuding, impossible to secure in writing*, 69; *youyinwuzi, sound without writing*, 24, 74, 89, 92. *See also* Chang; Hu

Walkowitz, Rebecca, 21, 32, 198n16

wen, wenxue, or *literature*, 42–43, 77–78, 181n39; contra *wu, substance*, 56–57

wenyan, literary classical Chinese: 44–45, 53–54, 65. *See also* vernacular

Wong, Shelley Sunn, 98

world literature: as aesthetic and literary praxis, 130–34 (Yang), 157–58, 198n16; as cultural institution, 6, 28; infrastructures of, 158; in world-systems and marketplaces, 6, 157–58, 198n14

xieyin. See harmophone

Yang Lian, 28–29; 126–28, 130–32; Chinese language as translingual, 138–42; Chineseness in question, 130, 134, 136–42, 150; on 'conceptual art,' 126–7; elegy as temporal erasure, 127, 134–38, 138–42; Holton and Chan, translators, 28, 131, 196n2, 197n11, 200 passim; ideographic inheritance, 127–29, 131, 134–38, 137–38; mourning in the wrong language, 128, 134, 138–142; poetry as concept, 126–27, 142–50; on Pound's *Cantos* and its Chinese translation as epic, *shishi*, 28–29, 127–32, 134–38, 199n23; read through translation, 131–134, 137; *Concentric Circles*, 28–29, 126–27, 130–132, 134, 139–50, 197n11. *See also* translingual erasure

Yao, Steven. *See* abstraction

Tze-Yin Teo is Assistant Professor of Comparative Literature and Translation Studies at the University of Oregon.